Cases on Worldwide E-Commerce: Theory in Action

Mahesh Raisinghani
University of Dallas, USA

 Idea Group
Publishing

 Information Science
Publishing

Hershey • London • Melbourne • Singapore • Beijing

658.84
C338

Acquisitions Editor:	Mehdi Khosrowpour
Managing Editor:	Jan Travers
Development Editor:	Michele Rossi
Copy Editor:	Jane Conley
Typesetter:	LeAnn Whitcomb
Cover Design:	Tedi Wingard
Printed at:	Integrated Book Technology

Published in the United States of America by
    Idea Group Publishing
    1331 E. Chocolate Avenue
    Hershey PA 17033-1117
    Tel: 717-533-8845
    Fax: 717-533-8661
    E-mail: cust@idea-group.com
    Web site: http://www.idea-group.com

and in the United Kingdom by
    Idea Group Publishing
    3 Henrietta Street
    Covent Garden
    London WC2E 8LU
    Tel: 44 20 7240 0856
    Fax: 44 20 7379 3313
    Web site: http://www.eurospan.co.uk

Library of Congress Cataloging-in-Publication Data

Cases on worldwide e-comerce : theory in action / [edited by] Mahesh Raisinghani.
        p. cm.
    Includes bibliographical references and index.
    ISBN 1-930708-27-0 (cloth)
        1. Electronic commerce--Case studies. I. Raisinghani, Mahesh S., 1967-

HF5548.32 .C366 2001
658.8'4--dc21   2001046332

British Cataloguing in Publication Data
A Cataloguing in Publication record for this book is available from the British Library.

NEW from Idea Group Publishing

- **Data Mining: A Heuristic Approach**
  Hussein Aly Abbass, Ruhul Amin Sarker and Charles S. Newton/1-930708-25-4
- **Managing Information Technology in Small Business: Challenges and Solutions**
  Stephen Burgess/1-930708-35-1
- **Managing Web Usage in the Workplace: A Social, Ethical and Legal Perspective**
  Murugan Anandarajan and Claire Simmers/1-930708-18-1
- **Challenges of Information Technology Education in the 21st Century**
  Eli Cohen, 1-930708-34-3
- **Social Responsibility in the Information Age: Issues and Controversies**
  Gurpreet Dhillon/1-930708-11-4
- **Database Integrity: Challenges and Solutions**
  Jorge H. Doorn and Laura Rivero/ 1-930708-38-6
- **Managing Virtual Web Organizations in the 21st Century: Issues and Challenges**
  Ulrich Franke/1-930708-24-6
- **Managing Business with Electronic Commerce: Issues and Trends**
  Aryya Gangopadhyay/ 1-930708-12-2
- **Electronic Government: Design, Applications and Management**
  Åke Grönlund/1-930708-19-X
- **Knowledge Media in Health Care: Opportunities and Challenges**
  Rolf Grutter/ 1-930708-13-0
- **Internet Management Issues: A Global Perspective**
  John D. Haynes/1-930708-21-1
- **Enterprise Resource Planning: Global Opportunities and Challenges**
  Liaquat Hossain, Jon David Patrick and MA Rashid/1-930708-36-X
- **The Design and Management of Effective Distance Learning Programs**
  Richard Discenza, Caroline Howard, and Karen Schenk/1-930708-20-3
- **Multirate Systems: Design and Applications**
  Gordana Jovanovic-Dolecek/1-930708-30-0
- **Managing IT/Community Partnerships in the 21st Century**
  Jonathan Lazar/1-930708-33-5
- **Multimedia Networking: Technology, Management and Applications**
  Syed Mahbubur Rahman/ 1-930708-14-9
- **Cases on Worldwide E-Commerce: Theory in Action**
  Mahesh Raisinghani/ 1-930708-27-0
- **Designing Instruction for Technology-Enhanced Learning**
  Patricia L. Rogers/ 1-930708-28-9
- **Heuristic and Optimization for Knowledge Discovery**
  Ruhul Amin Sarker, Hussein Aly Abbass and Charles Newton/1-930708-26-2
- **Distributed Multimedia Databases: Techniques and Applications**
  Timothy K. Shih/1-930708-29-7
- **Neural Networks in Business: Techniques and Applications**
  Kate Smith and Jatinder Gupta/ 1-930708-31-9
- **Information Technology and Collective Obligations: Topics and Debate**
  Robert Skovira/ 1-930708-37-8
- **Managing the Human Side of Information Technology: Challenges and Solutions**
  Edward Szewczak and Coral Snodgrass/1-930708-32-7
- **Cases on Global IT Applications and Management: Successes and Pitfalls**
  Felix B. Tan/1-930708-16-5
- **Enterprise Networking: Multilayer Switching and Applications**
  Vasilis Theoharakis and Dimitrios Serpanos/1-930708-17-3
- **Measuring the Value of Information Technology**
  Han T.M. van der Zee/ 1-930708-08-4
- **Business to Business Electronic Commerce: Challenges and Solutions**
  Merrill Warkentin/ 1-930708-09-2

Excellent additions to your library!

**Receive the Idea Group Publishing catalog with descriptions of these books by
calling, toll free 1/800-345-4332
or visit the IGP Online Bookstore at: http://www.idea-group.com!**

Cases on Worldwide E-Commerce: Theory in Action

Table of Contents

Preface i

Chapter I
GlobeRanger Corporation 1
     Hanns-Christian L. Hanebeck, GlobeRanger Corporation, USA
     Stanley L. Kroder, John H. Nugent and Mahesh S. Raisinghani,
     University of Dallas, USA

Chapter II
Implementation Management of an E-Commerce-Enabled Enterprise
Information System: A Case Study at Texas Instruments 32
     R. P. Sundarraj and Joseph Sarkis, Clark University, USA

Chapter III
A Three-Tiered Approach to Global E-Commerce:
Experiences of Nu Skin International 48
     David Paper, Utah State University, USA
     Kenneth B. Tingey, Opennet Corporation, USA

Chapter IV
E-Learning Business Models: Framework and Best
Practice Examples 70
     Sabine Seufert, University of St. Gallen, Switzerland

Chapter V
Growth and Consolidation in the Spanish-Speaking
E-Commerce Market 95
     Roberto Vinaja, University of Texas-Pan American, USA

Chapter VI
Inca Foods: Reaching New Customers Worldwide 113
    J. Martín Santana, Jaime Serida and Antonio Díaz,
    Escuela de Administración de Negocios para Graduados, Perú

Chapter VII
Reality vs Plan: How Organizational E-Commerce
Strategies Evolve 135
    David Gordon and James E. Skibo, University of Dallas, USA

Chapter VIII
Student Advantage Captures the College Market Through an Integration
of Their On and Offline Businesses 151
    Margaret T. O'Hara, East Carolina University, USA
    Hugh J. Watson, University of Georgia, USA

Chapter IX
Turning E-Commerce Theory into Action in Ireland:
Taming the Celtic Tiger 171
    Ira Yermish and Dale A. Bondanza, St. Joseph's University, USA

Chapter X
ENI Company 186
    Ook Lee, Hansung University, Korea

Chapter XI
SAFECO®: Leveraging the Web in a Knowledge-Based
Service Industry 201
    Debabroto Chatterjee and Leonard M. Jessup,
    Washington State University, USA

Chapter XII
E*Trade Securities, Inc., Pioneer Online Trader,
Struggles to Stay on Top 221
    Adam T. Elegant and Ramiro Montealegre,
    University of Colorado-Boulder, USA

About the Authors 250

Index 258

Preface

Wisdom grows in those who help others achieve greatness.
—— *Colle Davis*

Despite the fact that a quarter of the world's Internet population will reside in the United States by 2005, the U.S. share of the global market is predicted by Jupiter Research to drop from 36 to 25 percent by 2005 (*www.jup.com*, 2001). By 2003, according to research from IDC, an estimated 67 percent of Internet users will log on outside the United States; and the foreign share of e-commerce will reach 56 percent. Although e-business leaders at most companies recognize the need to develop a global strategy, unfortunately many have not yet put one in place. The focus of this book is to conduct and present research that is useful for both theory and practice. In theory, the Web can reach the world. In practice, U.S. e-commerce sites have largely limited themselves to North America. Although that is about to change as the use of the Internet matures in markets throughout Europe, Asia and Latin America, gaining a global foothold involves more than just translating content. Companies must decide which countries to enter first, how they will update and manage content globally, and what is the appropriate mix of central control and local flexibility. They must also decide whether to build a global Web presence alone or develop tight partnerships with companies based in their targeted foreign markets. The case studies illustrated in this book will provide rich insights into these critical management issues. The global perspective of e-business is highlighted throughout the book because the Internet is a worldwide network of networked computers and any business that moves its operations to the Web becomes an international business. Companies will increasingly need to look toward the global marketplace.

Chapter I is a decision-focused case study. GlobeRanger developed from the concept of using wireless technology to locate and track assets over a metropolitan, state, national or worldwide area. Although the initial value proposition focused on hardware-based mobile tracking systems that consisted of a GPS (Global Positioning System) receiver linked to the asset being tracked, software and data management seemed to be a much more viable niche in the location and tracking arena. This strategic shift from hardware to software, databases and information management is the major focus of this case.

It contains information that provided GlobeRanger management with insights regarding risks of pursuing a hardware strategy and, in turn, what caused them to shift in a new direction within the same field. Tracking is time- and information-sensitive. The logistics function of organizations is increasingly important, especially to those that are reengineering their supply chain and moving to just-in-time manufacturing, distribution and delivery. In effect, GlobeRanger shifted from the data gathering function to that of data mining and analysis with the attendant opportunity of offering proprietary solutions to clients by using advanced IT techniques and technologies.

GlobeRanger is a facilitator of B2B e-Commerce. Its products will add value to supply chain management initiatives. This company exemplifies global business on several levels:

• First, asset tracking and location is a worldwide challenge. As globalization increases, the need to track products grows in complexity. Raw materials may come from several different countries, manufacturing may be decentralized over continents and the customers may also be international.

• Second, the work force of GlobeRanger is international, with the attendant challenges of managing employees from many different cultural backgrounds.

• Third, GlobeRanger's business will be done, in part, through alliances with organizations and individuals from around the world.

Chapter II discusses the various stages of implementation of strategic ERP systems at Texas Instruments, from adoption to preparation and operation, and the performance metrics used to manage the process. The case study also provides an overview of how these performance metrics played a role in the implementation. A number of lessons for the broader community are detailed, such as practical issues that may need to be addressed when organizations seek to implement systems such as ERP and link them to customers via Internet and Web-based technology

This case study identifies the importance of enterprise-wide information systems to global e-commerce-based corporate solutions, explores the requirements for a single instance global implementation of an ERP system, provides some best practices and lessons learned to organizations seeking to replicate such an implementation program, and identifies possible research issues.

Chapter III illustrates the differences between global and transnational management requirements as organizations work towards making better use of resources
across networked, enterprise information systems. It uses a three-tier networked enterprise model developed to facilitate better understanding and management of global business requirements in e-commerce and describes how one organization, Nu Skin, deals with management of people and resources in the context of a global, networked enterprise.

Specific examples within the context of discussions with executives from one organization are used to contrast global and transnational systems. Rather than demonstrating characteristics of either "global" or "transnational" globalization models, Nu Skin exemplifies elements of both, along with "hybrid" combinations. Due to the complexities of the markets served by the organization and the differing requirements and capabilities brought on by the Internet and other information technologies, Nu Skin illustrates the process of adapting to the Internet by assimilating various globalization models between the home office and different parts of the world.

Chapter IV introduces the changes in the education market and the new learning paradigm, explains e-learning as the convergence of several forces, emphasizes the need for e-learning strategies, outlines a framework for e-learning business models for the implementation of the changes, and compares/contrasts best practice examples for the different e-learning business models.

New e-learning strategies, such as the E2B, E2E and E2C strategies that are needed to react to the changes in a competitive and global education market, are discussed within the context of customers increasingly demanding customized training in a modular and flexible way and the intense focus on content. Key success factors discussed are a well-known brand name that stands for a quality, differentiated service offering; large direct sales force; and strong partnerships across the value chain.

Chapter V aims to analyze, in some detail, the major challenges in the widespread adoption of electronic commerce in the Spanish-speaking population. It also provides a general overview of related issues in global e-commerce, specifically: language, localization, currency, cultural difference, export controls, payment methods, taxation issues, consumer protection, and legal issues. The case includes a description of the strategies followed by companies entering the Latin American market in order to illustrate some of the major cross-border issues and clearly exemplifies how localization involves a considerable financial investment and commitment. The chapter illustrates that while Latin America initially attracted many investors by offering one of the world's fastest growing online populations, the market was not large enough to accommodate all the new entrants. It describes the important factors that play a critical role in a global e-commerce initiative and discusses the different entry strategies used by companies entering the Spanish-speaking online market.

Chapter VI presents a discussion about the electronic business model developed by Inca Foods, which sells globally but distributes locally (within the country). Evidently this way of doing business marks a substantial difference from what retailers have been doing traditionally with regards to electronic business in Peru. One can also argue about the viability of this business model and about the possibility of its being copied in countries with less economic and social development on the one hand and less computer penetration and Internet access on the other. The discussion in this case study is centered within the social, economic and cultural environment in which Inca Foods operates. Its main focus lies in the unexpected and enormous opportunity of doing business with the community of Peruvian expatriates residing in different parts of the world.

The case study raises important questions about this subject, such as: How can its size be determined? How can these Peruvians be reached? How can an interesting and attractive offer be made? How can doing a transaction be made easy? How can these customers receive the necessary flexibility so that they can purchase what their family really wants? There are important lessons learned about the factors that influence the success in an e-business effort, the concerns of physical distribution of products sold by a virtual supermarket, the potential worldwide market for e-business initiatives, and the impact of electronic advertising through the Web.

Chapter VII takes the students through the structural evolution of several organizations entering into e-commerce. Initially the organizations exhibited rigid resistance to change, then adopted change accompanied by significant shifts in power. The driver for change was the desire to enter into e-commerce "now" rather than "later." It discusses organizational changes in strategy that result from entry into e-commerce and the approaches organizations take to successfully manage global e-commerce. It illustrates how change roles evolve within organizations undergoing rapid change in order to sustain their e-commerce enterprise and provides some insights into metrics of brick-and-mortar vs. e-commerce operations.

Chapter VIII highlights the strategic decisions involved in evolving from a "brick and mortar" to a "brick and click" organization; the challenges of attracting, enhancing, and retaining customers, i.e., the phases of customer relationship management (CRM); the nature of e-commerce business models; the use of partnering strategies and the strengths and weaknesses of web-facilitated marketing. After forming strategic alliances with AT&T and American Express, Student Advantage created an electronic community for college students, through in-house application development of technology, acquisition of competing companies, and further development of its relationships with business partners and universities.

Student Advantage has successfully transformed itself from the brick-and-mortar company it began as in 1992 into the leading online portal to the higher education community. It utilizes sophisticated software data mining applications, e-marketing campaign planning and CRM. Unlike many other "bricks to clicks" firms, Student Advantage very early on saw the advantage in fully integrating its online and offline databases to avoid inconsistencies in the data that might have resulted from multiple data sources, enabling more efficient data mining, and creating the basis for providing a more satisfying customer experience.

Chapter IX, explores entrepreneurial activity in the Republic of Ireland in the area of information technology (IT) consulting. The case is a hypothetical example of two young entrepreneurs seeking to capitalize their academic backgrounds into a business to provide consulting expertise to businesses looking to harness the power of the Internet. The issues of starting such an enterprise can be best understood by thinking from the perspective of these entrepreneurs and exploring these challenging issues in more detail. This case study could be an exercise in a capstone strategic management or global management course. From the IT perspective, readers/students should explore the general issues of outsourced e-commerce activity as a business model.

Chapter X is a good case study of how to conduct e-commerce in a country whose national IT infrastructure is not ready for it. ENI Company is an electronic commerce firm in South Korea that provides English news items and English lessons to the subscribers through daily e-mail service that includes free English news-related question and answer sessions via e-mail. This case study deals with the struggle of this firm to establish and sustain its business in a less-developed national information infrastructure. It describes the evolution and organizational structure of ENI Company and discusses the biggest challenge for the firm, i.e., marketing of ENI Company's products.

Chapter XI discusses how SAFECO, a large corporation in the insurance and financial services industry, is strategizing for and implementing technologies to exploit the Web. SAFECO was recently ranked as one of the leading innovative users of the Web technology in its industry. Since SAFECO's fundamental strategic driving force is the independent distribution system, this case study discusses the opportunities, implementation challenges and risks in adopting Web technologies in this competitive environment. It highlights critical management issues on how large organizations, particularly those that are knowledge-based and provide primarily information-based services, should strategize about, adopt, and implement Web technologies.

Chapter XII discusses the fierce competition and emerging ethical and operational problems faced by E*Trade, a company that revolutionized the securities brokerage industry by "creating" Internet trading. Although E*Trade's original strategy was to deliver cost savings to customers while amortizing fixed costs over a greater number of accounts, in 1997, several competitors established Internet sites and E*Trade was dethroned as the price leader. The case discusses the three general principles that guided the firm's service expansion: (1) attract new investors and fortify existing customer loyalty, (2) develop multiple revenue streams to protect against an extended market correction, and (3) increase customers' switching costs in order to prevent them from jumping to another online brokerage firm. Its management team introduced a strategic initiative to transform the company into a financial, one-stop shop for investors by expanding its information technology (this included the establishment of a popular website offering the convenience and control of automated stock options and mutual fund order placement at low commission rates), improving its marketing and advertising program, and developing new strategic alliances.

Mahesh S. Raisinghani, Ph.D.
Editor

Acknowledgments

The editor would like to acknowledge the help of all involved in the collation and review process of the book, without whose support the project could not have been satisfactorily completed. A further special note of thanks goes also to all the staff at Idea Group Publishing, whose contributions throughout the whole process from inception of the initial idea to final publication have been invaluable.

Most of the authors of chapters included in this also served as referees for articles written by other authors. Thanks go to all those who provided constructive and comprehensive reviews.

Special thanks also go to the publishing team at Idea Group Publishing. In particular to Michele Rossi who continuously prodded via e-mail for keeping the project on schedule and to Mehdi Khosrowpour, whose enthusiasm motivated me to initially consider taking on this project.

In closing, I wish to thank all of the authors for their insights and excellent contributions to this book. I also want to thank all of the people who assisted me in the reviewing process. In addition, this book would not have been possible without the ongoing professional support from Mehdi Khosrowpour, Michele Rossi and Jan Travers at Idea Group Publishing. Finally, I want to thank my wife and daughter for their love and support throughout this project.

Mahesh S. Raisinghani, Ph.D.
Editor

Dedication

To my angel daughter, Aashna Kaur Raisinghani

Kindness is more than deeds.
It is an attitude, an expression, a look, a touch.
It is anything that lifts another person.

- C. Neil Strait

Chapter I

GlobeRanger Corporation

Hanns-Christian L. Hanebeck
GlobeRanger Corporation, USA

Stanley L. Kroder, John H. Nugent and Mahesh S. Raisinghani
University of Dallas, USA

This case traces the dynamic evolution/revolution of an e-commerce entity from concept through first-round venture financing. It details the critical thought processes and decisions that made this enterprise a key player in the explosive field of supply chain logistics. It also provides a highly valuable view of lessons learned and closes with key discussion points that may be used in the classroom in order to provoke thoughtful and meaningful discussion of important business issues.

EXECUTIVE SUMMARY

GlobeRanger's business concept originated from the idea that wireless technology today allows for easy tracking of people, but that there are no means to comprehensively track assets and goods in real time as they move through the supply chain. Initial discussions about the value proposition focused on hardware-based mobile tracking systems as they are predominantly found in the market today. A solution necessarily would have consisted of a Global Positioning System (GPS) receiver chip linked to the asset being tracked, which in turn is connected to a wireless device that sends information to a central tracking center. Such a system would provide great benefits to those involved with the asset's transportation or dependent on its arrival.

After an extensive analysis, GlobeRanger made an early decision that hardware-based systems will substantially extend the time-to-market, tie-up resources, and limit the company's ability to adapt to its fast changing environment and unique customer requirements. Prior to funding, the executives decided that the greatest value was in location information and its derivatives that could add value in supply chain management. As a result, the decision, to drop hardware and concentrate on information, at a very early stage led to a novel and innovative business model that is, to this day, unparalleled in the market place. This strategic shift from tools to solutions is the major focus of this case.

GlobeRanger's management team's insights regarding risks and pitfalls of pursuing a hardware strategy and, in turn, its early shift in direction within the same field is the heart of this study. Tracking is time and information sensitive. An organization's supply chain management function is increasingly important in today's highly competitive environment with compressed business cycles. Many firms are reengineering their logistics operations and moving to just-in-time manufacturing, distribution and delivery. In effect, GlobeRanger shifted from the data gathering function to that of providing real-time data mining and analysis with the attendant opportunity of offering proprietary solutions to clients by using advanced IT techniques and technologies.

Today, GlobeRanger is a facilitator of B2B e-commerce solutions that add value to supply chain management initiatives by creating visibility in an area that has been largely overlooked. GlobeRanger's proprietary solutions offer its clients improvements in efficiency, effectiveness, customer satisfaction, and competitive advantage while creating barriers to entry.

One of the fundamental observations that led to GlobeRanger's current business model was that location information alone is of very limited value. Rather than settling for information about the mere location of an asset or goods, GlobeRanger has deliberately taken a much more comprehensive approach of integrating various other sources of information that provide context to location. For example, delivery trucks could be rerouted dynamically based on ever-changing traffic and road conditions. GlobeRanger serves as a facilitator in improving complex logistics systems. Traffic is getting more congested. Payroll and fuel costs are increasing, thus providing the needed business case for the GlobeRanger system named eLocate.™

GENESIS OF IDEAS

Several things came together rather serendipitously to bring GlobeRanger to life. As is often the case, the company originated as much from coincidence, right timing and luck, as it did from its founders' experiences and track records. Without several key individuals meeting at the right time, each one with ideas that ultimately melded into an innovative business concept, the company would have never been founded. A senior executive from Nortel Networks, a successful entrepreneur, and a seasoned IBM researcher put all of their experience and knowledge together to create the foundation for GlobeRanger.

It all started when George Brody left his post as Vice President at Nortel Networks to become an entrepreneur and founder of a company that was to operate in the converged areas of wireless and Internet technologies. He was contemplating several possible venture ideas. George met with Roy Varghese, a Dallas entrepreneur who also had ideas of starting a high-tech venture. The relationship between the two men had initially been formed when Roy invited George to meet an Indian government official for lunch. About a year later they met again to set off into what was to change the course of their lives.

Roy, at that time, had already worked closely with a third individual–Dr. Shrikant Parikh, a seasoned researcher at IBM–for several years. In early 1999, Shrikant started to think about novel applications of GPS technology that he felt would lastingly transform the way people live, work, and commute. At the time, he was studying novel telecommunications applications that would come to market several years later. Roy immediately grasped the vision and potential of Shikant's ideas. So he pitched them to George for his insight and thoughts. George, in turn, discussed his own ideas and where he wanted to go.

Once all three of them met, their thoughts quickly crystallized into the beginnings of a plan. It was George who first grasped the potential that lay in combining of his own ideas with those of Roy and Shrikant. During his years as a senior executive at Nortel Networks, he founded the wireless business of the company and, beginning in 1979, personally oversaw the development of wireless technologies that would forever change the way we communicate. In his role at Nortel, George had been actively involved in the development of the very first wireless standards and knew one thing that the others had overlooked. He knew that the standard ignored one critical piece of information–the precise location of a caller.

From the outset, George's vision for wireless communications had focused on an intelligent network. One that would locate callers no matter where they were, and would allow a person to carry a single phone number independent of where in the world he or she traveled. In addition, George envisioned a network smart enough to intelligently route a call to its designated recipient. This could be the case in a household with multiple potential recipients. The network would be smart enough to route a given call to its correct destination without involving all other potential recipients and members of that household. To a large extent, we now see George's vision materialize after more than 20 years. As George knew that the precise location of a caller had been lost or crudely approximated while developing the first wireless networks, he was aware that things like 911 emergency calls would not work since the network did not know to which police or fire station to transfer the call. Hence, when George talked to Roy and Shrikant, he immediately grasped the importance of locating not just a person, but also an asset such as a truck or a railcar.

George, Roy and Shrikant, the initial group of founders, decided to launch a company that subsequently leveraged wireless communications, the Internet and GPS technology to deliver value solutions to end-users and businesses. While it was immediately obvious that the combination of wireless and GPS technologies would lead to tracking something or someone, there still was a fairly large field of possible applications. Supplying the business-to-consumer (B2C) market with tracking or location devices similar to wristwatches, for example, at first seemed to have the advantage of sheer market size. At that time, B2C Internet businesses appeared to be taking off. Both factors argued for jumping in. It was George who quickly saw that the possible target market was narrower than they had originally thought, due to the fact that there only were few applications, such as tracking people within amusements parks. In addition, this business case would have needed substantial funding to cover the exorbitantly high marketing expenses. This conclusion drove the discussion towards a business-to-business (B2B) model that could eventually provide a much larger market size and thus, leave enough room to scale the company later on. In addition, it would allow the founders to initially concentrate on one segment, which is an essential criterion for any small company entering an existing market or creating a new one.

George's point of providing tracking capabilities to B2B customers had the added benefit of leaving few alternatives. While this may sound odd, it immediately focused the group on the area of tracking assets and goods as they move through a given supply chain. This foundation of the business model is shown in Figure 1. The new company would equip trucks, trailers, containers or railcars with hardware devices that included a GPS receiver chip and a wireless modem. As these assets move through the supply chain, their location can be reported back to a central database.

The founders then set out to discuss whether developing and manufacturing a device that housed a GPS chip and a wireless modem would make sense.

Figure 1: The business model foundation (© GlobeRanger, 2000)

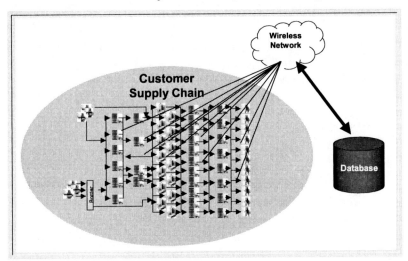

Again, it was George with his background in wireless telecommunications, who created an ingenious turn of events when he had the idea of being device independent. He argued that producing hardware would tie up considerable amounts of capital and require a lengthy development cycle. Rather, the new company should utilize any device in the market and readily deploy it based upon unique customer requirements. George's idea marked the most important strategic decision in the company's short life. It allowed GlobeRanger to enter the tracking market faster and with substantially less capital than any other player in this space. It provided a thread that would tie all ends together and create a business model that to this day is unique in this market space.

George's initial argument centered around the benefits to the new company, which mainly lay in a much shorter time-to-market and tailored customer solutions–versus the "one size fits all" model. Moreover, he saw great advantages for customers in that they could choose between different technologies and communication standards as their needs expanded while still being served by GlobeRanger's offerings. Unlike most of the world, where GSM is the prevailing narrowband wireless standard, the US to this day is characterized by a multiplicity of competing wireless communication standards leading to fractured coverage for many users. His point was that a customer could buy a satellite solution with full coverage within the continental U.S. while that customer effectively needed coverage only within one larger metropolitan area. Conversely, the opposite case could appear that a customer would buy a cellular solution and eventually miss out on location information whenever he was out of range. In addition, satellite communication is much more expensive than cellular or paging. In summary, there is no single, "one size fits all" solution for disparate classes of customer applications. As a result, GlobeRanger is now device and hardware independent. The company is able to sell different solutions to different customers based on their needs, while employing largely common software modules to all customers. In this way, there is an economy of scale that allows for "mass customization". Yet, George's idea had another equally important dimension. His approach allows "future-proofing" of existing customers. That is, GlobeRanger can provide its functionality by simply changing its interfaces to new hardware and communications technology. Customers can immediately replace older technologies with new ones as they become available. Last, his idea also proved to be a very strong competitive weapon since GlobeRanger was able to tap into the existing market of assets that already had devices deployed. George argued that they could literally take on a competitor's customer and use the devices installed by the competitor while providing all GlobeRanger services to that customer and thus, reaping the benefits of the true value creation.

A first market analysis led to the realization that there was a fairly large field of players in the tracking market, each one supplying its own hardware solution based on one communication technology or another. This effectively validated George's idea of independence from a given hardware platform. Now the founding group was convinced that its focus on supplying location information was a very attractive target of opportunity. In addition, the analysis turned up that almost all of the existing players sold proprietary client software that customers had to use in order to access information about the location of their assets and goods as they moved through the supply chain. This, too, was an initial concern to the group, and it readily decided on a fully Internet based solution and an Application Service Provider (ASP) model that would alleviate the need to buy software while making the information available and accessible anywhere and at any time. The approach also had a second advantage that potentially any authorized party could access information about the location of an asset or a particular shipment from any Internet connection–provided, of course, they had the appropriate security codes. This would enable transportation carriers to provide real-time monitoring of the goods being shipped to the originator and/or recipient and thus, drastically increase their level of customer service in a real-time environment. In addition, there was a seemingly simple but very powerful advantage in terms of time-to-market. While client software-based players had to ship literally thousands of CD-ROMs for every change in their functionality, GlobeRanger could change features and functionality virtually overnight and make it available to a single customer, groups of customers or to every user of eLocate™.

It was Shrikant, with the mind of a scientist, who saw a vitally important relationship resulting in an important differentiator between GlobeRanger and its main competitors. In his view, it was not enough to show the position of an asset or particular shipment on a map over the Internet. Rather, he argued, it would make sense to integrate location information into enterprise-level software such as Enterprise Resource Planning (ERP) systems. According to his vision, there had to be an advantage to the reduction of work steps, for a company to garner added value. Hence, if a given customer's employee did not have to look at an ERP screen for shipment details and then switch over to a second system and screen to access the current position of that exact shipment, this would provide a distinct competitive advantage and customer value add. Both George and Roy immediately bought off on the idea and established it along with hardware independence and full Internet access as the main pillars of service positioning for the new company.

The extensions to the business model foundation are shown in Figure 2. George's idea of being hardware and device independent is reflected in that the company was able to tailor the wireless network to specific customer requirements. Shrikant's idea of ERP integration is shown as a two-way link between the knowledge base and a cloud representing ERP software. In addition, the founders argued that the ubiquitous nature of the Internet would permit specific reporting and analysis capabilities that could directly feed into

Figure 2: Extensions to the business model foundation (© GlobeRanger, 2000)

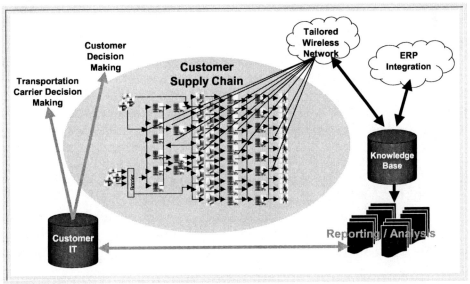

customers' systems. This would greatly enhance product offerings. These reports could be used by transportation carriers to enhance efficiency of daily operations and by customers such as originators or recipients of goods to provide better services.

Shortly thereafter, George and Shrikant had the idea of calling the company GlobeRanger to bring out the dimensions of being global and being a "trusted agent" for location-based services. The founding team then went out and convinced well-connected individuals to take positions on the board or as senior advisors to the company. For example, Ambassador James Jones, former Chief of Staff to President Lyndon B. Johnson, Chairman of the House Budget Committee, US Ambassador to Mexico and President of the American Stock Exchange, was asked to serve as Chairman of the Board of Directors. The team then created a first business plan and raised an angel round of over a million dollars to get the company off the ground. In addition, the founders brought in the first employees with software, marketing and supply chain management expertise to round out the senior team.

In addition to George, Roy and Shrikant, five employees worked at GlobeRanger to prepare for the launch. Rather than hiring all vice presidents right from the outset, with one exception George focused on hiring employees who had five to ten years of operational and management experience. This decision substantially helped him to save on salaries and also kept the team highly agile in terms of unanimously executing decisions once they were made. In early 2000, the core team started out with three key priorities in mind: 1) to secure seed and eventually first-round VC funding, 2) to define the value proposition and segment the market space, and 3) to evolve the founders' ideas into a first product release. It marked the beginning of a long and eventful journey, which led to highly competitive services and solutions for customers in diverse industries and with a variety of individual requirements.

EVOLUTION OF GLOBERANGER CORPORATION

Once the founders had assembled a core team, they started to focus on their three key priorities. All of the earlier work now merged seamlessly into the efforts that started in January of 2000. George knew that he needed what he called "smart money"–a funding source that would be able to provide much more than just capital. In addition to getting funding, he was looking for investors who could not only add value to corporate strategy through their deep-rooted expertise and business savvy, but who could also contribute substantial contacts to potential customers and to highly attractive alliance partners. In order to get funded, George turned to premier venture capitalists (VCs). He needed to provide a bulletproof business plan that consisted of a detailed market analysis and demand curve, a novel and hard to imitate business model, and rock solid financials to show a strong ramp through the first five years. In addition, George had to have the first customers lined up who were willing to take a bet on GlobeRanger's new technology and ideas.

For the market analysis, John Sweitzer was brought in as the VP of Marketing. John had more than 30 years of strong telecommunication and marketing expertise when he joined the team. Like George, John had spent a good part of his career as a senior executive at Nortel and had actually assumed some of George's responsibilities when George left. The two had been working closely together for a number of years, and so it was natural for both to immediately snap into a highly productive working relationship. John's first step was to identify the benefits of the product for prospective customers and to talk to as many of them as possible. Within weeks, he had contacted virtually everyone he knew that was affiliated with transportation or asset management. In these early days a passerby visiting John's office would see huge piles of market segmentation reports and analysis books on his desk. It made it almost impossible to spot John amidst of all of his reading. More often than not, his studies lasted well into the night and turned up an incredible wealth of information on how to "attack" the market. The core team, assisting John in his marketing activities, took his findings to create collateral, presentation slides and amend their ever-growing business plan document.

In regard to the business model, it was the team of Rakesh Garg and Chris Hanebeck, both in their early thirties and eager to add a lasting success to their professional experience, who worked closely with George to devise the next iterations to the business model. The two complemented each other in an almost perfect way. Rakesh came straight from Netscape with a strong background in Internet technologies and software architecture, while Chris covered strategy, ERPs and supply chain management after eight years as a senior management consultant on three continents. In addition, both had startup experience and knew all too well how much blood, sweat and tears it would take for the team to build a business like GlobeRanger from ground up. Especially in the early days, the two frequently seemed to have their heads glued together and cherished their daily exercise of bouncing ideas back and forth until they became so intertwined that no one was able to make out a single originator. One of their main tasks lay in defining key features and functionality around the extended business model as it is shown in Figure 2. Rakesh concentrated on the technical aspects such as the general architecture, partner software integration and finding a highly skilled team of developers to implement the first release. Chris, on the other hand, built a first business case based on the architecture, and constantly worked on presentations that were to be given to investors.

All along, the founding team was closely involved in everything that went on. George, as the most experienced senior executive, naturally had taken on the role of President & CEO. Roy, equipped with the most positive outlook on life that one could possibly imagine, was ideally suited to work on strategic alliances and key partnerships. Shrikant, too soon, had to retreat from his active duty as chief technologist for personal reasons, but has stayed close to the company as a senior advisor.

Once the first iteration of business plan and presentations was completed, George started to look for an incubator that could provide seed funding and help him establish relationships to top VC firms. During his tenure at Nortel, George had been instrumental in establishing STARTech, a Richardson, Texas-based incubator specializing in early stage seed funding and startup support. Thus, his first priority was to visit Matt Blanton, the CEO of STARTech. After hearing about GlobeRanger's extended business model and after providing several key inputs that were accepted, Matt agreed to take GlobeRanger on and run due diligence for seed funding. Together with one of his key principals, Paul Nichols, who, at the time, was responsible for operations, Matt proved instrumental in guiding and coaching the GlobeRanger team forward. They immediately liked the extended business model (as shown in Figure 2) for its applicability to logistics and, specifically, supply chain management.

Chris, who had been brought in for his expertise in supply chain management, had devised several application areas for GlobeRanger's technology. He quickly realized that the simple tracking solutions that were on the market would not suffice to win large customers. Mainly, Shrikant's idea of integration between GlobeRanger and enterprise-level applications such as ERP systems resonated well with his knowledge of the market. This integration could also be extended into more production and material management related systems such as Supply Chain Planning (SCP), Supply Chain Execution (SCE) and Event Management (EM) systems. The central question revolved around whether GlobeRanger could close the information gap that existed for material flows between companies. Throughout the nineties, companies had consolidated information within their own operations and across departments with ERP software. In the late nineties and fostered by the proliferation of the Internet, supply chain applications between companies became more available. Yet, they only covered sending documents such as orders and confirmations back and forth. No one had yet tried to create a system that was based on real-time information about materials and goods as they moved from one place to another. The obvious problem many companies experienced was that an information "black hole" existed in the supply chain with respect to physical movements of goods.

Just-in-time manufacturers, for example, will always schedule their production to maximize efficiency and then set up delivery times for all input materials as they become needed during production runs. Rather than solving the true problem of knowing where these necessary materials are, they often set up contracts with stiff penalties for missing the promised delivery date. While this practice has proven to enforce discipline, it has not addressed the underlying problem of uncertainty inherent in the physical deliveries. More precisely, if the manufacturer knew where all of his expected shipments were and when they would arrive, he could schedule his production runs more efficiently. This, in turn, would create flexibility and provide the ability to react faster to events such as truck breakdowns, cargo theft or simply traffic jams.

Furthermore, there was hardly any historical information about the quality and sophistication of transportation service providers that could be used to evaluate and rank them. A second opportunity in regard to historical information was that it could be used for business process improvements. Yet, historical information has not been available to manufacturers willing to invest in programs such as process improvements. George had already decided to offer advanced data warehousing and mining capabilities in GlobeRanger's product and had brought in a small team of outside consultants specialized in this area. This decision, once again, turned out to be a very visionary one as prospective customers looking for supply chain management services now were able to base process improvements and transportation carrier evaluations on historical data rather than intuition.

Once these ideas crystallized, it became apparent that previous efforts to track assets and goods throughout the supply chain had neglected a major component of the value proposition. They all focused on the asset owner rather than the originator or recipient of the goods being shipped. The result– they only provided very limited information such as pointing out an asset on a map. The existing companies in this field did not even provide an estimated time of arrival, which is crucial to a recipient of goods who is not interested in knowing about the specific location of an asset. To GlobeRanger's founding team and first employees, backed by the senior team at STARTech, this realization provided enough confidence to go into the first meetings with VCs. Again, it was Matt and Paul from STARTech who proved to be invaluable sources of knowledge about the ins and outs within the VC community. They tirelessly worked with GlobeRanger to provide feedback for presentations and carve out how to communicate a clear and unique value proposition. As it turned out, GlobeRanger, in addressing not only asset owners and operators with their tracking solution, but also the originators and recipients of goods, had found a market that was previously untapped. The value proposition resulting out of these meetings is described in the following section.

CREATION OF THE VALUE PROPOSITION

As the evolution of GlobeRanger illustrates, the founding team continually refined and enhanced the business model. This proved to be a crucial success factor as the company matured and sought initial customers. Yet, before the team was ready to deploy an initial release of its asset tracking and supply chain management services, by now named eLocate™, a precise value proposition needed to be shaped so that it could be communicated to VCs and prospective customers. This section provides a detailed overview of the resulting value proposition.

Definition of Location

Whenever we talk about a location that we have visited and appreciated, we have explicit and rather precise mental images. The location of that little restaurant in Rome or of the Eiffel tower in Paris are burned into our memories forever and are intertwined into a variety of other emotions that we have experienced while being in those exact places. Yet, much less romantic, vector coordinates of latitude and longitude can also define these very same locations. In the technical environment of logistics this would be the preferred way to describe and communicate information about a location. Independent of how we see it, a main question is whether the information about location by itself contains value?

A simple and straightforward answer is "No". Information about location by itself does not and cannot contain value. Only when location is put into a relevant context, does it become valuable and can it be utilized for a variety of purposes. Knowing precisely where we are on a highway is of little value unless particular knowledge about a traffic jam two miles down the road is overlaid. Likewise, it is of little or no value to know someone else's location in relation to our own unless a specific circumstance arises. For example, the location of a delivery truck is only relevant to the production manager who is holding up the manufacturing line and making a decision on next production runs while waiting for a critical part. To summarize, information about the location of a person or an asset is of little value unless circumstances or other information enhance and enrich it. With the above said, location is defined as a unique geographical position. This naturally translates into a unique and identifiable location for every spot on our planet.

In regard to the above, a classification for location information is presented in Figure 3 below. It is based on a differentiation between data, information and knowledge as three levels of increasing value.

As Figure 3 shows, there are three levels in the creation of value in conjunction with location. First, location data in and of itself does not contain value other than serving as the foundation upon which the next two levels are built. Second, location information results from adding facts to location data such as a street address that will increases its value. Third, location knowledge results from overlaying other relevant information such as traffic and road conditions that can be utilized to evade an unpleasant circumstance such as a traffic jam.

To broaden the concept of location knowledge, we can now begin to define all the areas in which other, relevant information can be overlaid to increase the value of location information. As previously stated, any information or knowledge that brings location data into a meaningful context for its user can be integrated. Figure 4 illustrates this point by a simple example of utilizing the precise location of a mobile asset such as a truck to flexibly adjust its path from origin to destination by adjusting to varying conditions along the way.

Figure 3: Levels of location value (© GlobeRanger, 2000)

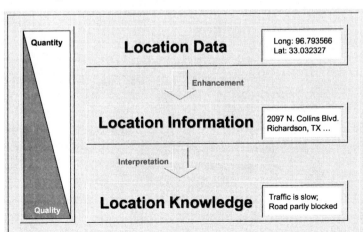

In Figure 4, basic tracking refers to the ability to identify and communicate the precise location of the mobile asset via GPS or triangulation in periodic time intervals. Seen in the light of our classification, basic tracking provides us with location data. On top of this, there are a multitude of combinations to generate and utilize other relevant information that lead to location information. In the above example, these are asset demand, asset status, geographical mapping, and automated regulatory and tax report generation. Geographical mapping relates to the ability to pinpoint and communicate the location of a mobile asset in natural language, such as a street address and an exact point on a geographical map. Based on available location data and information, location knowledge can now be created. The example in Figure 4 shows four possible combinations of destination address, traffic and road conditions, flexible rerouting and instant notification. In this example, destination addresses can be used to determine the distance between the truck and each of its drop-off locations. Based on these distances and their relationship to each other, software can then calculate the optimal route. Once we overlay actual traffic and road conditions, factors previously unavailable to us are taken into the equation to determine an optimum route. For example, there could be a slowdown or road closing along the way that would make it more efficient to change the order of destination addresses as the truck moves. The newly derived routing information is made available to the dispatcher who can then send an instant notification via text messaging to the truck operator. Of course, this process would repeat itself as often as

Figure 4: Example of location knowledge (© GlobeRanger, 2000)

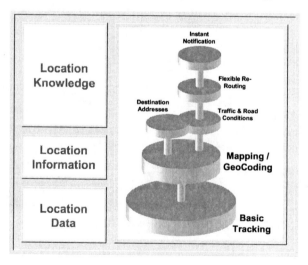

economically feasible and necessary. Moreover, because location information is known, such information can feed reporting systems such as
those required for regulatory reasons.

Leveraging Location for Intelligent Management

The above examples are very simple ones. There are, however, highly
interesting combinations of possibilities within the interface of location data
and Supply Chain Management (SCM). This holds especially true for the
latest developments of electronic exchanges enabled by the Internet. Most
prominent SCM software providers today are establishing electronic market
places that will enable the smooth and fluent integration of inter-company
business processes across the whole supply chain from producer of raw
materials all the way down to the retailer.

In terms of integration into logistics SCM software systems and
electronic exchanges, location information and location knowledge can
be applied and also be generated. As previously stated, location data needs
overlay information to be valuable. SCM software is one valuable source
and target for such overlay information. As a result, the relation between
SCM software and location information is two-fold: location information
creates value for SCM software and applications and at the same time,
SCM software provides overlay information that is extremely useful in the
creation of location knowledge. Figure 5 shows this relationship.

GlobeRanger's eLocate™ software interfaces with a variety of Internet-
based sources that can add value to location data. In addition, eLocate™
interoperates with SCM software to receive overlay information and transform it into location information and knowledge, which is fed back to the
SCM software. The very same relationship for eLocate™ and electronic
exchanges holds true. In the case below, overlay information could be detailed
scheduling or routing information, planned shipping dates and arrival times,
specific commitments to customers or simply generated bills of lading.
Internet-based real-time information services are flexibly deployable, as they
are needed. GlobeRanger's eLocate™ allows for maximum flexibility in the
sense that any service can be interfaced as long as it allows for access to its
data. If it is not directly available in real time, a cached source can be created
in the GlobeRanger database.

What becomes apparent in Figure 5 is that neither the originator nor
recipient of overlay information by itself can create the complex relationships
that arise from their integration. eLocate™ functions as a clearinghouse
between all parties involved so that efficient and effective aggregation and
retrieval of overlay information can be achieved.

Figure 5: Relation between SCM software and location information (© GlobeRanger, 2000)

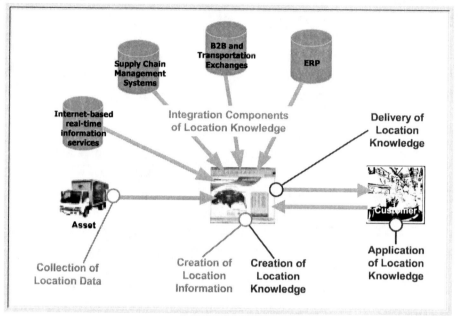

The following brief example, illustrated in Figures 6 and 7, will explain the interplay between overlay information and location knowledge in the case of a typical manufacturing process. Once a product such as a golf shirt is designed, it is offered to professional buyers who, in turn, take it to wholesalers or retailers for sale to consumers. These buyers will meet with their customers and receive orders that they pass on to the manufacturer. The manufacturer will already have established a Bill of Materials (BOM) based on the design of the golf shirt. The BOM specifies the quantities and qualities of fabric, thread and buttons that are needed for any given size of the shirt. Thus, as the manufacturer looks at the orders from buyers, it will be able to determine the materials needed based on the BOM to manufacture the golf shirts. Next, the manufacturer will start two parallel processes of Production Planning and Control (PPC) and Procurement. As Figure 6 below shows, both parallel processes have to be completed before the actual production can begin. It is intuitively apparent that the speed of procurement will determine the overall process from design to delivery. A closer look into procurement reveals that it consists of several steps, from a Request for Procurement (RFP) to a Purchase Requisition (PR) and finally a Purchase Order (PO) that is sent to the suppliers of materials needed to produce the golf shirt.

Figure 6: Location knowledge effects on inbound supply chain processes (© GlobeRanger, 2000)

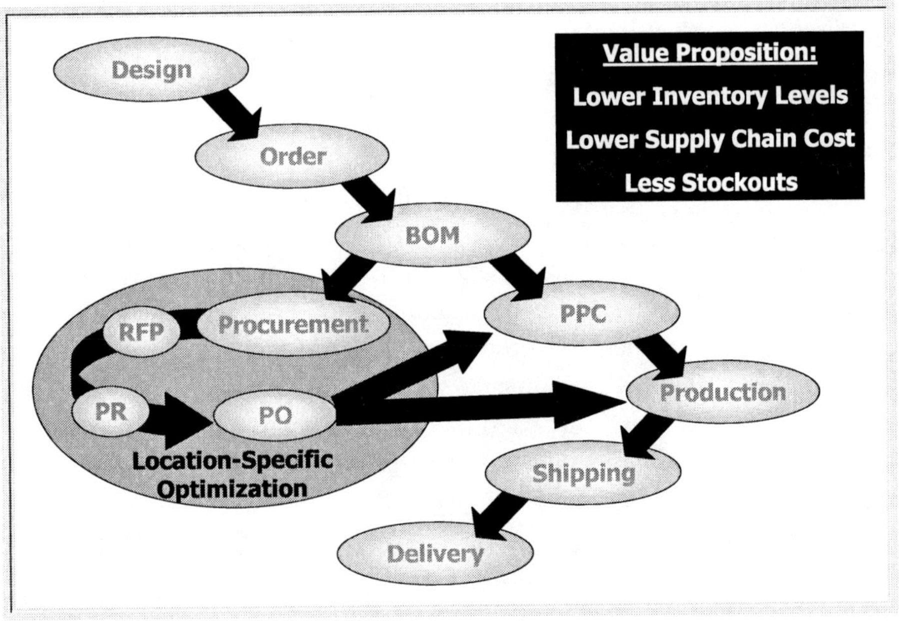

Location knowledge, as illustrated in the first section of this chapter, certainly has a strong impact on the efficiency of asset utilization by being able to transport goods along more effective routes, through less traffic and without delays typically caused by factors such as wait times or scheduling discrepancies. In addition, it is highly important to know the Estimated Time of Arrival (ETA) for all materials as the production process can only start when every needed part of the golf shirt is available on site. Knowing the ETA and integrating it into SCM software the shirt manufacturer uses will allow the SCM software to schedule and run production according to real-time information flows of how materials stream into the plant facility. This leads to lower inventory levels, an overall lower supply chain cost and less stockouts or prolonged manufacturing cycle times. There are also secondary saving effects such as cost savings from reduced warehouses, insurance, and personnel, as well as less rescheduling time due to accurate ETA information, and reduced capital expenditures.

In addition to cost and time savings on inbound material flows, location knowledge also leads to greatly enhanced efficiencies in outbound logistics as shown in Figure 7. The very same advantages that the golf shirt manufacturer captured during inbound logistics now become available to the manufacturer's customers during the outbound movement of goods. For the manufacturer, this leads to providing superior service to its customers, such as offering guaranteed deliveries, immediately notifying the customer when parameters change, or the ability to flexibly reschedule deliveries. It also leads to lower insurance premiums as the real-time tracking of assets and goods in transit will drastically reduce theft, especially when sensors for door opening, ignition or deviations from the scheduled route are deployed. Most important of all, the sharing of location knowledge between our manufacturer and its customers enables collaborative forecasting that, in turn, creates efficiencies on all ends.

Visibility into the movement and status of assets and goods throughout the supply chain brings savings of cost and time for all parties involved and, at the same time, raises the quality of the transportation process while enabling greater flexibility. The next section details these effects further by illustrating package tracking based on GPS and scanning technologies.

Visibility into the Supply Chain

As we had previously stated, knowledge of the whereabouts of a mobile asset such as a truck contains value in and of itself. It enables a scheduling and routing flexibility previously not possible. In addition,

Figure 7: Location knowledge effects on outbound supply chain processes (© GlobeRanger, 2000)

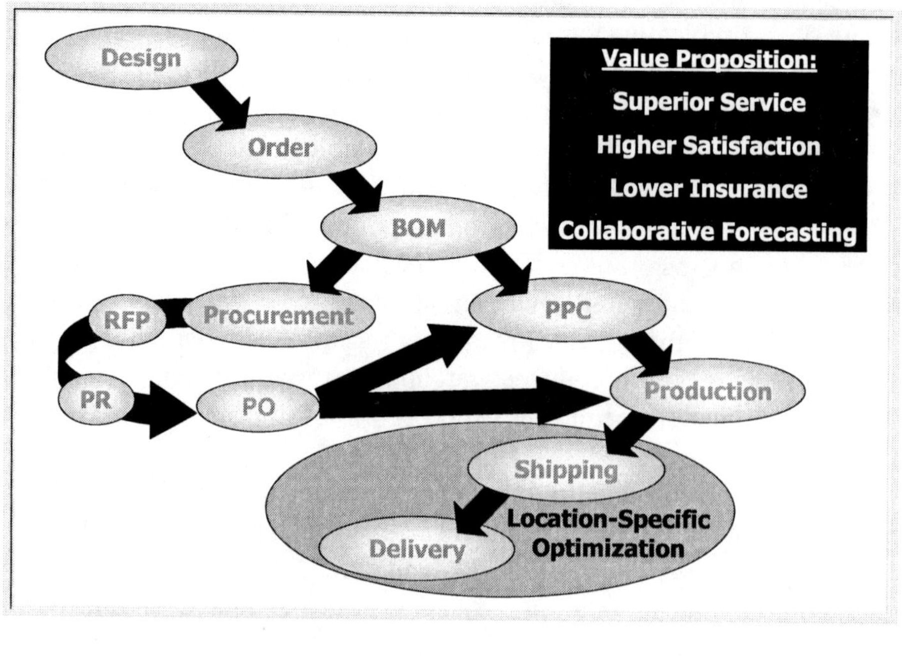

location information helps us overcome capacity bottlenecks, roadside emergencies, and even theft. Yet, there are limitations to tracking a mobile asset only. These limitations become apparent when we want to take into consideration that a truck, trailer or container is nothing more than a vessel that contains objects of interest such as materials or finished goods. A deeper look reveals that location information and knowledge are only relevant in the context of what is actually being shipped at any given point in time. Thus, the contents of a truck or trailer become overlay information just like traffic or road conditions.

Figure 8 illustrates a typical route from a west coast manufacturing facility to east coast retail locations. As packages are loaded into a truck at the manufacturers outbound warehouse in San Diego, they are scanned based on a bar code or using Radio Frequency Identification (RFID) tags. Should the manufacturer use RFID tags, a RFID reader would be installed within each of his trucks or in the staging area, eliminating the need to manually scan each package. The information about a trucks' content is then "married" to the truck identification number, which allows GlobeRanger's eLocate™ to instantly display both the asset location and content location. As the truck progresses towards the cross-dock in Dallas, users such as the manufacturer, freight agent and customer at the delivery location can immediately see where the goods are. Regular scheduled or unscheduled ad-hoc GPS readings can be taken by any authorized user of eLocate™ at any time. In addition, eLocate™ will provide the estimated arrival time (ETA) of the goods at the cross-dock

Figure 8: Example route for a package tracking application (© GlobeRanger, 2000)

and their delivery locations taking traffic and road conditions, as well as routing and scheduling information, into consideration.

Once the truck reaches the cross-dock, its contents are unloaded and scanned as they enter the cross-dock. This scan is necessary to ensure the complete arrival of all goods that were loaded onto the truck at its location of origin. It also provides GlobeRanger with the necessary information to "divorce" truck ID and contents in its eLocate™ database. The location of individual goods is now shown at the cross-dock in eLocate™ and may be entered into a Warehouse Management System (WMS). Usually, while at the cross-dock, whole truckloads and palettes of goods are disassembled according to their final destination and then put onto new palettes for their recipients. When they move out of the cross-dock, another scan is performed at the warehouse: the contents of a truck are "re-married" to another truck ID that can immediately be seen in GlobeRanger's eLocate™.

This second truck will now cover the remaining route between the cross-dock and the delivery locations. Just as on the first leg of the route, any authorized user can see the precise location of goods by simply requesting the location of the truck. As our truck delivers goods to the recipients, the truck operator will use a handheld scanner to report those goods that are "divorced" from the truck as they are unloaded. This information can be kept on the truck to be downloaded for later use or can be wirelessly transmitted into GlobeRanger's eLocate™ database in real-time. With RFID tags and a reader inside the truck, manual scans can be eliminated thus reducing the time and effort spent to deliver goods. Figure 9 shows the process and how GPS readings of the truck relate to content information about the goods onboard the truck.

The example process described above illustrates how a bill of lading can be applied as overlay information to enhance and interpret location data into relevant location information and knowledge. The way in which the necessary information is integrated into GlobeRanger's eLocate™ software is through application of devices that may use the wireless application protocol (WAP), Windows CE, JAVA, Palm OS or other platforms. These devices can be used for two-way text messaging communication with the driver as well as to send data such as package information to GlobeRanger's eLocate™.

Figure 10 shows how GlobeRanger's information technology components work together to enable seamless asset and package level tracking with integration of scanning or RFID technologies. A wireless device such as an enhanced Palm Pilot is used to scan package information. Once the device transmits data, it is received by a protocol server such as a WAP server for WAP devices, a Palm Server for Palm OS devices and so on. GlobeRanger's

Figure 9: Example process for GlobeRanger's package tracking solution (©
GlobeRanger, 2000

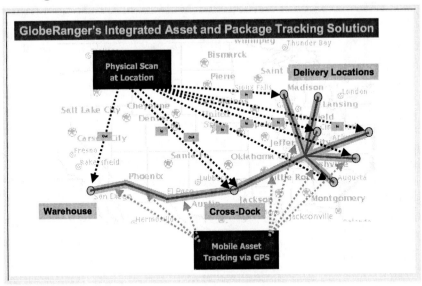

Figure 10: Package tracking integration in eLocate™ (© GlobeRanger,
2000)

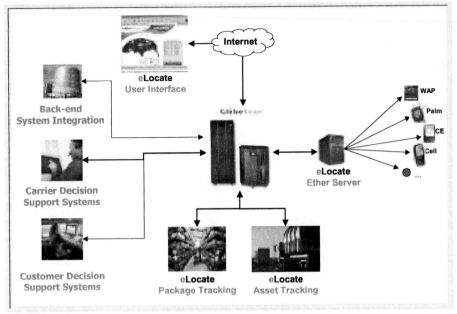

eLocate™ is fully device independent and, as such, can accommodate the device most suited for a specific requirement rather than a narrow choice of devices. The protocol server can be understood as a means of translating the data from a proprietary protocol language into one that Internet-based systems can understand. In this function, the protocol server sends the data to a Web Server, which in turn populates GlobeRanger's eLocate™ database. Once stored in eLocate™, package and mobile asset tracking knowledge is displayed through a standard Web browser so that users such as a dispatcher or materials manager and customers such as the recipient at the delivery location or the owner of the goods in transit can access it at any time. In addition, it might become necessary to intersect a separate package-tracking database. This could be the case when the warehouse and cross-dock scans are taken at each location and not via a handheld device. Should this be the case, a direct connection between these location scanners and a central package-tracking database is created. The database then feeds eLocate™ so that asset IDs and package tracking information can be flexibly "married" and "divorced" throughout the supply chain. GlobeRanger's eLocate™ database in Figure 10 also contains a link to decision support systems (DSS) that can be applied for later data mining and warehousing, as well as into back-end systems such as SCM software or Enterprise Resource Planning (ERP) systems.

Benefits Capture

The benefits of tracking packages are easily identifiable and range from enhanced customer satisfaction to security considerations and the ability to flexibly reschedule deliveries "on the fly." One of the biggest advantages stems from the difference between used and available capacity of mobile assets. Both freight operators and manufacturers can easily auction or sell available capacity of mobile assets if they have access to real-time availability data and an electronic exchange.

Location information and knowledge generated through a clearinghouse such as GlobeRanger will become a valuable addition to exchanges' offerings for their customers. One of the great potentials of asset and package tracking is the ability to learn from previous business processes by deriving improvements that can be implemented through a continuous process improvement cycle. It will, in effect, allow for optimization of a large part of Supply Chain Management features in real-time and with much more information than is available today.

MATURING OF GLOBERANGER CORPORATION

Once the detailed value proposition had been created, the GlobeRanger team was well prepared to present its ideas to the VC community. Paul Nichols and his team at STARTech set up a kick-off meeting to introduce GlobeRanger to several top notch VCs in their network–most notably to Centerpoint, Sevin Rosen Funds and HO2. During the presentation, George and his team showed the extended business model, market segments and supply chain applications. They also had a first demo of the product that the group of data warehousing experts had put together. Overall, the presentation was well received, yet only marked the beginning of the funding round. The VCs present at the kick-off meeting were very interested and grasped the novelty of GlobeRanger's value proposition immediately. Especially two of them, Terry Rock, the leading partner at Centerpoint Ventures and Victor Liu from Sevin Rosen Funds, took to GlobeRanger and agreed to schedule follow-up meetings. During the weeks and months that followed, George and his team worked relentlessly on preparing presentations, reworking assumptions and detailing the business plan so that it would meet the growth and market requirements set by the VCs.

For the complex task of establishing a detailed financial analysis and models, John Nugent, a professor at the University of Dallas and former President of several AT&T subsidiaries, was brought into the team as a consultant. John took on the role of acting CFO and chief financial strategist naturally and proved instrumental in steering through difficult financial terrain in all meetings extremely well. His lasting contribution to the company still remains, as he established the financial planning foundation throughout many meetings with George, John and Chris. Primarily, a five-year financial plan documented anticipated revenues over various customer segments and cost of goods sold, all the way down to depreciation and amortization. The company valuation was then tied into the financial plan and reached over the same period in time. From the outset, George and John Nugent strongly focused on a financial model that included a fast track to profitability and sound, yet defensive assumptions about the adoption of eLocate™ in the market. Both men knew all too well that the times when startup companies had to have large losses in their business plan were over. Once the senior team at GlobeRanger had bought off on the financial plan, each projected year-end result became an objective of financial performance for the years to follow.

It was not until three months later that George and his team finalized presentations to three leading VC firms in the Dallas area, as well as to Marsh McLennan Capital, the VC arm of Marsh Inc. in New York. During these last days of first-round funding, everyone at GlobeRanger had one single goal in mind–to conclude presentations and successfully close the first round of funding. Then, finally, came the day the whole team gathered in George's living room where George opened a bottle of champagne to share the news he had just received: four VCs, led by Centerpoint Ventures and Sevin Rosen Funds, had agreed to move ahead and several other parties willing to invest had to be deferred to a following round. Including the other participating investors–HO2 and MMC Capital–GlobeRanger raised $10.8 Million in its first round. This certainly was much better news than many on George's team could have hoped for, given that many technology startups were not being funded due to the drastic downturn of the NASDAQ and Internet-based companies during the first half of 2000. It marked the beginning of GlobeRanger's first strong phase of growth and provided enough financial stability to kick off the intense product and market launch in the months to follow.

One of the first initiatives after funding was to validate the extended business model as shown in Figure 2. With the help of Victor Liu, the well-known consulting firm McKinsey & Co. was hired and promptly set up a team of senior consultants at GlobeRanger's offices. Together with John and Chris, the consultants researched and tested all underlying assumptions of GlobeRanger's business model. Overall, they proved instrumental in detailing and communicating the market approach. As the discussion of GlobeRanger's value proposition had shown, the company differentiated itself early on by looking at supply chain solutions rather than simple track and trace applications. The strategy consultants set out to broaden the sales model into the two-staged approach of how GlobeRanger could identify possible sales targets, as shown in Figure 11.

As Figure 11 illustrates, GlobeRanger would go into a sales meeting with a two-staged approach. In the first stage, possible sales targets within the transportation industry are identified and can be chosen according to different criteria shown as two separate filters above. The main reasoning behind this first stage was that GlobeRanger obviously needed to deploy a hardware device on an asset or good. Thus, it made perfect sense to start out with the owners and/or operators of assets. During the second stage, the sales team would look beyond the transportation carrier and towards that carrier's customers. Here, a grid of four filter characteristics helps sales personnel to establish which carrier customers and industries to go after. The second stage

Figure 11: Strategic sales filters (© GlobeRanger, 2000)

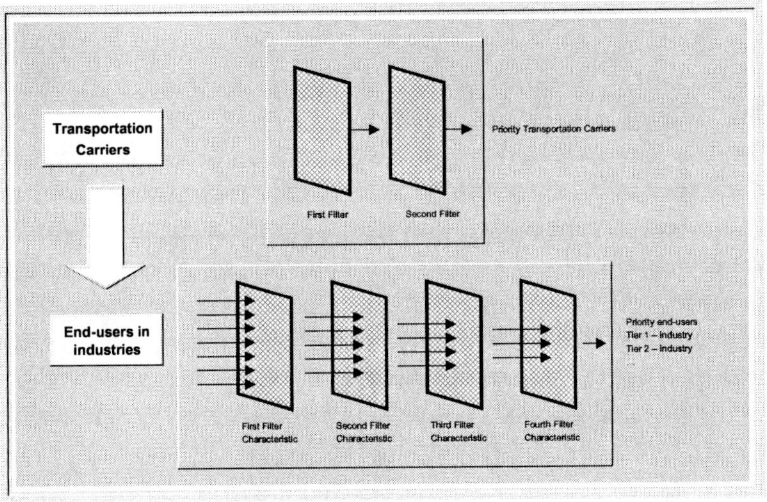

model is actually based on characteristics of the industry and of the goods being shipped.

While the strategic assessment went on, George was its most keen observer and prolific contributor. Yet, he also shifted his main focus to product development and to rounding out his executive team. It had been clear to him from the beginning that the development team needed much of his time, insight and experience. Together with Rakesh, he supervised many of the technology decisions and talked to most developers on a daily basis. During the months after first-round funding, the product grew from a software demo to a full-fledged first release for several different modes of transportation. One of the early adaptors had been a large US railroad company that used the eLocate™ service to monitor the utilization of its locomotives in real-time. In addition, several transportation companies became customers over time. With these customers, it became apparent that the strategic decision to custom-tailor solutions for each of them had been a very wise one. GlobeRanger was even able to replace an existing asset tracking system with the eLocate™ service, mainly due to its ability to listen and understand customers as opposed to merely arguing why a certain technology would be most beneficial for everybody in the market.

The hiring of executives took much more time since George wanted to ensure that each of them was not only highly qualified but also a good fit in terms of organizational culture. He knew well that his startup posed very different challenges from those his executives would face in any large corporation. In addition to high tolerance for ambiguity, all of his team members had to be very adaptive to the tight work environment where every member knew everyone else. In addition, executives had to do a lot of tasks for which they would normally have a support staff. To name just one trivial example, first class flights were and still are completely out of the question for everyone, including George himself. George felt it imperative that the leader "walk the talk," and serve as an example. George also fostered diversity right from the start. The first team at GlobeRanger was already comprised of members born on three different continents. He encouraged cultural ambiguity wherever he could and saw to it that people reached consent rather than obeying top-down decisions. Most of all, George knew that having fun can be a tremendous motivator and, equipped with a very intelligent sense of humor, certainly contributed more than his own fair share.

Another truly important issue for George was the clear definition of processes. Right from the outset, he had been very diligent about setting up structured lightweight business processes for GlobeRanger and has continued to foster this issue tirelessly. He had brought in Ramses Girgis, a widely known and acknowledged expert in performance and process management, as an outside trainer for the starting team, and continued to invite Ramses back at every major stepping stone. Every member of the senior team set out to define his or her own business processes, performance indicators and deliverables towards every other member of the team. This effectively proved to be of tremendous value since it structured activities and guided senior team members in their own actions, but in a manner such that all activities were integrated. At the same time, it depleted redundancy in processes and ensured that every activity was performed for a reason. To individual team members, having business processes meant that they were able to prioritize their tasks and tune their own work towards the overall goal and vision of the company.

As part of the process and performance training, George took a standard quadrant chart and organized it according to urgency and importance of a task, as shown in Figure 12 . He then explained that most people spend almost all of their time in the two Urgent quadrants, but hardly any time in the Not Urgent–Important quadrant. This very much reflects reactive behavior to things as they occur. Especially in a startup company, people tend to do fifty things in parallel, and they hardly ever have the time to sit down and reflect on what would make their work easier in the long run. Thus, everyone reacts to reality rather than actively shaping it. George went on to argue that truly successful managers would do the exact opposite. Most of their time is spent on preempting future work and requirements. Thus, everyone should be proactive and save time by anticipating future events, needs and requirements. This approach to management certainly was reflected in George's

Figure 12: George's time management chart based on the Covey Model

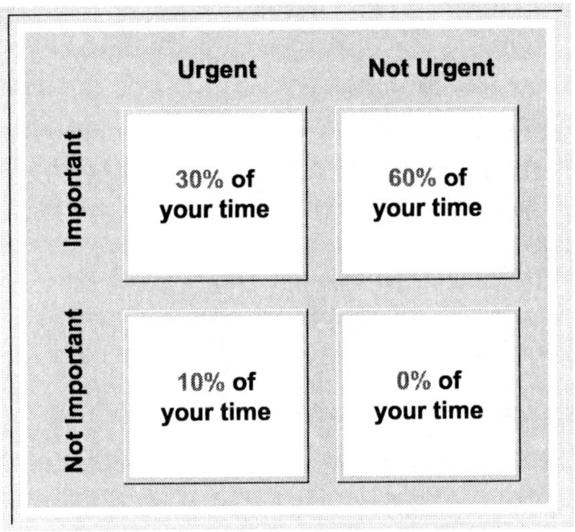

	Urgent	Not Urgent
Important	30% of your time	60% of your time
Not Important	10% of your time	0% of your time

insistence on structured processes, which he knew would help the company later on once the business grew more complex and less transparent than it had been when the team consisted of merely seven core members.

As a founder, Roy had naturally attended all funding meetings and was well informed of everything that went on within the company. Yet, he also aggressively drove his own responsibility of forming strategic alliances with a number of different companies forward. As the business model implied, there were a variety of different companies that would either supply goods and services to GlobeRanger or would foster the distribution of its eLocate™ service. Very early on, Roy drafted a priority list of possible alliance partners and put them into a priority order. He knew very well that some partners would automatically exclude others as they were competing in the same market space. Yet, his timing was crucial to keep new entrants out of GlobeRanger's market and to decrease the time to market for its service. Based on George's time management chart in Figure 12, Roy differentiated possible strategic alliance partners into three groups and then spent his time accordingly. The A-group of *not urgent*, yet *important* strategic alliance partners consisted of cellular network partners, device manufacturers and enterprise-level software vendors. Due to Roy's very early efforts and hard work, GlobeRanger today has a variety of marquee strategic alliances in place that cover some of the most prominent names in their respective industries.

Over time, a fourth type of partner entered Roy's A-group: insurance companies. Together with John Coghlin, a lawyer by training and Director at MMC Capital, Roy strove to utilize the ties that Marsh Inc. had in the insurance industry and to define the service offering that not only consisted of the value proposition described in this chapter, but also catered to insurance companies and underwriters. His reasoning was that the eLocate™ service would sell substantially better to GlobeRanger customers if he could offer clients a reduction in insurance premium. Roy's reasoning, of course, immediately made sense to the team at GlobeRanger. Yet, to insurers and underwriters there had to be tangible proof that GlobeRanger's eLocate™ would, in fact, reduce the number of claims due to theft and shrinkage. Together with Chris, he worked diligently on refining their pitch to the insurance industry, had numerous meetings with all sides involved in typical insurance transactions, and never rested to prove that his vision would eventually materialize. While his insurance-related effort certainly was one of the hardest tasks, it also seemed to motivate him the most in his daily work. Not a day went by in which Roy did not solve one issue or another to fully integrate insurance relevant features into eLocate™. In small and large steps at times, he continually strove to achieve his grand vision. GlobeRanger proved to be the first company in the asset and supply chain management market to truly integrate insurance companies into the definition of its location-based service.

As Figure 13 illustrates, GlobeRanger saw the development of its headcount increase more than six-fold during the second half of 2000. The executive team had been rounded out with seasoned executives from

Figure 13: Headcount development throughout 2000 (© GlobeRanger, 2000)

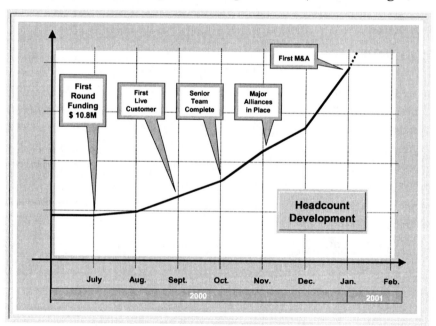

technology and transportation companies. In addition, several key directors had been hired for product development and management responsibilities. Both, the development and solution consulting teams had been fully staffed and everyone started to work tirelessly to achieve the vision of the three founders: to create a location-based asset management and supply chain visibility company.

Everyone had that sense of urgency that many large corporations lack– to build what had not been built in the decade since asset tracking first emerged. GlobeRanger's goal is now a reality, a fully integrated suite of services that allows customers to choose how they want their assets to be managed and that enable visibility throughout the supply chain.

CONCLUSION

The company GlobeRanger came to life when three individuals with different backgrounds and various ideas met. Each of the three founders had a unique perspective on business and technology. All three managed to bridge their diversity and strike a balance between vision and feasibility. They set out to create their own market and to change the rules of business in one area of supply chain management. Backed by the trust of their employees and investors, they are well on their way to succeed.

GlobeRanger's case is hardly the only one that has proven successful over a long run. It has not been the first such company and will certainly not be the last. It can, however, serve as an example in that some of the lessons learned are highly valuable. During the first year, the company saw its product architecture materialize, became familiar with its first set of supply chain applications, experienced its first round of VC funding and met its first real-life customers in a highly competitive marketplace. During that time, the core team learned several valuable lessons about how to build and grow a startup business. In summary, these nine lessons stand out as being extremely important:

- Establish the business model very early on, and keep improving on it.
- Assemble a team of very experienced and flexible people.
- Create a culture of continuous change, ambiguity and adoption.
- Provide strategic direction to the team continuously.
- Focus on "smart money" provided by VCs.
- Build lightweight and structured business processes early on.
- Complement technologists with strong management talent.
- Avoid politics, intrigues and infighting at all cost.
- Create and communicate a clear value proposition to customers.

In regard to the individual decision to join and augment the team of a startup company, it is true that some personalities get long better in situations of uncertainty and risk. Yet, there is hardly a typical startup personality. We have found that these companies are always comprised of people from many diverse backgrounds and with different ideas, dream, goals, and skillsets. One thing that all of them share is a unique enthusiasm for creating a new and better way of doing things. They are not afraid to venture far out of the ordinary, and they do not fear to believe in their dreams.

In summary, to be successful as a startup company, as Tom Hedrick, Senior Partner of the Dallas' McKinsey practice quoted one of his customers, all you have to do is:

"Think big, start smart and scale fast."

BUSINESS CASE DISCUSSION TOPICS

1) How important do you think a good management team and Board of Directors is in raising venture capital? Do you think GlobeRanger did a good job here?

2) How important do you think the founding members are in shaping the initial directions of the business? Did they have the right skill sets? Might this determine success or failure?

3) How important is it to recruit and retain a very experienced senior staff in a start-up? Do you think this was of particular importance to the VCs in making an investment decision in GlobeRanger?

4) Do you think it is very important to attract leading VC firms as investors, or is money just money? Do such leading firms contribute any other value? Expertise? Relationships? Access to customers?

5) Do you believe GlobeRanger made an appropriate decision to offer customized solutions, value propositions, to its clients by remaining technology agnostic? That is, by tailoring solutions to unique customer requirements by providing a service versus selling a hardware product.

6) Do you think GlobeRanger's vision regarding "technology refreshment" is important in today's marketplace?

7) With the information you have, how effectively do you believe GlobeRanger is in addressing the 4 Ps of Marketing (Product, Price, Promotion, Placement)?

8) Do you believe GlobeRanger is correct in offering its clients open interfaces to its solutions, accessible by the Internet, anywhere, anytime, versus closed, proprietary approaches taken by its competitors? How

important do you weigh this aspect relative to market demands and the enterprise's success?

9) Do you believe it is important, as GlobeRanger did, to reduce cycle times and time to market, as well as capital requirements and other costs by providing an integrated solution based on commercially available products? Is this similar to the U.S. Government's move to Commercial Off the Shelf (COTS) acquisition practices? What impact should such actions have on a start-up enterprise?

10) Did GlobeRanger appear to address Porter's Five Forces Model in its business case based on the information you have at hand?

11) How would you segment GlobeRanger's markets? Value of the goods? Perishable nature of the goods? Other segmentation or metrics?

12) Do you think GlobeRanger made the right decisions regarding its business case and direction concerning the imperfect nature of information available in a new market? What information would you like to have available in order to prepare a good business plan for a company in this market segment?

13) What skill sets do you think a founding team would be required to have in order to launch a successful company in GlobeRanger's market?

14) Do you think GlobeRanger is correct in its perception of the value of location information?

15) Do you agree with GlobeRanger that location "content" information is valued information? More so than geographic coordinates alone?

16) Would you integrate such technology solutions into your ERP systems if you had such a need? What do you foresee as potential downfalls of such a system? Do you see any additional benefits deriving from the deployment of such a GlobeRanger solution?

Chapter II

Implementation Management of an E-Commerce-Enabled Enterprise Information System: A Case Study at Texas Instruments

R. P. Sundarraj and Joseph Sarkis
Clark University, USA

This chapter presents a case study of an overview of the efforts of Texas Instrument's (TI's) internal and external ERP implementation, with a focus on linking its ERP system in a global e-commerce setting. This linkage is especially important since it had been stated in TI's strategic plan as an objective of this project to provide visibility of the ERP system to external constituents via Web linkages along with the objective of standardizing internal processes and important information technology systems to support market needs. Thus, its ERP system is central to managing its supply chain and B2B e-commerce linkages from both a customer and supplier perspective. Issues faced by TI are clearly outlined with future questions also posed in the final section.

INTRODUCTION

The integration of enterprise systems and the supply chain to an organization is becoming more critical in an ever-changing, globally competitive environment. As markets mature and customer preferences become more diverse and specific, quick response to those needs is required to maintain competitive advantage. This quick response will require close relationships, especially communications and information sharing among integrated internal functional groups, as well as the suppliers and customers of an organization. Texas Instruments (TI), headquartered in Dallas, Texas, is one organization that has come to realize this requirement for building and maintaining its competitive edge. One strategic decision made by the organization was to implement an enterprise resource planning (ERP) system with a focus on linking it with a global electronic commerce (e-commerce) setting.

This case study provides an overview of the efforts of TI's internal and external ERP implementation that led to over 70% of the transactions being conducted in a global e-commerce setting. TI's strategic goals include providing visibility of the ERP system to external constituents via Web linkages and standardizing internal processes and information technology to support market need. The e-commerce linkage is especially important in achieving these goals. Thus, TI's ERP system is central to managing its supply chain and Web e-commerce linkages from both a customer and supplier perspective.

In this situation there were a number of major players, including project management direction from Andersen Consulting Services, software vendors such as SAP and i2 Technologies, hardware vendors such as Sun Microsystems, and various suppliers and customers of TI. Part of the process involved outsourcing some of TI's internal information systems capabilities to these vendors, especially Andersen Consulting.

The various stages of implementation from adoption to preparation and operation are detailed as separate sections. At each stage of the implementation TI used performance metrics to manage the process. We also provide an overview of how these performance metrics played a role in the implementation.

STRATEGIC SYSTEMS IMPLEMENTATION BACKGROUND

Much research has been undertaken to develop a better understanding of IT implementation and to assess its contribution to improving organizational efficiency. A meta-analysis of IT implementation research (Lai &

Mahapatra, 1997) indicates that there is shift in emphasis from studying individual IT to organizational and inter-organizational systems. Since an ERP system has long-term and broad organizational implications, strategic planning is key to the successful management of such systems. There is an extensive body of literature related to strategic planning. Critical antecedents to developing a successful strategic plan are (Lederer & Salmela, 1996; Lederer & Sethi, 1992):
(1) external and internal environments,
(2) planning resources and processes, and
(3) an information plan that actually gets implemented.

These constructs provide a theory of strategic information systems planning and are important to both researchers and practitioners involved with planning.

By borrowing from the literature on the management of advanced manufacturing technologies (Meredith, 1987; Sarkis & Lin, 1994; Small & Yasin, 1997), a process-oriented framework for ERP management is presented (see Figure 1). As indicated in the figure, the process suggested by this framework is iterative, in the sense that it allows for higher level strategies and processes to be reformulated when they are discovered to be incompatible with lower level systems and configurations, and vice versa.

Figure 1. Timeline of TI's ERP implementation

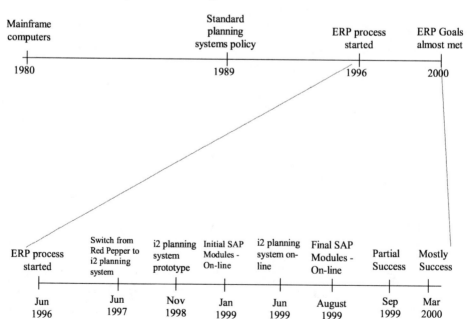

Strategy Formulation and Integration

Strategic justification frameworks should begin at the upper levels of management. The technology selected should fit within the vision, goals and strategic objectives of the organization. An organization should undergo a SWOT-MOSP process in which it assesses its Strengths and Weaknesses in the light of environmental Opportunities and Threats, then develops its Missions, Objectives, Strategies and Policies. One of the results of this step in the process is determination of an organization's core competencies that need specific technology support.

Process Planning and Systems Design

At the next level is the initiation of process plans that support the organizational competencies identified earlier and that in turn get supported by the chosen system (ERP or otherwise). Also known as the reengineering phase, three studies are usually undertaken at this stage, and they are named AS-IS, SHOULD-BE and TO-BE.

The AS-IS study provides baseline measures for later justification purposes and provides measures for post-implementation auditing. The SHOULD-BE study tries to exhibit how the current system should function after non-automation/non-hard technology improvements (e.g., total quality management) are instituted; a currently disordered system will lead to a disordered ERP system as well. The TO-BE study is used to define the system necessary to meet the objectives set forth by the strategic units.

System Evaluation and Justification

Here, analysis focuses on the economic, technical, and operational feasibility and justification of the system. The justification step should consider many different types of factors—tangible, intangible, financial, quantitative, and qualitative. Since the analysis of tangible factors (e.g., financial) is well-studied using methods such as Return on Investment (ROI), our focus will be on the evaluation of intangible factors.

System Configuration

An ERP system has some of the characteristics of packaged software such as Microsoft Excel and some of those of custom-built ones. It certainly is not designed and programmed for the exclusive use of one organization nor is its implementation and management as easy as that of packaged software. Each ERP software company is likely to have its own business model in the design of its package. As a packaged software system, there are likely to be discrepancies (at the detailed level) between the needs of an organization and the features of the software (Lucas, Walton & Ginzburg, 1988). Hence, a significant amount of effort can be expected to configure the system or the organizational processes in order to produce an alignment between them.

System Implementation

The implementation stage can be classified into: startup, project management and a migration handling the switchover from the old to the new system. ERP systems force large-scale overhaul of business processes and, therefore, their implementation needs to be supported by appropriate change management approaches (Markus and Benjamin, 1996). Another key concern of implementation is that of systems integration, in which multiple types of subsystems, platforms and interfaces must be integrated over diverse and dispersed geographic locations. Systems implementation involves:

- Acquisition and Procurement–Actual purchase of software, hardware and supporting equipment, and personnel.
- Operational Planning–The project plan necessary to bring up the system.
- Implementation and Installation–This is the actual implementation and startup step.
- Integration–Linking the systems to each other and other organizational systems.

Post-Implementation Audit

This last "feedback" stage, although very important from a continuous improvement perspective, is one of the more neglected steps. According to Gulliver (1987), for example, auditing should:

- encourage realistic preparation of investment proposals;
- help improve the evaluation of future projects as well as the performance of current projects that are not proceeding as planned;
- call attention to projects that should be discontinued.

As can be seen, the process suggested above can be arduous, but this necessary effort must be anticipated for the successful integration of complex and strategic systems into an organization.

IMPLEMENTING A GLOBAL ERP SYSTEM AT TI

Company Background

Texas Instruments Incorporated (TI) is a global semiconductor company and the world's leading designer and supplier of digital signal processing (DSP) solutions and analog technologies (semiconductors represent 84% of TI's revenue base). Headquartered in Dallas, Texas, the company's businesses also include materials and controls, educational and productivity solutions, and digital imaging. The company has manufacturing or sales operations in more than 25 countries and, in 1999, derived in excess of 67% of its revenues from sales to locations outside the United States. In the past few years, TI has sold several non-core businesses to focus on DSP solutions and analog technologies, where TI is the world leader. DSP and analog devices have more than 30,000 customers in commercial, industrial and consumer markets. TI faces intense technological and pricing competition in the markets in which it operates. TI's expectations are that the level of this competition will increase in the future from large, established semiconductor and related product companies, as well as from emerging companies serving niche markets. Prior to the implementation of ERP, TI had a complex suite of stand-alone nonintegrated marketing, sales, logistics and planning systems consisting of thousands of programs that were based on many independent databases and running on proprietary mainframe systems.

Overview

Since the 1980s, TI had used a highly centralized infrastructure utilizing proprietary mainframe computers for meeting its IT requirement. As the first step toward global business processes, certain planning processes and systems were standardized in 1989. However, the systems were independent of one another, and were, therefore, inadequate to meet changing customer demands. Market conditions dictated that TI must operate as a global DSP business, with greater flexibility, shorter lead times and increased productivity to meet customer demand. The company determined the need for dramatic changes in its technological infrastructure and its end-to-end business processes, in order to achieve these business goals. Starting in 1996, TI underwent a company-wide reengineering effort that led to the implementation of a four-year, $250 million ERP system using Sun Microsystems' hardware platform, SAP AG's ERP software, i2's advanced planning tools and Andersen Consulting's implementation process (see Figure 1 for a summarized timeline).

In 1998, Texas Instruments implemented the first release of the ERP system, which primarily consisted of a prototype implementation of the i2 system running on a Sun E10000 platform. This was the first step toward migrating the manufacturing and planning of TI's orders. In early 1999, TI began rolling out the second release. The initial deployment included the SAP Procurement and Materials Management module and the Financial Management and Reporting module. In the middle of 1999, TI completed the i2 Technologies software implementation as part of the third release. Finally, TI turned on the remaining financials, and new field sales, sales and distribution modules. Included in this release were the first Web-clients to be used with SAP and a next-generation, distributor-reseller management system, both developed in conjunction with SAP.

A high-level architecture of TI's pioneering ERP implementation consists of SAP, and the i2 system for advanced planning and optimization (see Figure 2). The system is a pioneering large-scale global single-instance implementation of seven modules (finance, procurement and materials management, logistics, planning, field sales, and marketing) for all of TI's divisions, and it is in use by 10,000 TI employees to handle 45,000 semiconductor devices and 120,000 orders per month. As shown in the figure, this solution also enabled global Web access to information for TI's 3,000 external users at customer's, distributor's, and supplier's sites. In total, over 70% of the business transactions conducted with TI by all customers and partners are now via the Web or electronic data interchange (EDI). In summary, the implementation:

- Institutes standardized process to support the market trend of order-anywhere/ship-anywhere services;
- Provides global visibility of the system to customers and suppliers, permitting them to conduct many activities via the Web

Figure 2: A conceptual model of ERP system, linkages

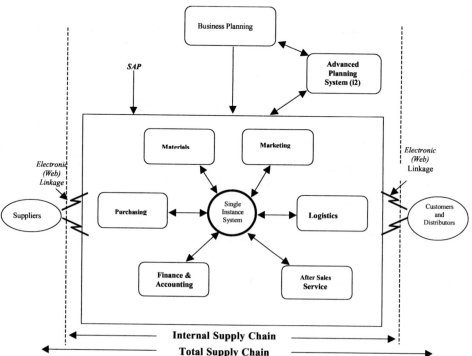

- Standardizes key information technology systems so as to support business goals.

The next two sections describe some of the activities involved in the substages of this large-scale implementation.

STAGES IN MANAGING THE GLOBAL ERP SYSTEM IMPLEMENTATION

We now describe TI's activities in each of the stages of the strategic framework that was generally described earlier in this case.

Strategy Formulation

Traditionally, TI was primarily running what was called a "commodity" business, wherein orders were received, manufactured and shipped as a batch. Throughout the 1980s and 90s markets evolved from the one-size-fits-all status to one in which customers started demanding customized products. This mass customization phenomenon, combined with the maturity of TI's business, caused it to reexamine its goals and strategies. TI started its shift towards a more customized product environment.

Within this new customized product environment, TI had a number of customer needs that could not be met easily. For example, a customer in Taiwan wanted to place all orders in California and then allocate a worldwide destination for the ordered products only at the time of shipping. This was difficult for TI to coordinate, because each of the regions was on a separate system. Other customers wanted to place orders for complete sets of devices that all worked together. Since its existing system could not handle such orders, TI had to enter the order for each device separately. The delivery of each of the devices was done at different times, implying that the customer will have to carry inventory while waiting for the remainder of the set. Manual workarounds and interventions were needed to handle these kinds of demands. Thus, the goal was to determine the appropriate processes and information systems that had to be put in place in order to support such agile design and manufacturing strategies (see, for example, Peters & Saidin, 2000, who describe the use of IT for supporting mass customization).

Another goal was a move toward supplier-managed inventory and customer-managed orders. Going beyond EDI and extending e-commerce meant that TI decided that leveraging the capabilities of the Internet to provide visibility of its systems to its customers and suppliers would be necessary. Finally, standardizing systems was another integrative corporate goal. TI's strategy was to ensure standardization of its systems as much as possible.

Specific areas such as factory automation were left to use custom solutions, but other areas such as planning were required to be on standardized open systems in order to support the other goals.

TI makes extensive use of metrics. Strategic goals are translated into tactical and operational quantifiable objectives. Key metrics are developed and used as a fact-based management approach that keep clarity in the project direction and manage the scope of the project. The metrics include standard operationally and organizationally strategic ones, such as Time, Cost, Flexibility and Quality. In addition, since TI's manufacturing equipment is very expensive, its management made it clear that it was also concerned with level of use—Utilization—of the organizational equipment.

Process Planning and Systems Design

TI conducted a massive reengineering effort for the whole organization with the goal of setting standard processes globally. The major result of this effort was to declare that all inventory and manufacturing management be done globally. This process change caused the practice of earmarking a production lot for specific customers to be discontinued. There were thousands of programs in use at that time, and this proliferation of stand-alone systems inhibited the implementation of global processes. Thus, a proposal to implement an ERP system was made to the president and other strategic business unit managers.

Many organizations find multiple-instance implementations more flexible and sometimes easier to implement. Yet TI decided to implement a single-instance ERP system so as to fully leverage the system's capabilities to support the flexibility and standardization demanded by global processes. After site visits by major ERP vendors, TI selected SAP, mostly because of its scalability to handle voluminous amounts of data. Yet, the actual selection and justification included the evaluation of a number of systems by TI. These systems were evaluated through a questionnaire that contained hundreds of detailed questions pertaining to capabilities, ranging from user friendliness to support of major functions. Many of these same questions were used in aiding in the system justification.

System Justification

A budget of approximately $250 million was set for the implementation. The justification of the system was done using a combination of tangible and intangible factors at both the enterprise and business-unit levels. Standard hard-justification measures such as ROI and IRR were used to ensure the financial viability of the project. In fact, if these were the only measures to be used, then the system would have been justified. Yet, the data for these measures were still forecasts and estimates. Strengthening the financial justification by evaluating other measures and factors helped to provide stronger foundation for managerial acceptance. In estimating financial measures, global capacity utilization as a result of the ERP system was also projected. The project managers kept in mind that such projections were only guidelines that could get offset or boosted as a result of other continuous-improvement activities that were ongoing in the company. These estimates ranged from 3-5% output improvements based on current assets, which although seemingly small, amounted to increased cost savings of several hundred million dollars. Some additional intangible and tangible factors included:

- TI's proprietary-mainframe-based ordering was incompatible with the goal of moving toward a Web-based e-commerce model.
- TI had thousands of programs that incurred huge maintenance costs such as integration among these software systems.
- Accurate global inventory was not possible without a "single-instance" ERP system.
- An ERP system would facilitate in cycle-time reduction, which would help TI compete effectively in the custom DSP market.

Through this business case justification, acceptable financial returns, along with strategic factors such as competing effectively within a given niche market, and operational factors, such as global inventory management, all played a role in ERP's justification at TI.

System Configuration

The goals and processes described above entailed a number of changes at the detailed level. Many of the changes are difficult to manage because of drastic changes needed to the ways of doing business (e.g., the business rules). The processes used to address the arising conflicts range from top-management-enabled dialogue among the participants to top-management-backed decisions that laid down the policy for TI. A few examples follow:

- All inventory is global. For example, inventory in Europe must ship, if needed, to any part of the globe, rather than be held for European orders that can potentially come at some time in the future.
- The number of levels of approval on a purchase order was standardized at four (there were some countries that had fifteen levels).
- Authorization amounts were standardized according to the level of the concerned person in the organization.
- An 18-character, globally accepted part number became an agreed upon standard. This standardization involved a huge IS and business effort because changes had to be made to the databases, programs supported by

them, and some manufacturing procedures, in addition to having to communicate the changes to the customers.

- All systems were mandated to be in English except for customer-specific information such as addresses, etc., used for external communication with them. In general, English was used when information was to be shared among multinational facilities, while local data, specific to a facility, could be in the local language.

Implementation

In this phase, concepts and goals are translated into tangible action, and as a result, it is perhaps one of most difficult phases of the project. General principles such as global processes and standard systems need to be backed up by convincing and deploying the right people to implement the processes.

We briefly describe TI's implementation phase in the following categories, startup, project management, and "going live". This description contains the manner by which problems were addressed in each category.

Startup. A number of key personnel, along with their families, were expatriated to the US and stationed in Dallas for a few years. About 250 people were transitioned from TI to Andersen Consulting (i.e., put on Andersen's payroll) which became the main provisioner of services with respect to the ERP system. IT outsourcing in this case involved Andersen Consulting taking over the employment and management of former TI people.

Project Management. Change management played a large role in this stage. The roles of training, planning, and communicating were of equal importance. All management levels were involved in this process, as were various vendors and suppliers. Some of the practices included:

- On-site experts were made available to new users of the system.
- A help desk was set up to handle problems that could not be addressed by these experts.
- A ticketing system for managing and prioritizing problems was also established (e.g., a system stop was a high-priority ticket that would get round-the-clock attention).

Handling Go-Live. To get prepared for "go-live", the key managers who were stationed in Dallas were sent back to their territories for educating the next level of users. Using selected experts, user-acceptance scripts were defined and tested, with problems, if any, being resolved as per one of the schemes outlined above. Daily conference calls were set up for thirty days prior to go-live to obtain status checks on progress and on the tickets.

Based on the results of these checks, a risk analysis was conducted weekly to determine the effects of various potential failures. The implementation plan was to have a few go-live dates one after another, but in relatively quick succession. Except for the planning system, in all the other stages, in this case a direct conversion was employed. That is, with a downtime of about two to three hours during a weekend, the old system was turned off and the new one turned on.

Post-Implementation Status

The system met most of its goals nine months after the complete implementation. Response time for the system has exceeded expectations, with 90 percent of the transactions worldwide getting a response within three seconds. There are around 13,000 users (10,000 TI + 3,000 outside) on the system, with concurrent users ranging from 300 to 1,700. The integrated system allowed TI to better manufacture and deliver its 120,000 orders per month involving 45,000 devices.

Some of the key performance measures and parameters evaluated were:

Productivity Dip. There was a period of reduced productivity. Given the voluminous changes involved, this was to be expected. TI expected this and discussed with Andersen methods to ameliorate this problem.

On-time Delivery. TI was not hitting its goal of on-time delivery. In addition to the new system, market conditions caused more orders than they could deliver. They were falling short of capacity.

Single-instance, global system. The single-instance, integrated, global model was successful, fundamentally transforming how business is conducted at TI.

Better response. Because of its Web capability, the system is used by TI's external constituents as well, namely, distributors, customers, suppliers, and field sales people worldwide. This Web capability allowed easier-to-use order management systems for customers. Customers no longer had to use TI-specific software applications and/or costly point-to-point connections.

Inventory reduction. Some TI factories reported output increases of 5-10%, and up to 15% reduction in work-in-process inventory.

MANAGERIAL IMPLICATIONS

This case study of a successful ERP/e-commerce implementation offers and reiterates a number of lessons for the management of these systems. The following lessons are summarized:

Conduct a Thorough Strategic Plan - The case illustrated how market forces had compelled the company to make radical shifts in its organizational environment and culture.

Align IT Plans with Business Plans - Conduct reengineering studies and develop strategic IT plans to align key IT needs with those of the business.

Get Top Management Support - The prescription of top management support has been made ever since early IT implementations (O'Toole & O'Toole, 1966) to the present. Strangely enough, as stated by Jarvenpaa and Ives (1991), it also remains to be one of the prescriptions that have been regularly ignored. In this case, TI's president and the Chairman of TI's Board communicated the importance and status in their quarterly satellite broadcasts to the company. The president sat in on quarterly meetings, and even stipulated that if anyone wished to "customize" aspects of the system that they would have to personally explain it to him and show why TI would get more profit out of this change.

Change Management - Set realistic user expectations such as the initial productivity dips. User involvement is critical. Andersen Consulting's process helped to ensure that such was the case. Make sure that the user is supported to help improve user satisfaction.

Strong Champion Characteristics - In TI's situation, the manager of the ERP project had over two decades of experience in various levels of the organization. This manager had broad knowledge of Corporate operations since he was in charge of the previous business process reengineering programs that formed the foundation of the new ERP system. Previously he was a vice president of one of TI's divisions.

Rationalize Business Models and Processes - Make sure the business models and processes fit within the strategic direction and goals of the organization. Time, mass customization, and flexibility concerns led to a global model. Part of this rationalization was also completed after the SAP system was agreed upon, since SAP required business processes to be completed as specified by them or significant customization of the system would be required.

Manage External Enterprises - Appropriate and well-planned involvement of consultants is important for keeping the project on a tight schedule. Further, with the advent of e-commerce, companies are more likely to ship and order goods on the basis of Web-based inputs (Kalakota & Whinston, 1996). A training program must encompass such constituents as well, an aspect that seems to be ignored in the research literature. Managing external enterprise relationships (and systems) is not something that many organizations have had experience completing. This makes the e-commerce setting more complex, especially when organizations seek to integrate inter-organizational systems.

Manage Using Metrics - TI and Andersen Consulting have a corporate culture and policy that requires the stringent and formal use of metrics in the management and evaluation of projects. They attribute this policy adherence as one of the key reasons for success of the ERP implementation.

CONCLUSION

Traditional information systems are often implemented with the goal of improving the internal productivity of an organization. In contrast, modern enterprise and inter-enterprise systems have supply chain integration as an additional and an increasingly critical goal. This makes their management and implementation a very time-consuming and difficult task. TI's ERP implementation with an e-commerce perspective compounded these inherent difficulties by requiring additional features.

- It is a single-instance system, providing access to the same data, irrespective of the geographic location of the user.
- It provides access to 3,000 external users (customers and suppliers), thereby enabling 70% of the transactions to be conducted electronically.

Management did see some problems in this implementation process and tried to address the issues. Some of the major problems included:

1. The software for supply chain management (Red Pepper) that was initially chosen did not meet expectations of TI. This system had to be scrapped; this resulted in a multimillion dollar cost. The i2 system was then implemented.
2. A productivity dip did occur. The implementation had to address this issue for all managers throughout the organization who had some stake in the performance of the system. The expectations that this would occur were communicated through newsletters and messages. Consistent and continuous communication helped to mitigate a situation that could have caused a major project failure.
3. Getting buy-in from internal functions not directly associated with the implementation process was difficult. This occurred with the marketing function. This function needed to be on board for the e-commerce linkage with customers to work effectively. Training and pressures from upper level management helped to ease the transition for the global marketing group.
4. Engineering is still not fully integrated into the ERP system. The e-commerce linkage incorporating product design with the ERP system was not feasible for management. For such a technology driven organization, the lack of engineering function integration with the ERP system may need to be investigated.

Key Questions to consider:
1. Can a large multinational organization implement a single instance global ERP system without the aid of an outside consultant? Could they manage this process even after implementation? Is outsourcing the IS function for ERP a good idea?
2. Which functions are critical within a global ERP system? Why would engineering not be considered a central function for E-commerce? Why should it be?
3. What metrics could be considered for system selection, system implementation, system auditing? Would these be the same metrics? Can e-commerce based metrics be used? What type of e-commerce based metrics may exist?
4. What lessons could be learned from TI's implementation process that could be used for future module integration? How much inter-organizational system integration is required for TI in the ERP/e-commerce system linkage?

REFERENCES

Gulliver, F. (1987). Post-project appraisals pay. *Harvard Business Review*, 65, 128-132.

Jarvenpaa, S. and Ives, B. (1991). Executive involvement in the management of information technology. *MIS Quarterly*, 205-224.

Kalakota, R. and Whinston, A. (1996). *Frontiers of Electronic Commerce*. Reading MA: Addison Wesley.

Lai V. and Mahapatra, R. (1997). Exploring the research in information technology implementation. *Information and Management*, 32, 187-201.

Lederer, A. and Salmela, H. (1996). Toward a theory of strategic information systems planning. *Journal of Strategic Information Systems*, 5, 237-253.

Lederer, A. and Sethi, V. (1992). Root causes of strategic information systems planning implementation problems. *Journal of Management Information Systems*, 9, 25-45.

Lucas, H., Walton, E. and Ginzberg, M. (1988). Implementing packaged software. *MIS Quarterly*, 537-549.

Markus, M. and Benjamin, R. (1996). Change agentry—The next frontier. *MIS Quarterly*, 385-407.

Meredith, J. (1987). Manufacturing factory automation projects. *Journal of Manufacturing Systems*, 6, 75-91.

O'Toole, R. and O'Toole, E. (1966). Top executive involvement in EDP function. *PMM and Co-management Controls*, June, 125-127.

Peters, L. and Saidin, H. (2000). IT and the mass customization of services: The challenge of implementation. *International Journal of Information Management*, 20, 103.

Sarkis, J. and Lin, L. (1994). A general IDEF0 model for the strategic implementation of CIM systems. *International Journal of Computer Integrated Manufacturing*, 7, 100-115.

Small, M. and Yasin, M. (1997). Developing a framework for the effective planning and implementation of advanced manufacturing technology. *International Journal of Operations and Production Management*, 17, 468-489.

Chapter III

A Three-Tiered Approach to Global E-Commerce: Experiences of Nu Skin International

David Paper
Utah State University, USA

Kenneth B. Tingey
Opennet Corporation, USA

Access to the world enabled by the Internet facilitates internationalization as never before. However, lack of a coherent global Internet strategy can relegate any company to a strictly provincial "neighborhood" status. Globalization strategies and tactics should therefore be of central concern to all enterprises. To research the strategic issues involved in Internet-based globalization, we embarked on a case study. Our goal is to explore how the Internet and its related technologies can serve to help organizations better deal with the challenges of conducting global business. Our research enabled us to identify a set of heuristic "rules of thumb" that might be used to support Internet-based globalization efforts. In our study we discuss the many challenges to establishing successful global enterprises. We then introduce a model for understanding global business requirements in the e-commerce age. We conclude by analyzing a case study to initially validate our theoretical model and summarize our findings.

INTRODUCTION

Many organizations look to the Internet as an instrument to support their global aspirations, to allow them to enter new markets, to extend their brands and offerings geographically, and to use increasingly pervasive Web access to enter global markets. The hope is that instant worldwide access to information via the Internet can serve as a global "calling card" in consumer and business-to-business environments alike. The current global climate of peace and openness appears to be conducive to global business. The Cold War is over. China is moving toward being an "open" trading partner with the world (Weeks, 2000). Moreover, access to the Web is relatively inexpensive as compared to the past.

The Web appears to be the new vehicle to global business exchange. It seems that Web merchants are satisfied if they can get credit card money verified in real-time while leaving other business processes to a complex maze of emails, sticky notes, and off-system paper trails. However, basic business principles should still apply in e-commerce. Successful global e-commerce requires more than a Web site and simple data interchange functionality. The way of the Web has been to slide through fulfillment requirements. Few Web-based tools provide much in the way of inventory control, for example. As a result, organizations face a continental divide between whatever systems they have used in the past and new Web-based technologies. ERP, the hoped-for "do all" and "be all" of the mid-1990s, didn't meet expectations (McNurlin, 2001)—the long-term implications of which are still to be determined in the marketplace.

The question confronting large-scale organizations around the world is how these two technological worlds–the Web and internal enterprise computer systems–can and should come together. The Web is of necessity directed outward at customers and markets and collaborative partners. Traditional enterprise systems, from ERP to older legacy systems, are by their very nature mostly inwardly directed, focusing on the need to coordinate employees and manage materials according to financial, tax, and operating imperatives.

Furthermore, immediate access to the world as enabled by the Internet forces the internationalization issue as never before. Lack of a coherent global Internet strategy can relegate any company to strictly provincial "neighborhood" status. In the face of such challenges, globalization strategies and tactics should be of central concern to all enterprises. We therefore embarked on a study to explore how the Internet and its related technologies can serve to help organizations better deal with the challenges of conducting global business. Moreover, we want to identify a set of heuristic "rules of thumb" that might be used to support Internet-based globalization efforts. We begin by discussing the challenges to global enterprises. We then introduce a model for understanding global business requirements in the e-commerce age. We continue by analyzing a case study to initially validate our theoretical model.

BACKGROUND

Agency and Delegation Challenges For Global, Networked Enterprises

Global business opportunities did not start with the Internet. Drucker (1973/1993) outlined a mature international business environment decades ago. He drew attention to important strategy and delegation issues that continue to elude executives and managers of international organizations. Drucker believes that global enterprises cannot be managed wholly at home or abroad because top executives do not have the requisite local knowledge to make all decisions and oversee all projects. Furthermore, locals tend to optimize solely on their national or regional operations, many times causing sub-optimization of the overall company effort. We believe that the answer lies in an enterprise approach. The question remains whether the Internet and its related technologies can serve to support the global organization as a holistic enterprise. We believe that the existence of the Internet provides an opportunity for organizations to greatly expand their business initiatives.

Global e-commerce introduces massive delegation problems and broad-scale agency challenges in spite of the open, friendly nature of the Internet. Success in international business requires that organizations groom their message to match preferences and characteristics of local audiences. As such, people (agents) with knowledge and experience in local markets and local customs must be enlisted in the cause, armed with knowledge of and commitment to the primary mission of the organization (Victor, 1992). However, success in foreign markets may be stymied by behavioral challenges such as pecking orders set up between managers at headquarters and those in local markets restricting effective cooperation, delegation, and integration.

The business model at headquarters tends to follow established patterns related to the country of origin and past experience. Hence, financial procedures, models, marketing, sales, and associated systems will naturally follow edicts dictated by the home office. Production, manufacturing, and sourcing procedures are typically established to meet specific requirements of the home market based on standard products and processes. Global organizations also attempt to establish norms and procedures for employment and outsourcing requirements based on known patterns.

To extend a traditional business model to world markets, home office agents and foreign agents must engage in a comprehensive study of the existing model to apply it to new and different environments (Victor, 1992). Delegation and the associated power given to agents must therefore be carefully balanced to match headquarter objectives to local ones.

Matching corporate strengths with global requirements, however, can prove unproductive due to a number of reasons. The sheer number of agents increases so dramatically that communication difficulties arise due to complexity alone (Collins, 2001; Sklar, 2001). Diversity is also greatly increased due to different cultures. Diversity opens such problems as collective action due to the difficulty of establishing consensus and cooperation.

Obstacles to collective action come from a tendency by agents to maximize local self-interest (Kiewiet & McCubbins, 1989). As such, agents often behave "in ways that are inimical to the interests of the community as a whole." Coordination may also suffer where "[agents] become uncertain as to which strategies other members will pursue, and coordination may never be achieved" (Kiewiet & McCubbins, 1989, pp.1-2). Traditionally, collective action is often achieved through manifestations of leadership on the part of managers (Drucker, 1998). Digital systems can remove communication barriers and assist agents at all levels if such systems are strategically deployed.

Three-Tiered Approach to Global Business Requirements

St. John and Young (1999) distinguish between two kinds of global companies. First, the "global enterprise" attempts to find economies of scale by placing standardized products into local markets. This reduces the need for delegation because decisions come mostly from a centralized authority. Agents are less likely to have high degrees of autonomy. Second, the "transnational firm" has dispersed specialized national units that provide differentiated market offerings through integrated worldwide operations. Delegation is widespread and agents are given high degrees of autonomy in their local markets. Consistent with Drucker (1973/1993), St. John and Young underscore a need for complex and flexible systems to support unpredictable requirements of global systems that must be responsive to local markets.

The "global" model is differentiated from the "transnational" model as delegation is considered from an entirely different perspective. With a global model, delegation is minimized. Local authorities are charged with deployment of the office model with little modification, coupled with a general understanding of the overall global system. Local agents follow home office directives with little room for discretionary decisions. In the transnational model, business and systems policies are highly delegated to local agents, as they are in the best position to understand diversity in language, currency, and customs. Thus, agents have a lot of discretionary power.

Walton (1995) discusses the value of the transnational model, that is, one that allows a "structurally fluid and ever-changing" paradigm to meet market demands.

Take the example of a high-technology company moving toward globalization. Initially, the challenge was stated as a financial goal: increasing nondomestic revenues. Despite a lot of attention and specific financial targets, progress was slow and inadequate. Executives concluded that the strategy could not be enacted with the current [global] organizational structure and that the company needed to move to a transnational organizational architecture ... empowering local managers was the implementation strategy ... the old structure was unaware of, or filtered out, the regional limitations it had placed on people and market development (Walton, 1995, p.125).

Even before the Internet, Castells argued in favor of a transnational model that he termed the "network enterprise."

Under this strategy [transnational] ... companies relate to a variety of domestic markets ... rather than controlling markets from the outside, they try to integrate their market shares and market information across borders ... in the old strategy, foreign direct investment is aimed at taking control ... Under the [transnational] strategy, investment is geared toward the construction of a set of relationships between companies in different institutional environments. Global competition is greatly helped by "on the spot information" from each market, so that designing strategy in a top-down approach will invite failure in a constantly changing environment and with highly diverse market dynamics (Castells, 1996, p. 165).

Information technology plays a major role in facilitating the transnational model, as it enables a flexible, adaptive model to actually work (Castells, 1996). "With adequate levels of [local] information and resources [organizations can] handle errors better than fragmented, decentralized networks, provided they use adaptability on top of flexibility" (Castells, 1996, p. 166). Castells argues that the organization must integrate the logic of the corporate system with the business process logic of the organization into a digital, networked format so that managers can obtain and use information to meet the unique needs of the organization in its various markets. However, there may be a "reverse effect" in terms of agency and delegation levels. Central agents may want to delegate powers to the local agents, but local agents may not elect to accept them. For delegation and agency to work, local agents must use their agency powers to generate desired objectives typically localization, market adjustments, and lateral cooperation (Nadler and Tushman, 1997). Nadler and Tushman also promote information technology as a means of accomplishing this objective.

> Rather than seeking designs that emphasize coordination and control, what organizations need now is speed, innovation, customer focus, and radically improved productivity... information technology ... makes it possible for companies to make timely information available ... no matter where [agents] are located. Not only does information technology demolish traditional constraints of time and geography; it enhances collaboration and teamwork, eliminates the need for entire levels of bureaucracy ... the innovative use of teams [allow] people to use their collective knowledge, judgment, skill, and creativity to perform a variety of jobs and functions, rather than just one, in concert with their colleagues (Nadler and Tushman, 1997, p 9).

Organizations must also take into account localization issues such as currency, taxes, culture, etc. (Sklar, 2001). By all rights, conditions will not be constant across-the-board (Cannella & Monroe, 1997). However, the transnational model provides delegation powers to make decisions at the local level and agents are given latitude in establishing and executing their own objectives. Delegation and agency powers give local managers the ability to interact more effectively with their customers especially if they are "natives" to the culture. Our theory focuses on the agency and delegation levels with networked enterprise systems because we believe that localization issues cannot be controlled from headquarters. Therefore, our model controls for these factors. However, financial standards, general company policy, and production techniques can be better controlled centrally.

Organizations may demonstrate elements of the global and transnational models depending on levels of delegation, flexibility, and adaptability. A more realistic scenario would account for some combination of the two—a hybrid model in which some system elements retain centralized features, while other factors are open to local interpretation and implementation. While organizations may prefer one of the three—global, transnational, or hybrid— we posit that they should be expected to exhibit features of all three. The effects of Internet technologies on variations of these models are of particular interest to organizations wishing to use the Internet to extend their missions worldwide.

The "global" model is characterized by limited agency with minimal delegation in which local agents are wholly responsive to home office mandates. Agents are given very little autonomy and are charged with carrying out orders. Decisions are made at the top and "trickle" down to the bottom. Agency initiative is not considered important. Agents in the "transnational" model are trusted to use their initiative to coordinate activities at the local level and make lateral connections as deemed appropriate (i.e., to be proactive). Cross-functional and cross-geographic interaction is encouraged. The home office realizes that complexity alone minimizes its ability to control the business at the local level and has come to feel comfortable with control mechanisms—largely embedded in the information architecture of the firm (Castells, 1996). Authority is granted to agents to make decisions that cannot be made effectively in a top-down paradigm. Delegation is maximized in transnational environments wherever possible.

The "hybrid" model is a compromise. Agents are recognized (by the home office) for special skills, perspectives or implementation ideas. Agents are given authority to make decisions within limited functional areas based on customs and localization factors. However, delegation between the home office and local organizations is limited to agreed-upon boundaries. Agent initiative is valued, but tempered by careful planning and analysis of each market and each business function by the home office.

Our model is not intended to be comprehensive. We are now focusing on agency and delegation because these factors emerged from our case study. Other factors that require future consideration may be compensation structures, corporate cultures, cultural factors in the home office and in locations

Figure 1: Three-tier networked enterprise model of global e-commerce

	Agency	**Delegation**
Global	Responsive	Minimized
Hybrid	Negotiated	Situational
Transnational	Proactive	Maximized

throughout the world where the organizations function (Cannella & Monroe, 1997; Zacharakis, 1997).

MAIN THRUST OF CHAPTER

Research Focus

To explore the nature of agency and delegation problems faced by global competitors where technology plays a major role, we embarked on a case study of Nu Skin International (NUS), a global direct sales leader. To collect data, we interviewed managers responsible for overseeing global implementation of Nu Skin's systems. We also corresponded with our contacts by telephone and email. We maintain current relationships with our contacts. Our theoretical model (Figure 1) helped provide a theoretical lens to frame the case. We looked at Nu Skin's global systems development strategy (given its relationship with the company's Internet and global systems strategy), the company's intensive use of ERP systems (SAP, in particular), its commitment to Internet technologies, and its continued dependence on legacy systems of various types. Case analysis provided valuable information to aid in understanding the requirements of global enterprise competitiveness in the era of the Internet.

Nu Skin

Nu Skin is committed to providing compelling business opportunities and superior products and services. It is a leader in the direct selling industry. For more than 15 years, it has extended its business model and products around the globe, identifying and capitalizing on important demographic and business trends. Nu Skin global sales are at nearly $900 million a year. It does business in 31 countries and has been an active global competitor for over a decade. The organization oversees the activities of over 500,000 independent distributors, who may choose at any time to participate in business opportunities in any region and country in the world through use of a fully integrated global structure that existed long before the Internet became a public phenomenon. Every month, the company calculates and remits bonuses and other rewards to its distributor force that entails tens of millions of dollars of disbursements in a country/currency mix that is based on rules, regulations, and incentive structures of tremendous complexity.

To manage such requirements, Nu Skin has brought together technological resources, people, and information systems on a global scale. As an early implementer of advanced computing tools, Nu Skin has been on the forefront in the use of distributed systems, global networking and communications technologies, large-scale, multilingual database implementation, integration of heterogeneous systems, and global ERP rollout.

Key Players

Top management support is strong and responsive to the management team charged with global Internet management. That is, Boyd Blake, Joel Erickson, and Shane Moss have responsibility for all projects in this area and report to top management periodically.

Boyd Blake is the ERP manager at Nu Skin. According to Mr. Blake, Nu Skin's recent attempts at making use of state-of-the-art technologies, including the Internet, to expand globally have provided the company with early-stage knowledge and experience as to the strengths and weaknesses of available technologies and models. In Nu Skin's move toward globalization and integration, careful attention has always been given to local business and technological issues, lending an interesting view as to how a successful global competitor addresses its various markets.

Boyd Blake manages the overall ERP, but Joel Erickson oversees new ERP and Internet development. One of Mr. Erickson's main concerns is to manage Nu Skin's global Internet presence. Therefore, he is very concerned about customer perception of its Internet sites around the world. When Nu Skin customers complain about navigation problems on the Web and other unsatisfactory process issues, Mr. Erickson is charged with reconciliation. He must keep the Web customers satisfied, in addition to his non-Internet ERP development duties. He must also keep abreast of foreign Web sites using English to make sure that they adhere to Nu Skin standards.

Shane Moss leads the financial integration team in Japan. Mr. Moss exhibits some patience with the home country language in finance because there is a language problem. For example, accounts payable is all in Japanese because many clerks do not speak English. However, final reporting must be in English because this is a requirement from headquarters in the U.S.

Issues, Controversies, and Problems

Nu Skin has high hopes with respect to its global Internet initiatives. The company plans to achieve a leadership role in what it has defined as "e-direct marketing" and "e-direct selling". With several country-specific sites on the Internet, Nu Skin plans a major effort to bring its off-line community to the Internet. As such, it hopes to provide instant access to its global tree of distributors, to achieve real-time information retrieval, and to seamlessly provide access to up-to-date inventory information around the world.

Such plans, however, do not revolve around a monolithic site—a global 'nuskin.com', if you will. Although such a site does and will continue to exist, the major global Internet effort will take place on a more loosely integrated country and regional site scenario. Although Nu Skin's e-direct plans are very ambitious technologically, it has no overt mandate for integrating diverse technology platforms around the world. As such, Nu Skin is faced with a tremendous technology integration and implementation challenge. However, the social aspects that come with such radical change may prove to be an even greater challenge.

Nu Skin has experience meeting individual local market needs while establishing a global presence. It also has a mature understanding of the capabilities and limitations of traditional ERP tools. Nevertheless, management realizes that they need to begin thinking "out of the box" because their global presence was brought together without considering the Internet's potential to integrate and streamline processes and social challenges that surface when working in a variety of different cultures. Nu Skin management is thus attempting to keep all of its options open until a specific solution set proves its merit in a given market. In this, the company's plans are similar to the "transnational" model. As we will see, however, the requirements of effective globalization do not allow for a single delegation style for the entire company because elements of a "global" model as well as elements of a "hybrid" environment exist within the overall corporate structure.

Many Internet users may perceive that a corporate Web site with language-based buttons for the non-English-inclined and perfunctory but functional links to back-end systems is all that is needed for successful implementation of e-commerce on a global scale. When a global enterprise like Nu Skin that already services hundreds of thousands of distributors establishes e-commerce strategies as Nu Skin has done, "e-anything" would seem to be an easy proposition at any level. The enterprise, after all, has an existing community and it already serves the function of a "portal", albeit largely offline. Nu Skin thus has a basis to command the kind of traffic that is the lifeblood of an all-encompassing e-commerce organization. However, successful global e-commerce requires much more than what initially may appear to be required.

Boyd Blake is the ERP manager at Nu Skin. According Mr. Blake, Nu Skin's recent attempts at making use of state-of-the-art technologies, including the Internet, to expand globally have provided the company with early-stage knowledge and experience as to the strengths and weaknesses of available technologies and models. In Nu Skin's move toward globalization and integration, careful attention has always been given to local issues, lending an interesting view as to how a successful global competitor addresses its various markets.

I think that there is a split that depends on your market size and the growth potential in a market. I think it is different for a small market than it is for a large market. Japan is our largest market. They are very autonomous. They tell us what to do and we try to give them a framework to work with. A lot of it is driven by our divisions, as well, and not all divisions are in all countries, so as a division goes in we are very new in this division model. We struggle with "does the division own this, or does the country own this?" But if you look at a small market, like a Guatemala, they look to corporate for direction, how do we do this, what would you like us to do, how do we need to do this so that we will be successful, so that we will take off? So it's a couple of different models [large and small]. Your mid-sized markets, probably [require] a little of both, but I don't think its a "one size fits all." Not all small markets shun corporate [however]. They'd like corporate to do everything for them because they don't have the resources, they don't have the talent and skills, etc. (Boyd Blake, personal communication, July 14, 2000)

The state of the art for Internet globalization is typically considered to be a one-tiered approach, that is, there are really no new business models in this "new" economic arena (Collins, 2001). The typical business model extends the home country site with some language and content localization (Sklar, 2001). Information portals have introduced a high degree of sophistication in a similar manner (Meyers, 1999). Nu Skin's experience, however, points to a much more stylized approach, depending mostly on the dynamics of markets in individual countries and regions such as market size, resources, and local expertise.

Heuristic Rules of Thumb

The first rule of thumb is that a multitiered environment can make use of e-commerce tools and technologies to improve its position in the global e-commerce arena. Not only does Nu Skin constitute an example of how companies in various industries, particularly consumer-related sectors, can globalize, but it provides a unique means of understanding relations between organizations that function on a global level and their intended audiences. In most cases, unsatisfied Internet visitors simply abandon sites when their global e-commerce experience is less than satisfactory. In Nu Skin's case, they complain to the company. Joel Erickson, says, " . . . when foreign Web sites come up in English, we hear about it very fast and work toward making our site(s) more efficient and effective" (personal communication, July 14, 2000).

The second rule of thumb is that language is critical in dealing with country-specific issues. Although Shane Moss indicates that there is some patience with home country language in finance, he remarks "we hear about it in the finance realm, but it is not as important, I don't think." He indicates that overall it becomes quite critical, even in underlying communications within the firm.

> Well, take accounts payable, for an example. That needs to be all in the Japanese language because they have many clerks that do not speak English. There's only a few that speak English, but a lot of the reporting that we provide to them comes out in English, mainly because it is required because we are a U.S., or a centralized U.S.-based company and we require that information in [English]. Most areas you are going to find are going to be in Japanese, but there are some areas where [it is not], but it is still important. It is very important to them that its in their language just as it would be for us if we were here and we had a foreign country coming in and telling us about English. (Shane Moss, personal communication, July 14, 2000)

The third rule of thumb is that market tiers are important strategically in a global networked environment. In Nu Skin's 31 markets, there is a great deal of variation, from large-scale market penetration in Japan (one of the largest consumer markets in the world) to participation in smaller markets in Latin America and throughout the world. The model utilized by Nu Skin in Japan and in parts of Asia, where language elements are more critical and the scale of operations is substantial, would correspond to a "transnational" structure. Latin American markets, as outlined by Nu Skin representatives, would follow a "global" strategy similar in some sense to a "cookie cutter" approach. Latin regions follow the edicts of the home office more closely than larger markets because they have substantially less resources and they lack the technical and marketing expertise that larger regions like Japan have in abundance. Resource availability is a critical factor in global Internet business (Garten, 2001). Interspersed are many mid-tier markets in which significant requirements for local investment and modification of business issues may not be necessary. This type points toward a hybrid strategy. We believe that market size is a critical factor influencing choice of model. Of course, we understand that Nu Skin is only one case that cannot be generalized until we gather data from other organizations (which we are in the process of doing).

The fourth rule of thumb is that offline business activities can be successfully converted to online if the capabilities and limitations of technology and the dynamics of the market are well understood. Nu Skin's experience is beneficial in large part because we believe that the company is working to achieve the reverse of most global Internet organizations. Nu Skin's goal is to bring its world to the Internet to accomplish a number of things electronically that the company has traditionally achieved offline. Many organizations wish to use the Internet to gain access to markets in which they do not now participate (Collins, 2001). Nu Skin's experience in converting an existing population of affiliates provides an interesting kind of feedback that should help all global Internet-based e-commerce hopefuls. Basically, its approach is to adapt to the scope and requirements of local markets while working toward technology integration with its affiliates in specific functional areas.

The fifth rule of thumb is that flexibility and adaptability are critical when integrating Web and ERP technologies into plans for global business deployment. Nu Skin was not able to translate its ERP system screens into several desired languages due to overstatements of an overzealous ERP vendor. Interestingly, this may have aided its efforts at internationalization and localization at its current stage in the development of its global infrastructure. Nu Skin bought its ERP system based on representations that the technology supported double-byte characters at that time, but during later implementation activity, it discovered that the vendor's beta-stage product did not meet Nu Skin's requirements. As a result, Nu Skin did not attempt to develop multi-language functionality within the ERP structure as the company had originally planned. Fortunately, company managers feel that they now have more flexibility and adaptability in terms of translation options than if they had begun full language integration within the original ERP structure. As stated by Mr. Blake and Mr. Erickson,

> **Blake**: . . . when we bought the [ERP] system in '96, we found out very quickly that it was not easy to do that [support double-byte characters], and in some cases, not possible at all to have different combinations of languages.
>
> **Erickson**: We had to make some choices as to which languages we wanted to combine. We were at the forefront of those issues and really helped push SAP into further development and evolution to where today, they have a much better solution and [the] answer to that is much better today.
>
> **Researcher**: So, at this point, in the process of extending, or of making choices to [implement] those three or four key languages, did you find that it helped to have had experiences in working with multiple languages or did it restrict you? In other words, did the [language] choices you made restrict you as you tried to expand to other languages?
>
> **Blake**: I think it would have restricted us if we had been successful in taking the system to other markets. But it wasn't a problem since we

didn't do much outside of the U.S. [using ERP] and then, when we finally did get approval to go do something in another language [Japanese] in Japan, the problems were that we didn't see anything else on the horizon past that point. So we took the path to do English and Japanese and now we can do almost anything we'd like (personal communication, July 14, 2000).

The sixth rule of thumb is that the Internet infrastructure should be integrated with head office data before connecting with other countries. In other words, it should be thoroughly tested with internal processes and systems before international deployment. With limited commitment to a fixed environment, Nu Skin is free to consider many options for Web-based, front-end integration worldwide. Nu Skin was also fortunate in that it developed its Internet infrastructure to integrate and process data very well within its U.S. headquarters before connecting its core business processes to other countries. Nu Skin had the advantage of streamlining and refining the Internet infrastructure before moving it global.

The seventh rule of thumb is that experience in global markets is critical to success when moving to a global Internet paradigm. Other than with respect to the monthly global bonus calculations and some material management functions that have always been managed centrally, offices outside the U.S. have operated more or less autonomously. By the time corporate management decided to expand its Web-based initiatives to support globalization objectives, Nu Skin was a seasoned competitor in many diverse markets. The company had already proven successful in deploying global strategies making use of various sized markets – small, medium, and large. Hence, Nu Skin developed proven business models that it was able to adapt in its efforts to incorporate the benefits of the Internet on a global scale. The major task of company executives and managers was to develop an overall globalization model that would fit the company's basic business model and that would allow the company to take advantage of the Internet phenomenon.

Analysis of the Three-Tiered Model

The three-tiered globalization model serves as a guideline for selecting desirable markets around the world for entry and for evaluating strategies and tactics for improving performance of ongoing initiatives. Requirements brought on by internationalization are as old as commerce, of course, but the Internet's existence does affect the costs and benefits of doing business in various countries by making information available more cheaply, more quickly, and with less effort than could be achieved in the past.

At the high end, it should come as no surprise that large markets require more attention and resources than smaller locales. In the Nu Skin case, such larger markets would include Japan and Taiwan. In the latter case, local management spearheaded a separate computer environment altogether in order to meet local needs. Also, a higher level of autonomy by local representatives is warranted because of the sheer size of the markets themselves, as it is difficult to maintain a "command and control" structure in large markets (Drucker, 1973/1993).

Nu Skin supports many "global" market tiers, such as Guatemala, which, as Mr. Blake indicated, are happy to get anything and everything from the home office that they can. In the case of Nu Skin, many markets would fit into the "hybrid" category, where there are varying levels of autonomy and delegation, including Australia, New Zealand, and several Asian and European markets.

Achieving a balance between local and home office controls may be easier now that the Internet and related technologies exist (making a transnational strategy more attainable) (Castells, 1996). However, dissemination of information by means of the Internet cannot compensate for lack of skill or judgment on the part of local managers or employees. Employees who are charged to make critical localized decisions and otherwise represent the organization to local authorities, employee populations, and market players are not automatically endowed with the requisite experience and skill just because the Internet is available to them. Furthermore, a transnational strategy is likely to be beyond the reach of an organization with an Internet presence, but no other physical resources or connections in the market in question (which size tends to provide).

Medium-tier, hybrid markets may be the most difficult of the three to manage. In the face of uncertain potential outcomes, such environments may have unique requirements that levy costs in line with major markets, but with population demographics or lack of size and robustness in related industries and markets that make equivalent investment less compelling, even questionable. In other words, medium-tier markets typically cannot attract resources in similar ways as large-tier markets. Fulfillment and localization activities are determining factors as to whether participation in this type of market is worthwhile to the organization. By the same token, penetration into smaller markets may be more feasible if the organization overall is able to achieve transnational-like characteristics that allow for lower costs overall as a result of intelligent collaboration by local agents in position to see opportunities for optimizing the resources of the firm within local and regional areas. This is a major objective of Nu Skin in its efforts to centralize back-end systems, where materials must be deployed on a large scale while the company follows a three-tiered strategy in its Internet-centric distributor interface to meet the demands and characteristics of local markets.

Lightweight products of high value, with limited trade restraints and high relative prices, are ideal for medium-tiered markets because their return on investment can be considerable. Such products are more conducive to Internet-based globalization than heavy, low margin items that face local restrictions, trade barriers, and competition. If language and other localization issues are not consequential, medium-sized market opportunities can be very compelling.

The Internet globalization challenge was brought out by Nu Skin management when the company, as a matter of strategy, decided to expand on its initial U. S. based Internet experience with an integrated, worldwide enterprise network. As is the case with all companies that trade in goods, Nu Skin must function with some kind of physical presence in every market in which it conducts business. The relationship with physical and virtual worlds is where globalization models based on the Internet alone become problematic. Tangible items do not benefit from blanket exemptions from trade, customs, communication restrictions, and even gravity that are enjoyed in the virtual, networked world. In large part due to these conclusive limitations, it remains to be seen whether the Internet can revolutionize and significantly modify goods-based markets that in some cases have existed for centuries and longer.

Medium-tier markets may be most conducive to hybrid globalization systems that borrow from both global and transnational systems structures. Moderate market opportunities with low-level localization and fulfillment requirements will likely provide the basis for many global Internet success stories. Meanwhile, a similar market and localization environment with minimal dependence on physical product fulfillment is in line with the "global" strategy as outlined in our model. The ideal "global" product, of course, is anything that can be converted to digital form—words, music, movies, and documents. Such products do not face the logistics problems associated with physical goods.

Solutions and Recommendations

The Nu Skin experience is that a broad category of physical, personal care products breaks down to the three tiers simply as a function of the markets themselves. The same product line in Guatemala takes on very different characteristics when taken to Taiwan or Japan or the countries of the European Union. Thus, regardless of other factors that make the decision to be involved in local markets valid, three market tiers as indications of Internet strategies on a country-by-country basis are useful criteria.

Treatises on Internet commerce seldom deal with inventory control issues or materials management systems, though these factors have a great deal of bearing on whether success is to be achieved when doing business around the world. In the case of Nu Skin, the requirements of global fulfillment, forecasting inventories, and other mainstays of business—not often emphasized in the glitzy world of the Internet—occupy a major part of its efforts. Globally, the firm clearly follows a transnational strategy in the area of materials management and fulfillment. As outlined by Blake,

> We've seen a need to centralize our forecasting and get sales information from a central source, so we use SAP to do local forecasting and we do that by taking feeds from all of our different systems, orders systems, [and] sales systems around the world to give us a rough inventory picture … and I say rough, because it's rough, it's not timely, it's not integrated, but [the system works] through interfaces. We bring that data in and project our forecasting through SAP.
>
> In doing that, we have also pushed out some SAP functionality to seven markets, mainly in Asia, because those are our biggest markets, but they have SAP access. They enter goods receipts when they receive shipments, and we are in the process of trying to even upgrade what they do a little more all in an effort to give us a better more timely picture of global inventory so we can forecast better.
>
> So we've been through some initiatives [where] we've dealt with rolling bits and pieces of [information accessible] to those seven markets. We also embarked, about two years ago, [on] a project for Japan after we failed to put SAP in Taiwan. We were looking for what we should do next and Japan needed a new finance system. There was some thought that we ought to upgrade their inventory and could use a warehouse management system, but with the volume that we do in Japan, it became very apparent that we should put the whole package there because of the tremendous ordering volume … and so the ordering piece at that time started to become separated and we started to look at SAP as more of a fulfillment vehicle. We embarked on a project to do part of the inventory management [with] the full suite of financials in Japan (Boyd Blake, personal communication, July 14, 2000).

Even now, the relationship between these two worlds—the Web and the front-end world (as seen by outsiders) along with ERP and operating require-ments behind the scenes necessary to make it come together right—is far from fixed. Apart from the marketing concepts and the promotional representations of these various technologies, the efforts of those charged with making them work are critical to sustained competitiveness. As stated by Nu Skin's Blake,

... Our new wave or next generation of systems is being driven by the Web and e-commerce. We would like everything to be available via the Web, especially our ordering piece and what the distributor sees. We would like to push our ordering out to the Web from the call center model. So you can see even a bigger break between our ordering system, our back-end fulfillment system, and our commission system [although this] is still the core functionality that we've had in the past... But we've seen a break away from using it as everything and you'll see more of a break as we take a Web e-commerce solution out worldwide, or at least we think we will take it worldwide. At least that's the plan now. The plan is to have it live in the U.S. towards the end of this year. Japan and Taiwan and a couple of other countries already have their own solutions, but the plan is to replace it with this, so we are very similar to where we were four years ago saying that SAP would be our ERP around the world. Now, we are saying [that] this fancy front-end e-commerce solution [is our Web strategy and] we are going to [it] take worldwide.

I think the two projects parallel each other and I think for some of the same reasons we didn't do SAP everywhere, I doubt [that] we will do this e-commerce solution everywhere. But that's kind of the picture of what we have around the world and how we got there (Boyd Blake, personal communication, July 14, 2000).

Back-end, front-end, market tiers and local requirements are the elements of a successful strategy, whether for local or global e-commerce efforts. Although organizations may carve out capabilities for their existing, local business efforts without much effort, they may find that extending these capabilities to a global sphere is an onerous task—even if underlying products and services are otherwise well suited to global requirements. Figure 2 depicts our theoretical model with revisions taken from Nu Skin's experiences with global electronic commerce.

Small-scale markets are more conducive to a "global" strategy because in these environments, corporate leaders can exert higher levels of control. Small markets have less resources and typically less expertise. They are also easier to control because the absolute number of employees, facilities, complexities, and technologies is much lower than large markets. In addition, IT capabilities do not have to be as sophisticated in a localized environment because the number of clients and processes is much reduced. In contrast, large-scale markets are almost impossible to control, making them much more conducive to "transnational" strategies. IT capabilities in transnational settings must be many times more sophisticated than required in "global" environments in order to be responsive to the various players. IT resources must exhibit higher levels of

Figure 2: Revised three-tier networked enterprise model of global e-commerce

	Agency	Delegation	Market Nature	IT Capabilities
Global	Responsive	Minimized	Small-scale	Localized
Hybrid	Negotiated	Situational	Mixed	Mixed
Transnational	Proactive	Maximized	Large-scale	Integrated

integration to allow corporate executives and managers to assimilate what is happening in the disparate markets being served. Integration within small markets is much less complex, of course. Medium-sized markets are also more difficult to manage—not unlike large industrial and consumer settings. In many cases, intermediate environments are not large enough to warrant investment on the scale of large markets, but they are still much more complex than small markets (making hybrid strategies very problematic).

The Nu Skin experience is that there are no easy fix, off-the-shelf solutions. Its efforts to make the Internet work in support of its other globalization imperatives are ongoing and are not conclusive. Rather than demonstrating characteristics of either "global" or "transnational" globalization models, Nu Skin exemplifies elements of both, along with "hybrid" combinations. Thus, due to the complexities of the markets served by the organization and the differing requirements and capabilities brought on by the Internet and other information technologies, Nu Skin is adapting to the Internet by assimilating various globalization models between the home office and different parts of the world. Nu Skin is experimenting with various tiers in the context of market size and IT configurations, not unlike our theoretical model.

FUTURE TRENDS

The requirements of operating on a global scale are multiplied in large part by capabilities and demands brought on by computerized networks—most notably the Internet. "Going global" requires that organizations master the art of localization. Globalization by commercial enterprises and other institutions is a critical delegation and agency problem. Authority must be delegated in order to enter the global marketplace, but not too much, and not in all areas. Use of digital, networked systems shows great promise in this vein, but there are significant limitations that make globalization and support of attendant systems-based delegation awkward and inefficient. One such limitation is the technology itself. For instance, Asian countries must use 'double-byte' files because of the numerous characters inherent in languages like Mandarin Chinese. This causes difficulties when transforming, storing, and translating information between languages.

Drucker and others outlined two delegation models. Typically, these models represent opposite ends of the spectrum. The "transnational" model tends to push decisions out to people in the various countries and markets in which business is conducted. Limited delegation (and limited customization to meet local differences) is represented by the "global" model, in which the home office structure is duplicated as widely as possible. Herein, we have identified a "hybrid" globalization option, where a balance is struck between transnational and global systems structures. As such, empowerment is encouraged for many operational activities while strategic issues, like company standards for excellence in customer service, adopts a global decision-making approach.

CONCLUSIONS

We have expanded our hybrid structure to outline a globalization model for organizations in the Internet age that incorporates the three-tiered market structure with delegation, agency, market nature, and IT capabilities factors. This model's primary purpose is to provide a vehicle to assist business decision makers and organizational theorists in overcoming the global "collective action" problem faced by organizations as they attempt to make use of the Internet and e-commerce technologies to penetrate markets on a global basis.

In the case of Nu Skin International, the process of sorting out local, home country, and global issues is a challenging task, managed in tune with market conditions and other factors on a case-by-case basis. As a result, the company exhibits features of all three models. In countries and regions where high growth has been achieved or is imminent, more latitude is granted to local managers and systems administrators—following a "transnational" mode. In certain cases, technology acquisition decisions have been altogether localized for improved efficiencies. A delegation strategy that requires proactive behavior on the part of local agents and high levels of interactivity in order to achieve transnational performance should not be a separate activity from the global mix of the overall organizational activities. That is, it should not be an island apart from the rest of the enterprise. Language requirements play an important role in the process, but logical imperatives play a part as well.

Central to Nu Skin's concerns is a need to function on a centralized, "global" basis for managing products and materials. The company tends to accomplish this task in a "transnational" manner, however it attempts to coordinate activities in a way that takes local and regional issues into account.

A further central management requirement of its business is to oversee compensation disbursements globally due to the integrated nature of its global distributor corps. Home office personnel manage this task exclusively—truly a function that follows the "global" systems model by not delegating at all.

Centralization at Nu Skin is tempered in many cases by a process of delegation that allows for differences in market conditions, management expertise, and strengths and weaknesses of technologies that are available to the firm and its subsidiaries around the world. Agents, depending on resources and expertise, are given autonomy in many activities as long as their actions do not sub-optimize central business objectives. The Internet is a powerful tool for the firm, but not a definitive answer to all of its systems problems. The Internet does facilitate communications, but it cannot "magically" make business processes more effective. Transforming offline processes to the Internet is a major challenge that will take Nu Skin many years to master. As one example, the simple function of verifying inventory at the point of sale is a challenging task when extended around the globe. Technology alone will not solve the problem. The Internet must become even more central to strategic plans. The three-tiered, market-based delegation and agency process—coupled with centralization of certain specific, worldwide tasks—is therefore a fundamental tool to enable Nu Skin to develop more cogent plans for Internet globalization.

Our next task is to further refine our theoretical model by exploring agency theory in more depth (with more cases) and revisiting our Nu Skin contacts. We have already sent drafts of this chapter to Nu Skin as they requested. In the future, we hope to be able to gather more relevant and timely data to test the model and assist Nu Skin management in its efforts to meet its global objectives.

REFERENCES

Cannella, A. A. and Monroe, M. J. (1997). Contrasting perspectives on strategic leaders: Toward a more realistic view of top managers. *Journal of Management*, 23(3), 213-238.

Castells, M. (1996). *The Information Age: Economy, Society, and Culture: Vol. I. The Rise of the Network Society*. Malden, MA: Blackwell.

Collins, P. (2001). Internet business executive conference. *Management Services*, 45(3), 6-11.

Drucker, P. F. (1973/1993). *Management: Tasks, Responsibilities, Practices*. New York: HarperBusiness.

Drucker, P. F. (1998). The next information revolution. *Forbes ASAP*, August, 1-3. Retrieved September 27, 2000 on the World Wide Web: http://www.forbes.com/asap/98/0824/046.htm/.

Garten, J. E. (2001). The Internet. *The Journal of Business Strategy*, 22(2), 6.

Kiewiet, D. R. and McCubbins, M. D. (1989). The spending power: Congress, the president, and appropriations. *National Science Foundation Grant SES 8421161*. Washington, DC: National Science Foundation.

McNurlin, B. (2001). Will users of ERP stay satisfied? *MIT Sloan Management Review*, 42(2), 13-14.

Meyers, J. (1999). Mission accomplished. *Telephony*, 237(5), 18-21.

Nadler, D. A. and Tushman, M. L. (1997). *Competing By Design: The Power of Organizational Architecture*. New York: Oxford University Press.

Sklar, D. (2001). Building trust in an Internet economy. *Strategic Finance*, 82(10), 22-25.

St. John, C. H. and Young, S. T. (1999). Coordinating manufacturing and marketing and internal firms. *Journal of World Business*, 34(2), 109-128.

Victor, D. A. (1992). *International Business Communication*. New York: HarperCollins Publishers, Inc.

Walton, A. E. (1995). Generative strategy: Crafting competitive advantage. In Nadler, D. A., Shaw, R. B. and Walton, A. E. (Eds.), *Discontinuous Change: Leading Organizational Transformation*. San Francisco: Jossey-Bass Publishers.

Weeks, A. M. (2000). PRC trade strong in first half. *The China Business Review*, 27(6), 34-35.

Zacharakis, A. L. (1997). Entrepreneurial entry into foreign markets: A transaction cost perspective. *Entrepreneurship: Theory & Practice*, 21(3), 23-40.

Chapter IV

E-Learning Business Models: Framework and Best Practice Examples

Sabine Seufert
University of St. Gallen, Switzerland

According to several forecasts given by Gartner Group or International Data Corporation, for example, e-learning as a new buzzword for Web-based education and its commercialization seems to be a growing market in the digital economy. This case study will analyze this new and dynamic e-learning market and the corresponding changes on the education market. A framework of the different education models that have already developed on the e-learning market will be introduced and their benefits and risks discussed. Several cases demonstrate the new e-learning models in action. Therefore, this contribution consists of several smaller cases that can be used for getting an overview of the e-learning market and for a discussion about e-learning as a promising e-commerce application on the Internet.

INTRODUCTION AND MOTIVATION

The globalization of education is increasing rapidly. Students attend courses from all over the world, employees work and study globally in multinational companies. Due to the interactivity and ubiquity of the Internet, learning is possible without space and time barriers. The students and instructors are connected through a digital medium, which replaces the physical, geographically delimited meeting space. Education around the world is becoming strongly networked, and we are beginning to see fundamental changes taking place in the organization of education. We no longer have geographical isolation at the college and university level. The long-term implications are a worldwide network and a real marketplace for university and college level education. This will expand naturally into vocational and adult training as well. Education might become a major export factor between countries (Seufert, 2000). The competition between universities is increasing more and more, and universities are under pressure to find "new strategies and business models" to produce and deliver educational products.

Similarly, company training is influenced by the dramatic changes. The business environment is going through a dramatic transformation due to the increased complexity and uncertainty of the radical changes in information technology, globalization, changing customer demands (and customer knowledge), increased expectations for social responsibility, and other changes that are placing new stresses on the organization and its people (Glotz, 1999). Multinational companies already train their employees via online learning networks globally. E-learning as a new buzzword for Web-based education and its commercialization (e.g., business strategies, technologies, applications, etc.) is a growing market. Companies are spending more than ever on training to respond to a growing need for new information and knowledge required to cope, manage, and drive the new-mega mergers, new business models, re-engineered and reinvented organizational forms, and other changes of the business environment. The rise of the cyberconsumer has shifted power from producers to consumers, radically altering the nature of industries. Training, especially connected with knowledge management strategies, is a central activity of the successful 21st century firms.

New e-learning strategies are needed to react to the changes in a competitive and global education market. This will fundamentally reshape the role of training and education and create enduring advantages for firms, universities and institutions that adopt the new learning paradigm. The purpose of this chapter will be (a) to introduce the changes in the education market and the new learning paradigm, (b) to explain e-learning as the convergence of several forces, (c) to outline a framework for e-learning business models for the implementation of the changes, and (d) to demonstrate and compare best practice examples for the different e-learning business models. Thus, this chapter encloses several smaller cases instead of one big case study.

E- LEARNING AND THE CHANGING EDUCATION MARKET

E-learning is a very broad term for internet-based learning in general. Technology-based education, online learning, e-learning – all of these terms are becoming synonymous with the latest approach to providing high quality educational offerings (Seufert et al., 2000). E-learning may be defined as internet-based learning where the student and instructor are not necessarily face-to-face. Interaction with the instructor and with other students may occur via videoconferencing or teleconferencing. When using computers, interaction may take place in asynchronous (email or bulletin board) sessions or synchronous (chat room) sessions. Still other technologies for distance education include the more traditional methods of closed circuit television or mailed videotapes. The intent of the instructor in these long distance environments should be to create a community of learners where students interact with each other and the instructor just as if they were together in reality. In summary, there are many avenues through which e-learning may take place. E-learning might be defined as net-based learning on the basis of electronic media including commercialization aspects (Bullinger, 2001).

E-learning has been established as a new "buzzword" created and pushed by marketing strategists and by educational institutions to boost the e-learning trend. The Internet has allowed colleges, corporate universities and for-profit businesses to begin offering degrees and executive education via the Web. In fact, this segment of the education market appears to be the fastest growing when compared to the traditional market. International Data Corporation estimates that the online corporate education market may total $11.4 billion by 2003, up from $234 million in 2000 (Schneider, 2000). John Chambers, president and CEO of Cisco systems promotes e-learning on the corporate Web site (www.cisco.com): "There are two fundamental equalizers in life: the Internet and education. E-learning eliminates the barriers of time and distance creating universal, learning-on-demand opportunities for people, companies and countries." E-learning is seen by many experts as the future "killer application" of the Internet. Peter Drucker said "Online continuing education is creating a new and distinct educational realm. There is a global market here that is potentially worth hundreds of billions of dollars."

Why do all forecasts agree on the dramatic growth of e-learning? Firstly, technology drivers, pedagogical advances and changing learning patterns, the demands of corporate training and the business aspect of e-learning as "window of opportunities" are causative factors. Secondly, the experience with the "dot.com revolution and later disillusion" shows that one should be careful to trust such forecasts. Perhaps they might only correspond to the pure wishful thinking of educational organizations and companies on the wave of a new hype – e-learning as the killer application of the Internet.

BUSINESS MODELS FOR E-LEARNING STRATEGIES

Convergence of the Educational Market

E-learning represents the convergence of many factors from different fields, for example technological drivers, changes in society, changing corporate training and the new learning paradigm in the context of lifelong learning which describes the shift from training to learning. Conversely, the growth of e-learning has an converging effect on the educational market (see Figure 1). The once almost visible line between corporate training and higher education is blurring. Distance education is causing this convergence. Kaeter (2000) suggests that this convergence is creating a common battlefield for colleges, corporate universities and for-profit education businesses. The development of corporate-college partnerships around online learning offerings is opening up new roles for academic institutions to play. Students benefit from being able to choose from among the best programs in the country (or world), instead of being limited by geography and time.

What are the challenges and strategies for universities and for companies? Who are becoming competitors in an converging education market? Who are the key players of e-learning? What are the new business models in this converging market?

First of all, the term "business model" has to be clarified. The literature about electronic commerce is not consistent with the usage of the term "business model." Timmers (1998) gives the following definition of what is meant by a business model:

Figure 1: E-learning convergence

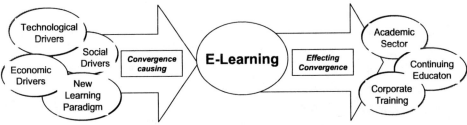

- An architecture for the product, service and information flows, including a description of the various business actors and their roles,
- A description of the potential benefits for the various business actors, and
- A description of the sources of revenues.

Based on this definition the different business models for e-learning will be introduced and explained in the following.

Framework of E-learning Business Models and Best Practice Examples

The educational market landscape has developed several models to produce and deliver educational products. Some have their roots in the academic sector, some in the business sector. But as noted in the previous section and as the following figure illustrates, the line between both sectors, academic education and corporate training, is blurring. As innovative e-learning business models, one may distinguish between "the Alma Mater Multimedialis" which describes a ''traditional university'' in the transformation process focusing on implementing the new learning paradigm and new ways of delivering education such as "Virtual Universities," "University Networks," "Corporate Universities," "Education Providers" and "Education Consortiums."

Figure 2: Educational market landscape

The E-Learning Universe

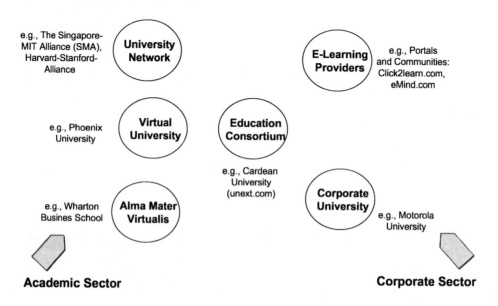

New entrant e-learning players have developed mostly by deconstructing the traditional educational value chain. With reference to e-commerce terminology, one may distinguish between three different categories:

- E2B = Education to Business (corporate e-learning): target groups are companies and their training institutions.
- E2E = Education to Education (university e-learning): target groups are universities, professors and other educational institutions.
- E2C = Education to Consumers (private e-learning): target groups are private consumers, students who learn with online courses and materials.

Alma Mater Multimedialis

"Traditional" universities, the classic "alma mater", might likely exist in two different forms in the future. First, only a few elite institutions–Centers of Excellence–will be concentrated on the global market specialized in a certain area. Education will be considered as customized learning provided by the best "masters" in a field. Second, the alma mater will survive offering a lower quality education confronted with global competition from the academic and corporate sector. The traditional university can develop into an "Alma Mater Multimedialis" by creating a learning and community platform for its students and developing a library of online courses (Palloff and Pratt, 1999). The term *Alma Mater Multimedialis (or Virtualis)* stands for a campus-based university that uses new media and communication technologies for teaching and research in innovative ways. Hybrid-concepts are used for teaching in the form of method mix and a combination of face-to-face seminars and self-conducted online course components ("dual mode institutions"). The benefit for the university lies in better study conditions and the improved personal contact of the students to their professors and tutors.

The business actors are mainly universities and private students which means that the "Alma Mater Multimedialis" represents a typical form of E2C business. E2B-business plays a role mostly in the field of executive education. Especially the elite institutions will offer and deliver executive education modules to companies and to other universities (E2E Business). The sources of revenue are mainly university fees and fees for courses and e-learning products. Five models are suggested as a framework for "traditional universities" to use to develop online courses and to act on the e-learning education market:

Classic Approach

The classic approach follows the traditional tuition reimbursement model in that students apply for a particular degree or set of course offerings, are admitted, and register for their courses. Students take courses from the college's standard curriculum, but take their courses at a distance. In this model, *at a distance* usually means that students are sent videotapes of faculty members' lectures in "live" classes or in an empty TV sound stage. Courses usually have a synchronous component, where students discuss topics in chat rooms, or critique papers and projects in a team setting. The benefit for the university in this model is that it develops a library of courses it can literally "pull off the shelf" for course delivery. Also, universities can bring in "guest lecturers" from academia or industry via videotape or live video feeds.

Cooperative Approach: Cooperation with Educational Providers

Educational portals, or use of a Web site to offer curriculum, gives students access to a variety of coursework offerings, regardless of the originating source (Kaeter, 2000). Oftentimes, a commercial education provider or broker (the third party) hosts the Web site and works with a number of universities to offer course work. The third party supplier benefits by being able to leverage its "off the shelf" courseware and technology to a number of corporate clients. Until recently, the courseware in this environment was minimally customized. Corporate clients and executive education seem to be the main focus of this delivery system. However, more than 200 universities, including Johns Hopkins and the University of Pennsylvania, have contracted with portal providers, such as HungryMinds.com or Ecollege.com (Kaeter, 2000). Ecollege.com offers a platform for courseware delivery and supports Internet-based education. Now educational institutions are crafting their own curricula and using companies like Ecollege.com as the portal provider. The business model of educational providers will be explained in section 3.2.5.

Tailored Training Approach

While the first two models proposed tend to involve large-scale libraries of online courseware, the tailored training approach allows the university to offer a curriculum that is focused to the needs of the corporate client. Certificate programs allow students to master a specific piece of information, and usually use that information at work the next day. Accountability and demonstrable achievement are important tenets of this model. Pat Postma, Assistant Dean of Degree and Nondegree Executive Education at the University of Tennessee's College of Business, stated that certificate degrees benefit both the student and the corporation. "Companies want more certificate programs because it shows that people have mastered something...Employees want it too because they can show competence on a resume" (Kaeter, 2000, p. 120). Duke University uses this approach, and rounds out its executive education program offerings by putting basic information (like reading a balance sheet) on the Web. Then students who need that resource can access it, others who don't can ignore it (Kaeter, 2000; Schneider, 2000).

For-Profit Approach: Education Providers
This model involves the university spinning off business ventures to pursue the market. In Bloomington, Indiana, a company named Wisdomtools.com was founded when the Indiana University's Center for Excellence in Education decided that its research had produced a viable commercial product for student interaction in a distance classroom (Kaeter, 2000). Duke has also spun off Duke Corporate Education, Inc. in order to run its custom executive education program (Schneider, 2000). Duke's plan is to repackage the materials it creates for executives into online courses and market courses to the general workforce. Babson College in Wellesley, Massachusetts will also create a company to put content on the Web that will support part-time M.B.A. students and corporate clients. As the market for online education grows, and it will by all accounts, more universities will consider for-profit options as a serious alternative. In the end, the business model is the same as education providers and will be analyzed in detail later in this chapter.

Cooperative Approach: University Approach
Traditional universities have the option to cooperate with other universities in developing course material and e-learning products. The benefits of this approach are sharing costs and reaching a critical mass of students for a specialized study program. This approach leads to the business model "University Networks" which will be explained later in this chapter.

In the U.S. more than two-thirds of universities offer online courses for their students (Wilbers, 2000). Some Web sites have already been established to function as "clearing houses". They catalogue available courses that are offered worldwide over the Internet. The World Lecture Hall (http://www.utexas.edu:80/world/lecture/), for example, lists several hundred online courses. Another Web site is Ed/x (http://www.ed-x.com) as a global resource for information about e-learning and online courses.

Wharton Business School of the University of Pennsylvania in Philadelphia (www.wharton.upenn.edu) serves as a best practice example. Wharton is one of the leading business schools worldwide and has initiated several Internet-projects to strengthen its leading position and to become the leader in technology for academic research (Aragon, 1997). Wharton IS manager Kendall Whitehouse built the desktop environment and intranet-based information service "Spike" for students (Aragon 1997). Spike isn't an acronym, and the name doesn't have any kind of hidden meaning. Students can download course materials and class notes, gain access to the university library and its electronic resources, bid for a seat in a Wharton course, send email, chat in Spike's Webcafe and explore the Internet and other areas on Wharton's intranet. Furthermore, Wharton developed the research database "knowledge@wharton" and the internet-based business data service "Wharton Research Data Services (WRDS)."

Table 1 compares potential benefits and pitfalls of this e-learning model "Alma Mater Multimedialis."

Table 1: Potential benefits and pitfalls of Alma Mater Multimedialis

Potential Benefits	*Potential Pitfalls/Risks*
For Universities	*For Universities*
- Enhancing potential customers: (non-regional) students studying from a distance, cooperations with companies and other educational organizations.	- Hybrid Solution: expensive, how to combine the virtual and the real world?
- Higher flexibility in organizing study programs.	- High risk of technological problems and access problems.
- Marketing aspects: innovative approach for universities, high competition in a global market	- Professors are not used to new media technologies, high investment at the beginning.
	- Quality system, evaluation measurement, more difficult in an online environment.
For Students	*For Students:*
- Increased communication: more channels to communicate with professors, tutors	- Less social contact, professors have more possibilities to escape and to delegate (to tutors, for example).
- Higher flexibility: if self-study components are integrated into the curriculum.	- Information overflow: students are lost in "hyperspaces"
- Learn skills needed to self-organize studies, how to learn with new media, better support for self-study, good preparation for life-long learning.	- Higher fees for the technological infrastructure.

Virtual Universities

The term "virtual university" is often not clearly defined (Porter, 1997) and is used for a wide range between "conventional" campus-based universities offering online courses ("hybrid" institutions) and virtual universities in a "pure" form in the sense that all their activities are delivered online via the Internet. A virtual university may be defined as an institution that is involved as a direct provider of learning opportunities to deliver its programs and courses and provide tuition support (Ryan et al., 2000). They belong to the academic sector, are often accredited, and core activities are the same as in conventional universities. The business actors are the universities and their students, privately employed people, who are mainly studying part-time (E2C-business). The benefit for the universities is that they can unite the whole program of conventional universities under one "virtual roof". Students benefit from virtual universities because they can learn anytime and anywhere in a very flexible way to guarantee their continuing professional education (Maehl, 2000). E-learning environments guarantee access to digital libraries and to student teams and tutors to support their learning processes. Sources of revenue are similar to traditional universities and are mainly university fees and tuition fees for online courses. Four models are suggested as a framework for "virtual universities" to use to act on the e-learning education market:

Model 1: "Pure" Virtual University

The virtual university exists instead of a conventional presence campus-based university. This is the model of a *pure virtual university*. All core activities are delivered online.

Model 2: Additional Virtual University

The traditional university has, in addition, a virtual university that offers online courses or course components within a curriculum program. This model is very similar to the Alma Mater Multimedialis model. The e-learning strategy is organized university-wide and the program is complementary to the conventional university.

Model 3: Cooperative Approach: Virtual University Networks

Several traditional campus-based universities are the founding partners of an additional virtual university. This model is a special type of university network that will be explained later.

Model 4: Cooperative Approach: Cooperation with Educational Providers and/or Consortiums

In this scenario, the virtual university cooperates with partners from the corporate sectors, e.g., with educational providers, or as a member of a consortium which will be analyzed in the following sections.

Virtual universities are already widespread in Great Britain where they have a long tradition. The Open University (UK) (http://www.open.ac.uk), was formed as one of the first Virtual Universities in 1989, offering a distance study programme to a group of students. The target group of the Open University is working adults seeking continuing professional education, mainly in the subject fields of business administration and information technology. It currently enrolls more than over 20,000 online students and is the largest educational institution in Great Britain. Students work with self-study material in a structured way and in small groups of three to four students who correct the weekly homework mutually before it is given to the instructors. High-quality study material is one of the leading goals the Open University tries to achieve and cooperates with companies like BBC and its TV studios. The personal support by online tutors is another crucial success factor that is facilitated by worldwide networks and residential schools. The development of modular e-learning components for mass production leads to flexible study programme structures.

In the meantime, almost all over the world virtual universities have been founded: for example, in Hong Kong, Singapore, Moscow, Australia, Colombia, Costa Rica, Finland, Israel, the Netherlands, Pakistan, South Africa, and Venezuela. They are especially important in countries with huge territories and difficult to reach regions because they make access to education easier.

University Networks

E-learning affects networking among universities in a global market. For long-lasting competitive advantages universities form university networks. The members of the network have access to a pool of e-learning products. Usually, the networks practice a hybrid-concept for teaching (Seufert and Seufert, 1999). Online learning environments are used in combination with face-to-face teaching. Courses and certificates are mostly compatible. The business actors are universities who offer their courses to other university members within the network (E2E business). The multimedia format of the products is usually not of the same high quality standard as in institutions from the corporate sector (e.g., corporate universities). Therefore, the fees of the online courses as the main source of revenue are much more affordable for the partners. The university networks also discovered the continuing professional education market, but they mainly offer their courses to small and medium-sized enterprises (E2B business) that can't afford the development of online courses on

Table 2: Potential Benefits and Pitfalls of Virtual Universities

Potential Benefits	Potential Pitfalls/Risks
For Universities: - Investment in technological infrastructure is cost-efficient (saves salary costs). - Focus on Virtual world: easier to implement and to organize university-wide, no resistance by professors. *For Students:* - Higher flexibility and individualized learning: The Online program is designed to benefit working adults: they can study at any time, anywhere, at his or her own speed. There are no semesters, so students can begin a course of study any month of the year. - Good preparation for life-long learning skills, students learn new media and communication competencies.	*For Universities:* - High investment for tutors and coaching to support students (necessary for a high quality program). - Danger: just putting books and course material online instead of using the internet as interactive medium for innovative teaching methods (Berge 1998). - Quality system, evaluation measurement, more difficult in an online environment. - "Brand" of virtual university degrees only vaguely clarified, some positive examples exist. *For Students:* - Less social contact, difficult environment for community building, students might miss not being able to study with permanent peers (difficult to develop friendships). - High motivation and self-discipline is necessary, might lead to a higher drop-out-rate.

their own. At present, the main focus of existing university networks is the development of specialized study programs such as an MBA program in electronic markets or media informatics. The benefits for the universities are sharing the development costs of online courses (economies of scale) and gaining a competitive advantage in a highly competitive market.

A few months ago, Harvard Business School and Stanford University founded a strategic alliance to strengthen their market position in the field of executive education. Another case is the SMA University Network (the Singapore MIT Alliance) (Web.mit.edu/SMA). The Singapore-MIT Alliance (SMA) was founded in 1998 and is an engineering education and research collaboration among the National University of Singapore (NUS), Nanyang Technological University (NTU), and the Massachusetts Institute of Technology (MIT). A primary goal of SMA is the creation of a Center of Excellence for graduate

Table 3: Potential Benefits and Pitfalls of University Networks

Potential Benefits	Potential Pitfalls/Risks
For Universities:	*For Universities:*
- Sharing the development costs of online courses (economies of scale).	- High investment at the beginning to establish the organization and infrastructure.
- Gaining a competitive advantage in a highly competitive market.	- Coordination costs and problems, overhead costs.
For Students:	- Technological problems, cultural communication problems.
- Easy access to a different culture: exchange programs, study with peers in a different culture.	*For Students:*
- Double degree programs are sometimes included.	- Coordination, technological and cultural communication problems.
- Learn new media and communication competencies.	

education and research in engineering, which features the most technologically advanced distance learning facilities available. The Center will provide opportunities for private-sector organizations to share in SMA's research, collaborate with its students, and recruit potential employees.

Corporate Universities

While the first corporate university was founded over 40 years ago with the launch of General Electric's Corporate University in 1955, the real surge of interest in launching a corporate university as a strategic umbrella for managing an organization's employee learning and development began in the late 1980s (Meister, 1998). Over the last ten years, the number of corporate universities has more than doubled from 400 to 1000.

Companies as well as their training departments can be considered business actors which might have–depending on their type of corporate universities–internal (all employees, work groups, top management) and external target groups (suppliers, customers). The sources of revenue are dependent on the type of corporate university as well. The benefit for the companies is the flexible and fast concept of e-learning. Conventional training is usually too procedural and fragmented to deal with the demands of fast knowledge turnover (Aubrey, 1999). Just-in-time learning and learning-on-demand are needs of corporate training. In the words of Douglas McKenna, General Manager, Executive and Management Development at Microsoft: "Learning is the most valuable benefit we can offer employees, and our ability as a company to learn faster and better than competitors is our most valuable competitive resource. The implications of this combination are quite staggering. When it comes to learning, what's good for employees is the same as what's good for the company".

In literature, many typologies of corporate universities have already been introduced. Based on the common frameworks developed by Aubrey (1999), Fresina (2000) and Deiser (1998), five models are suggested in the following:

Model 1: Training Department, Qualification Center
- Target group: all employees, internally focused,
- Strategic goal: reinforce and perpetuate (evolution),

Table 4: Potential Benefits and Pitfalls of Corporate Universities

Potential Benefits	Potential Pitfalls/Risks
For Corporate Universities:	For Corporate Universities:
- Development of online courses for many students in a multinational and global company (economies of scale).	- High investment at the beginning to establish the organization and the technological infrastructure.
- Quality of online courses are usually higher than university online courses.	- Corporate University = very often nothing else than a trainings department under a new label.
-Human Resource Development: innovative approaches, certification and degrees as incentives for employees.	- Difficult to connect with corporate strategy: implementation problems.
For Students	For Students:
- Higher flexibility and individualized learning, easy access, study any time, anywhere, at his or her own speed.	- Less social contact, less face-to-face seminars for informal idea exchange and come-together events.
- Certification and degrees as incentives to join a company.	- High self-organization on the job: environment is not a learning culture, employees are not able to organize their self-studies.
- Good preparation for life-long learning skills, students learn new media and communication competencies.	

- Business logic: incentives for professional education, certificates for the employees,
- Curriculum focus: technology development, service development,
- Knowledge aspect: general, fundamental knowledge and enterprise specific knowledge,
- E-learning aspect: learning anytime and anywhere, just-in-time, innovative learning methods.

Model 2: Top Management Lessons

- Target group: top management,
- Strategic goal: manage change (revolution),
- Business logic: incentives for the top management, cooperations with top business schools,
- Curriculum focus: people development, customized executive seminars at top business schools,
- Knowledge aspect: general and brand-new management knowhow,
- E-learning aspect: interactive discussion forums, face-to-face seminars, virtual cooperation partners and networks.

Model 3: Standardization Engine

- Target group: all employees, customers, suppliers,
- Strategic goal: reinforce and perpetuate (evolution).
- Business logic: Economies of scale, costs are reduced as more people are involved in the corporate university,
- Curriculum focus: technology development, service development,
- Knowledge aspect: transfer of work practices,
- E-learning aspect: development of mass products, interactive learning systems for a broad target group, standardized programs.

Model 4: Profit Center, Education Vendor

- Target group: all employees, customers, suppliers, other companies, consumers,
- Strategic goal: reinforce and perpetuate (evolution),
- Business logic: profit, revenues (e.g., corporate fees, fees for online courses, etc.),
- Curriculum focus: technology development, service development, enterprise specific knowledge
- Knowledge aspect: transfer of knowledge, content delivery
- E-learning aspect: killer application on the internet, mix of educational products, interactive and innovative learning forms, learning anytime

and anywhere, just-in-time, marketing of e-learning products (e.g., education portals).

Model 5: Learning Lab, Strategic Change Engine
- Target group: all employees, customers, suppliers,
- Strategic goal: drive and shape (vision),
- Business logic: sustained competitive advantage on the basis of a learning culture, strong relationship to knowledge management,
- Curriculum focus: not extremely focused, technology, service, people development, certificates are not relevant,
- Knowledge aspect: creation of new knowledge, initiate innovations,
- E-learning aspect: workout programs as knowledge exchange and creation places, direct communication, interactive learning processes.

As a well-known example, Motorola University represents a combination of a qualification center and a learning lab. Motorola University was established in 1981 and designed as a "center for strategic thinking and a major catalyst for change" (Aubrey, 1999). Therefore, the effort required the strong commitment from the top. At present, 130,000 employees and a huge number of customers and suppliers in five continents are users of the Motorola University. Motorola manages what it considers a strategic competency of the company—the learning strategy that includes customer satisfaction, manufacturing supervision, negotiation and communication. Teaching methods range from face-to-face classroom training led by professional instructors to original coursework developed by line managers to "learning on the job concepts" of shop-floor workers teaching their peers essential job skills. The media-based environment builds the Internet, CD-ROMs (as just-in-time lectures technology) and the Web-based training administration system (TAS). Despite the term "university", fundamental education is not the focus of Motorola University. One best practice example of the curriculum is Motorola's leadership development program—China Accelerated Management Program (CAMP)—where learning is always tied to a real business issue and includes case discussions and action-based exercises. Underlining the strategic importance of learning, Motorola University has its own board of trustees, which includes Christopher Galvin and the heads of the company's major businesses.

Education Providers

Commercial suppliers or education providers represent e-learning ventures mostly as new entrant e-learning players. As mentioned previously, e-learning has the potential to become the killer application of the Internet. Financial capital to launch new ventures comes from the corporate sector. Companies are investing in the e-learning market as it is a business field of dramatic growth. The business actors are the education providers; both companies and universities can take the role of suppliers or customers. The whole portfolio of e-learning business categories is represented in the following:

- *E2C-Business*: The target groups are students and adults interested in supplemented learning. For example, GEN.com (Global Education Network) is a content factory and service provider seeking to provide a strong core curriculum in liberal arts. The content is supplied by acclaimed professors but GEN provides the technology to video tape and disseminate courses.

- *E2E-Business*: Customers are universities and university professors as the example of WebCT.com (www.webct.com) demonstrates. WebCT's main area of business is providing Web packages that allow faculty to develop, deliver and administer Web-based courses.

- *E2B-Business*: E-learning ventures provide corporations with interactive Web-based training courses affiliated with universities (e.g., Quisic.com) or not affiliated with any universities (Emind.com).

Sources of revenue range from advertising, fees for courses, books, subscriptions to university fees and corporate fees. New entrant e-learning players have developed by deconstructing the traditional educational value chain as the following figure demonstrates.

Different Internet-based education business models which have emerged seeking to offer the benefits of the Internet and three basic models are suggested in the following.

Figure 3: Examples of new entrant e-learning players

Educational Value Chain

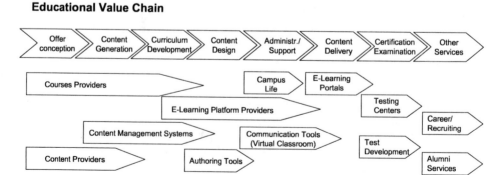

Table 5: Potential Benefits and Pitfalls of Education Providers

Potential Benefits	Potential Pitfalls/Risks
For Education Providers:	*For Education Providers:*
- New business models and cooperation forms with universities are promising, e. g., University delivers content, education provider specializes in media production.	- High competition and sources of revenue are limited, very dynamic market.
- Gaining a competitive advantage, a well-known "brand" in a highly competitive market.	- High investment in technological infra-structure is necessary for high quality products.
For Consumers:	*For Consumers:*
- New business models for Universities: easier access to high-quality material.	- Difficult decision process: who has the right material, high-quality products? Is "brand" the only decision instrument in a dynamic and intransparent market?
- Higher flexibility and individualized learning for their students, easy access to courses and material, study any time, anywhere, at his or her own speed.	- Integration in the "real" world: how to im-plement the online courses and material into the existing curriculum.
- Good preparation for life-long learning skills, students learn new media and communication competencies.	

Model 1: Integrator

Similar to a virtual university or an online business school, the educa-tional provider of this model develops and delivers every single process of the educational value chain from offer conception, to content and curriculum development, content design and delivery, to other customer services.

Model 2: Broker

An education broker collaborates together with other partners along the educational value chain. In this model, the value chain is deconstructed and the broker has the function of coordinating the different processes. Usually, this model represents a strong network of academic and corporate partners (Wilbers, 2000). Corporate universities, traditional universities, other education providers belong to the partners who can be both customers and suppliers. In this sense, the brokerage form of e-learning providers might be identical to education consortiums which is explained in the following section.

Model 3: Specializer

Some e-learning companies concentrate on a specific service within the educational value chain, e.g., authoring tool developers, e-learning platform providers or testing centers.

As a promising case, the e-learning site Quisic (www.Quisic.com) demonstrates a corporate content provider. Quisic is a content factory that provides education products mainly to corporations (not yet available to the individual). University professors help to develop the content and Quisic offers corporations tailored programs or pre-MBA programs. Quisic's strategy is to provide the best quality of on-line education. Quisic has won more than 50 awards for educational excellence. The site provides a full range of products from a library of books and articles to undergraduate, graduate and corporate courses. The sources of revenue are mainly university or corporate fees and institutional funding. In the education market for four years, Quisic continues to grow as it recently purchased IEC, a 17-year-old custom corporate training development company. Quisic is also planning to deliver courses with E-ducavia through a $ 96 million joint venture with Cisco, IBM and Telefonica. The partners plan to create an online business school for Spanish, Portuguese and Latin American markets.

International Education Consortium

The international education consortium is a group of companies who come together to pool their training resources and together offer these to working adults. Consortiums act as training brokers, acquiring content from traditional institutions of higher education or even corporate universities, and then offer this back to the open market in the form of an electronic education mall, with reference to Timmers' business models (1998). Brand information is common across many suppliers in the mall, which means that a well-known brand functions as a common umbrella. In this scenario, corporate universities as well as traditional universities become both customers and suppliers to the consortium.

The building of a consortium can be motivated differently. The following example is based on a concept that brings together companies with common interests to create an educational solution for an entire industry (Meister, 1998). The Global Wireless Education Consortium (GWEC) was formed in late 1996 by the founding partners Ericsson, AT&T Wireless Services, Lucent Technologies, AirTouch Communication, and Motorola, along with Mankato State University, South Central Technical College, and the University of Texas at

Table 6: Potential Benefits and Pitfalls of Consortiums

Potential Benefits	Potential Pitfalls/Risks
For Consortiums: - Sharing the development costs of online courses (economies of scale). - Gaining a competitive advantage in a highly competitive market: building a well-known "brand" based on strong partnerships with top business schools. - Quality of online courses are higher than conventional university online courses. *For Students* - Higher flexibility and individualized learning, easy access, study any time, anywhere, at his or her own speed. - Certification and degrees based on material from top business schools as incentives. - Good preparation for life-long learning skills, students learn new media and communication competencies.	*For Consortiums:* - High investment at the beginning to establish the organization and the technological infrastructure. - For high quality products cost-intensive online tutors and coaching programs are necessary. *For Students:* - Less social contacts, decreasing motivation in an online environment, higher self-discipline necessary, perhaps higher drop-out rate. - Is the "brand" really a good indicator for efficient learning and didactic appropriate settings?

Dallas. Each company in this network had been confronted with the same problem: a great deal of difficulties with recruiting and retention because of a huge and growing need for wireless technicians and engineers in an industry that is growing exponentially. Misty Baker, executive director of GWEC, stated: "This is a people problem and we can either sue each other, like the software industry is doing, or we can collaborate to solve the problem". The industry decided for a collaborative solution. GWEC represents an education model where corporations and academia come together as partners to solve a common problem. The consortium has been established as a means of effectively creating a pool of skilled wireless technicians. Additionally, the advantage of this collaboration is that the participating companies can share their costs for training development and high quality multimedia courseware.

Another case represents the international education consortium UNext.com (www.unext.com). UNext stands for the "Next Generation University" and was created to deliver world-class education. Whereas GWEC was initiated by companies to collaborate together and solve a common problem (internally focused), UNext offers e-learning products to the open market (externally focused). UNext was founded in 1997 and is 20 % owned by the company "Knowledge Universe" - a company which establishes and invests in companies delivering education services in all different areas (higher education, corporate training, consumer training, etc.). Under the brand name "Cardean" or "Cardean University" unext.com offers "next-generation" business courses online, mainly to companies in association with academic consortium members, leading top business schools such as London School of Economics, Stanford University, Columbia University, University of Chicago and Carnegie Mellon. Members of the academic advisory board are Nobel prize winners Arrow, Becker and Miller. The Internet is the basis

Figure 4: E-learning business models

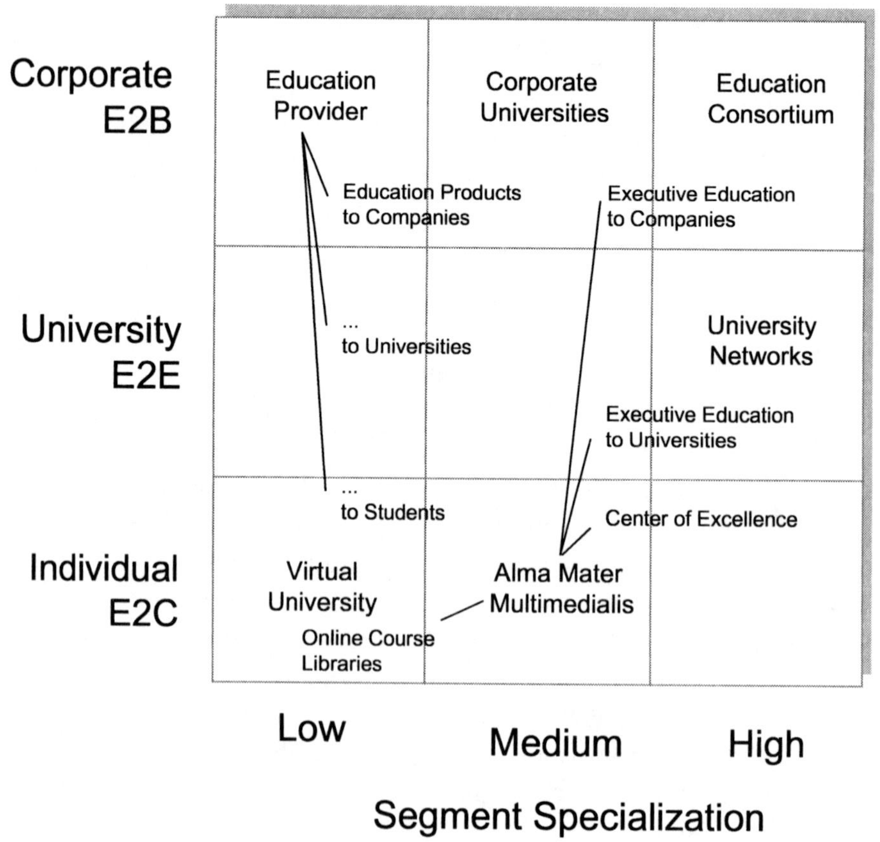

for the learning processes and the knowledge transfer. The learning environment allows a combination of self-study and interactive team work. Integrated feedback and performance control systems as well as the support of group work should help to provide a user- and student-centered learning environment.

CONCLUSION

The e-learning market is still small, but rapidly growing in all customer segments and geographies, if one trusts the forecasts. The current e-learning landscape is concentrated on the U.S. and the corporate segments, especially the IT training which is the largest subject segment in corporate training, where competition is already fierce but still fragmented (Brockhaus et al., 2000). "Content is king" has become a famous expression to demonstrate the growing importance of content creation as the largest supplier market segment. Customers are increasingly demanding customized training in a modular and flexible way. The impact of Internet needs greatly vary by segment. Key success factors are a well-known brand name that stands for quality, differentiated service offering, large direct sales force, and strong partnerships across the value chain.

Several e-learning business models coming from the academic and corporate sector have been introduced and could be grouped into E2B, E2E and E2C-strategies. The landscape of the education market is still changing, converging and the line between academic and corporate sector is blurring. By deconstructing the educational value chain, new key players have entrance to the education market. Figure 4 compares the different e-learning business models by analyzing in which field it is positioned (E2B, E2E, E2C) and the intensity of specialization and concentration on certain content subject segments.

Increasing global competition, rapid technological advances, demographic changes, and the emergence of a service- and knowledge-based economy, force organizations to train and retrain their workforces in new ways. Companies that deploy and effectively utilize e-learning will have a distinct competitive advantage. The Internet presents companies with numerous possibilities for leveraging knowledge and education resources. It redefines e-learning in terms of current, dynamic educational content, individualized and personalized, relevant learning experiences, and more collaboration with globally dispersed experts and peers (Schreiber, 1998).

However, shortcomings of e-learning exist as well. Human interaction is a critical component for learning. There are situations in which classroom training cannot be replaced. Certain content because of its nature, relative value, or importance, is not suitable for technology-based delivery. It is still an open question how efficient soft-skills can be trained in an online environment. Certain groups of employees do not want to miss the "edutainment value" of live experience and desire total interactivity with a human trainer. Others are simply uncomfortable with computers. For a number of individuals, technology-based training is not the most efficient learning method, as their learning style is kinesthetic as opposed to visual. The classroom also provides guidance and structure. These elements are important for individuals who lack the motivation and confidence to succeed in a self-study-only program. E-learning may require more dedication and discipline. Frequently, it also does not yet yield the degree of interactivity and collaboration offered by classroom training. However, for many companies seeking a reputable continuing education, this is not an issue anymore. Many of them are happy to put up with insufficiencies of distance learning in order to enjoy its unparalleled convenience. E-learning may not be perfect, but it is practical. While technology-based learning is unlikely to completely replace the school and university experience, it offers a lot of opportunities for corporate training and continuing education.

The most promising market within the education industry might be corporate e-learning, the E2B market. Companies face more economic and social pressures to find new ways of training delivery, and have fewer regulatory, bureaucratic, financial, and technical barriers to the implementation of e-learning than other segments of the education industry. The most successful e-learning models of the future will likely be hybrid e-learning networks that are combinations of academic, professional and corporate content.

REFERENCES

Aragon, L. (1997). Wharton's information spike. Case study: Collaboration between students, IT spawns intranet app that simplifies mundane tasks. *PCweek*, 14(41), 3-6.

Aubrey, B. (1999). Best practices in corporate universities. In Neumann, R. and Vollath, J. (Eds.), *Corporate University*. Strategische Unternehmens-entwicklung durch massgeschneidertes Lernen, Ahrendt et. al.: A&O des Wissens, 33-55.

Berge, Z. L. (1998). Conceptual frameworks in distance training and education. In Schreiber, D. A. and Berge, Z. L. (Eds.), *Distance Training. How Innovative Organizations are Using Technology to Maximize Learning and Meet Business Objectives*, 19-36. San Francisco: Jossey-Bass.

Brockhaus, M., Emrich, M. and Mei-Pochtler, A. (2000). Hochschulentwicklung durch neue medien-Best-practice-projekte im internationalen Vergleich. In Bertelsmann. (Eds.), *Online Studium*, 137-158.

Bullinger, H.-J. (2001). Einsatz neuer Medien in der Personalentwicklung, Einführungsreferat des IAO-Forums "Betriebliche Weiterbildung mit digitalen Medien" am 22.02.01, Fraunhofer Institut, Stuttgart.

Deiser, R. (1998). Corporate Universities-Modeerscheinung oder Strategischer Erfolgsfaktor? Organisationsentwicklung, 1, 36-49.

Fresina, A. (2000). The Three Prototypes of Corporate Universities, www.ekw-hrd.com/3_Prototypes.pdf, 23.07.2000.

Glotz, P. (1999). Die beschleunigte Gesellschaft. Kulturkämpfe im digitalen Kapitalismus, München: Kindler.

Kaeter, M. (2000). Virtual cap and gown. *Training*, 37(9), 114-122.

Maehl, W. H. (2000). Lifelong Learning at its Best: Innovative Practices in Adult Credit Programs, San Francisco: Jossey-Bass.

Meister, J. C. (1998). Corporate Universities. Lessons in Building a World-Class Work Force, New York: McGraw-Hill.

Palloff, R. M., & Pratt, K. (1999). *Building Learning Communities in Cyberspace: Effective Strategies for the Online Classroom*. Cambridge: The Jossey-Bass Higher and Adult Education Series.

Porter, L. R. (1997). *Creating the Virtual Classroom: Distance Learning with the Internet*. New York: John Wiley

Ryan, S., Scott, B., Freeman, H. and Patel, D. (2000). *The Virtual University*. London: Kogan Page.

Schneider, M. (2000). Duke's B-School goes into business. *Business Week*, June 30.

Schreiber, D. A. (1998). Instructional design of distance training. In Schreiber, D. A. and Berge, Z. L. (Eds.), *Distance Training. How Innovative Organizations are Using Technology to Maximize Learning and Meet Business Objectives*, 37-65. San Francisco: Jossey-Bass.

Seufert, S. (2000). Trends and future developments: Cultural perspectives of online education. In Adelsberger, H., Collis, B. and Pawlowski, J. (Eds.), *International Handbook on Information Technologies for Education & Training*, Berlin, Germany: Springer.

Seufert, S., Back, A. and Häusler, M. (2001). e-learning. Weiterbildung via Internet. Das "Plato-Cookbook" für internetbasiertes Lernen. Kilchberg: Smartbooks.

Seufert, S. and Seufert, A. (1999). The genius approach: Building learning networks for advanced management education. *Proceedings of the 32nd Hawaiian International Conference on System Sciences*, Hawaii.

Timmers, P. (1998). Business models for electronic markets. *EM-Electronic Markets*, 8(2), 3-8.

Wilbers, K. (2000). Lernportale, universitäre Aktoren, Business Intelligence und m(obile)-Learning: Vier Herausforderungen des e-learning. In Esser, F. H., Twardy, M., and Wilbers, K. (Eds.), E-learning in der Berufsbildung. Telekommunikationsunterstützte Aus- und Weiterbildung im Handwerk, Köln: Eusl, 396-431.

Chapter V

Growth and Consolidation in the Spanish-Speaking E-Commerce Market

Roberto Vinaja
University of Texas-Pan American, USA

This case aims to analyze, in some detail, the major challenges in the widespread adoption of electronic commerce in the Spanish-speaking population. The case also provides a general overview of related issues in global e-commerce, specifically: language, localization, currency, cultural difference, export controls, payment methods, taxation issues, consumer protection, and legal issues. The case includes a description of the strategies followed by companies entering the Latin American market in order to illustrate some of the major cross-border issues. The case clearly exemplifies how localization involves a considerable financial investment and commitment. The chapter illustrates that while Latin America initially attracted many investors by offering one of the world's fastest growing online populations, the market was not large enough to accommodate all the new entrants.

A GROWING MARKET

Analyst studies in 1999 pictured Latin America as one of the world's fastest growing online populations; Internet access was growing faster in Latin America than in other regions of the world (Vidueira, 1999). The number of new websites in Spanish was rapidly increasing. This explosive growth rate was attracting investors and newcomers into the online Spanish-speaking market (Vidueira, 1999).

All new entrants were looking after a share of the "potentially" huge Latin American market (Fattah, 2000b). Latin America seemed an attractive market with huge growth potential (Anonymous, 2000c). More and more U.S. e-tailers were offering Spanish versions of their own websites, while others were establishing alliances with companies with existing websites in Spanish in an effort to reach the online Spanish-speaking market.

Many U.S. companies, especially those run by U.S. Latinos, were targeting Spanish speakers. Forrester predicted the development of more ethnic portals from expatriates who retain ties to the motherland, Americans who opt out of using English as their primary language, and residents of emerging Internet markets (Mand, 1999).

Many U.S. e-tailers were realizing the revenue potential from Latin American markets (Slover, 2000). Many U.S. companies were implementing dynamic plans to direct their e-commerce efforts to reach Hispanic or Latin-American Internet users (Anonymous, 2000e; Oldham, 2000; Werner, 2000). 1-800-Flowers.com inaugurated a Spanish version of its site called 1800-LasFlores.com. Sears was also pursuing the Spanish-speaking community and opened its Spanish-language site in early 2000 (Rutledge 2000).

According to e-Marketer, the overall Internet Hispanic population is around 14 million, and almost half of those are Hispanics in the U.S. (Zoltak, 2000; Azios, 2000). StarMedia estimated the worldwide online Hispanic community at 20 million, about 5% of the overall potential market.

THE HISPANIC POPULATION IN THE U.S.

According to the 2000 census data, there were approximately 34 million Hispanics in the U.S. In addition:

- The Hispanic group was the fastest growing group in the U.S. growing at a yearly rate of 2%.
- The Hispanic population was expected to double by 2025 (Trujillo, 1998).
- Hispanics would become the largest minority in the U.S. by 2010.
- Hispanic youth would be the largest non-white population in the U.S. by 2025.
- In 1998, the Hispanic purchasing power within the United States was over $383 billion.
- There was a 50% gap in home computer ownership between the general population and middle-class Hispanics (Trujillo, 1998).

- 19.4% of Hispanic households owned a PC, compared to 40.8% of White households (Anonymous, 1998).
- 27% of Hispanics were planning to buy a computer in the short term.
- 20% of U.S. Hispanics had Internet access at work.
- 75% of U.S. Hispanic households with incomes above $75,000 owned computers, of which half had Internet access.
- About half of households with incomes between $35,000-$74,999 owned computers, and a quarter had Internet access (Trujillo, 1998).
- In 1999, Internet access among US. Hispanics was around 4.5 million users.
- 50% access the Internet (includes any location).
- 23.4% of Hispanics not accessing the Internet cited monthly service costs as the major obstacle.
- From the bilingual Hispanic group, 47% of those who own a computer also had Internet access.
- The estimated PC purchases by U.S. Hispanics in 2000 were more than 1.5 million, equivalent to the whole U.S. college student market (Rutledge, 2000).
- Approximately 61% of US Hispanics online made a purchase in 1999, and 74% of those purchasers accessed the Internet on a daily basis (Rutledge, 2000).
- 12% of U.S. Hispanics have bought something over the Internet (Zbar, 1999).
- U.S. Hispanic shoppers were predominately male; the average age was 32, and the average annual income was $51,600.
- Younger Hispanics (13-17) tend to use the Internet more for chatting, music, etc., while those age 18-35-plus use the Internet for information and news, etc. (Anonymous 2000d).
- The average shopper bought six items and spent an average of $547 during 1999.
- 86% of the shoppers bought music and 45% bought books (Rutledge 2000).

CAG (Cultural Access Group) claimed, based on a study conducted in 2000, that the Hispanic Internet was becoming as important as Spanish language TV, radio, and print as an advertising medium.

THE HISPANIC POPULATION
IN LATIN AMERICA

- The Latin American market as a whole had 500 million potential Internet users and $2 trillion in GDP (Shetty, 2000).

- Internet use in Latin America was growing at a fast rate. The number of Latin America Internet users grew from 4.8 million in 1998 to 10.6 million in 2000 (2% of the population) and was expected to grow up to 19.1 million users by 2003 (Disabatino, 2000) or up to 38 million in 2003 according to the most optimistic estimates (Oberndorf 2000).
- Jupiter forecasted up to 66.6 million (12% of the population) in 2005 (Ebenkamp 2000). Jupiter report was based on number of Internet users, not households, because Latin Americans were more likely to access the Web at kiosks, a friend's house, at Internet cafes or at computer rental shops.
- The e-commerce market in Latin America was expected to grow from $167 million in 1998, up to $8 billion by 2003 (Oberndorf, 2000, Disabatino, 2000) of which more than $6 billion would be business-to-business e-commerce. More optimistic estimates forecasted $82 billion by 2004, out of a global Internet economy that would reach nearly $7 trillion by 2004. Brazil will register $64 billion in online sales, and Argentina, $10 billion (Anonymous, 2000c).
- According to Jupiter Communications, Latin America's online sales would reach $8.3 billion by 2005 (Ebenkamp 2000). This was an optimistic estimate that assumed that companies would find solutions to current impediments.
- The majority of Internet users were in Brazil, Argentina, and Mexico.
- Internet penetration in Latin America was only about 2 to 3% (Fattah, 2000b).
- The number of Internet users in Mexico was 500,000 and 350,000 for Colombia (Zoltak, 2000).

ANALYSIS OF CHALLENGES

As electronic commerce in the region was growing in popularity, cross-border issues in Latin America were critical factors in the success of online ventures. Despite the expected growth, entrants faced many obstacles. Some of the obstacles for the expansion of Internet access in Latin America were:
- poor PC penetration and low Internet usage (Graves and Nucete 2000);
- a nascent and not highly reliable delivery infrastructure;
- low credit card ownership among consumers (Ebenkamp 2000);
- weak credit card processing infrastructure;
- high costs of access;
- antiquated back-office computer systems;

- inefficient distribution networks;
- expensive phone charges;
- widespread credit card fraud (Petersen, 2000a);
- tariff barriers;
- high shipping costs;
- distrust of mail-order shopping;
- preference to pay cash (Ebenkamp 2000);
- distrust of online transactions; and
- the need to handle multiple currency payments.

In the U.S. the major barriers for Hispanic widespread use of the Internet were the price of computers, high monthly Internet access fees, and lack of familiarity by the less acculturated Hispanics

Making e-commerce happen in Latin America would require overcoming some serious obstacles (Petersen, 2000c). Major challenges needed to be addressed before the Latin American market potential could be capitalized. Computer ownership and Internet usage was highly correlated with income. However in Latin America, relatively few people own computers. Although a growing number of Hispanics were online, only a small percentage was purchasing online. (Ebenkamp, 2000).

Financial-related websites were facing the challenge that access to financial information had always been restricted (Schmerken, 2000). The logistics infrastructure and the postal service were less than 100% efficient, and order fulfillment was really challenging. Just as in the U.S. the most successful players would likely be retailers that use the Web as an extension of their stores (Ebenkamp, 2000).

Given the current obstacles, Internet companies moving into the Latin American online market had to implement several strategies in order to be successful. Some of the strategies included adapting Websites to cultural differences, the use of localization services for translation of Websites into new languages (instead of using machine language translation) (Dodd and Graves, 1999), protecting brands via local domain registration, understanding local business customs, and implementing payment mechanisms in multiple currencies.

Language

Some companies mistakenly thought of Latin America as a homogeneous region; nothing was so far from the truth. Although all countries (but Brazil) shared a common language, Spanish was spoken in so many different ways across the continent. The Latin America population was composed of many nations with different backgrounds and cultural values. Some U.S.

retailers had committed the big mistake of just mimicking their English Websites and were offering a translated carbon copy of their English language Websites. The Latin American market had very unique characteristics, and in order to conquer the market, companies needed to implement new strategies and creative business models. There was no cookie cutter solution for the region. Indeed, Latin America was not one country and one language, but many countries and two languages (Schmerken, 2000). A report by CAG showed that English was the preferred language for U.S. Hispanics, Spanish was preferred only when U.S. Hispanics visited Latin American Websites. However, older U.S. Hispanics were more concerned about content in Spanish, and they thought that more Websites in Spanish were needed. By 2000, only about 2% of the Internet content was in Spanish (Shetty, 2000). The same reports showed that U.S. Hispanics teenagers tended to use the Internet more for chatting, and music, while the rest of the U.S. Hispanic population used the Internet for information and news. Recent studies showed that U.S. Hispanics refer to Websites from their home country when accessing information in Spanish. Web portals such as StarMedia and Terra were taking this fact into account when offering content. Websites were targeting audiences of each nation and culture.

Companies entering the Latin American online market were aware of language differences when building their websites. Many businesses today are involved in Electronic Commerce. It is important to understand that communication can be a major barrier in regards to cross-border negotiations among countries. It is also very important to provide information in the local language. Although, English is the major language of business communication in the world, many local Latin American customers would not understand any other language than that of their native country (Fridman, 2000). Websites offering information in the local language were having a selling edge over the competition not using the local language. Consumers were more likely to buy from a Web site with content in the local language. Every nation in Latin America had special characteristics and had to be considered individually. The Latin American market was culturally rich and diverse; in addition to Spanish many dialects were still in use. Winning the battle for the Latin American market meant winning a series of battles in each country. A multilingual Web site with icons that feature different language options would cater to more markets.

However, offering multiple versions of the same website was an expensive alternative. Major problems experienced by startups were the costs of creating multiple websites, and customizing/adapting to different cultural tastes and suit language variances. Latin American startups were very expensive to run because they were organized as micro-multinationals. The cost involved with maintaining multiple regional offices and developing separate flavors of a website was tremendous.

Legal Issues

Economic activities need regulations and laws; however, most legislation was only applicable within the borders of every specific country (Mosquera, 1999). There are many legal issues that needed to be considered (Engler, 1999). Some of the legal issues included customs, laws and regulations, privacy, copyrights, jurisdiction issues, export/import regulations, and compliance with intellectual property, cryptography and security contracts (Drake, 1998). Only a few countries had established committees or initiatives for the development of domestic and global legislation to facilitate global electronic commerce.

Currency

Currency varied from country to country. Local currency included pesos, bolivares, quetzales, cruceiros and sucres, to name a few. Because of currency devaluation, some country's currency may be of a higher rate or lower rate than the hosting website's currency. Because currency exchange rates were different, the value of the currency could increase or decrease in different countries. Purchasing in different Latin American currencies was a potential barrier, as exchange rates could literally change every minute. However, major credit card companies operating in the region provided their customer with automatic currency exchange services for multiple currencies.

Infrastructure

The region's IT infrastructure varied from nonexistent to rudimentary to adequate. Many regions in Latin America were still lagging behind in terms of infrastructure. However, major telecommunications providers were reluctant to invest in less profitable parts of the continent and preferred to focus on closed loops to selected cities. For example, 70% of the overall connectivity market constituted traffic between Brazil and Argentina, and many companies were focusing their efforts in this region.

International connectivity was a critical factor to provide Internet access for the nascent Latin America's e-commerce economy. However, a major hindering block in Latin America was the high cost of international half circuits. Telecom Argentina charged $71,351 per month for 2Mbps leased lines. Chile's Entel charged $26,600 and Brazilian Embratel charged $20,109 per month. One of the reasons for these high tariffs was that while many new ISPs had been entering the region, the supply market was highly concentrated (Shetty, 2000).

There were several obstacles to achieving universal coverage for businesses all over Latin America. An alternate solution to the current obstacles was the use of the Wireless Application Protocol (WAP) to enable Internet access through wireless devices.

Cultural Differences

Companies entering a new market must get to know the culture of that country. Countries may have diverse views on e-commerce regulations. A few countries in Latin America did not have defined electronic commerce initiatives, and therefore they lacked a established body of regulations. Credit card penetration was extremely low. The estimated card ownership was as low as 10% in some regions. Concerns over credit fraud and a cultural preference for price haggling and face-to-face transactions were prevalent (Pereiera, 1999). According to Francisco Ramirez, sales director with Mexico City reseller Getronics: "Mexicans do not even make purchases by phone because merchants insist on verifying credit card signatures. It's not a technology issue, it's a cultural issue."

Building customer loyalty and trust in the region would require additional efforts. Many Latin American customers were not used to catalog shopping, store returns or exchanges. Many Latin Americans were also distrustful about the security of online transactions and were reluctant to buy products they had never seen or touched. In order to overcome this attitude, many companies were exploring alternative payment methods and others were implementing alternative Web currencies and extensions of their traditional services (Ebenkamp, 2000).

In the Latin culture, community features such as chat rooms, personal pages, email and shopping were strongly emphasized. The average Latin American user spent a considerable amount of time chatting or sending e-mails (Fattah, 2000a). According to Fernando Espuelas, founder of StarMedia, there is a difference in Internet utilization in Latin America. Whereas the U.S. user has a greater focus on information retrieval, the Latin American users places more emphasis on communication.

New Initiatives

Many obstacles had hindered e-commerce in Latin America; however, the situation was beginning to improve. Many countries in Latin America, such as Mexico, Brazil and Argentina, were opening their economies and markets to the new globalization trend and facilitating the development of global e-commerce.

Electronic commerce in Latin America was expected to rise after a slow start. Although Latin America was still lagging behind North America in technology, many Internet trading partners were investing in the region in key technologies, such as phone lines, computers, Internet hosts, and cell phones.

The trend of increasing local content and regulatory cooperation would pave the way for economies of scale that would drive the growth of e-commerce in the region. Optimistic forecasts expected a continuous drop in computer prices, the proliferation of satellite and wireless technology, a growing number of free Internet service providers, the issuance of new e-commerce legislation, and new developments in telecommunications (Gower, 2000). One of the benefits of Latin America as an emerging market was that entrants were able to learn from success and failure stories from their experienced counterparts in more mature markets.

Many analysts expected the index of PCs per head of population to grow. Many ISP were trying to provide alternative and affordable options for Internet cccess. The number of Web-based applications was also increasing at a fast rate (Shetty, 2000).

There were many projects underway. Approximately, 15 new fiber projects were close to completion. Major projects totaling 170,000 kms of cable were under construction. The new improvements in infrastructure would likely decrease the price of Internet connectivity.

According to the Americas Telecommunications Indicators 2000, released by the ITU, in some of the large markets, the incumbent carriers had anticipated the Internet growth and captured a large share of Internet subscribers. For example, in Argentina, Telecom Argentina's Arnet and Telefonica Argentina's Advance shared 43% of the Internet subscribers in the country. In Chile, incumbents CTC's and Entel's Internet service had left only a 5% market share to independent ISPs. Likewise, in Mexico, Uninet, the official ISP of Telmex had taken 50% of the access market and in Venezuela, CANTV Servicios had 35% of the market.

Many local governments were encouraging Internet service providers and telecommunications companies to offer Internet access at affordable prices and, if possible, offer free access (Oberndorf, 2000). The Chilean government mandated interconnection among Internet service providers and a national peering exchange was established so that Chile's bound Internet traffic would stay within the country, rather than traveling through outside networks before reaching a neighboring city. Other countries were imple-menting innovative measures to provide Internet access to the general population. Colombia's Minister of Communications, Claudia de Francisco Zambrano became a champion of universal Internet access through an elaborate program called Comparatel. Plans were to take the Internet to all Colombian municipalities, the poorest of which would receive free access. In addition, the Colombian Ministry of Education was planning to wire 2,000 schools. The plan was ambitious and many analysts were skeptical about the cooperation of the national carrier, EBT (Shetty, 2000).

Despite the major challenges, many improvements, mostly resulting from the ongoing privatization of telecommunications were underway (Pereiera, 1999). The number of Spanish language Internet sites was constantly growing, and the number of Spanish-speaking users was also increasing.

MAJOR PLAYERS AT THE END OF 2000

Many Web portals were offering localized content and local Web brands for every specific country. Some portals were targeting the U.S. Hispanic population, others focused on the Latin American population and still others were trying to reach both groups. Each company was trying to target Latin America in many different ways. Many sites were targeting specific niches among U.S. Hispanic Internet users and those in Latin America (Zoltak, 2000). Each Web site was trying to differentiate their style and offerings, both in terms of content and community. Some portals specialized in content, while others were emphasizing community.

Table 1 lists the major players and whether they were targeting the U.S. Hispanic population, the Latin American population or both. Table 2 indicates which sites emphasized content versus those emphasizing community features.

Starmedia.com

StarMedia was founded in 1996 by Fernando Espuelas, a former AT&T executive and Jack Chen, a securities analyst (Katz, 1999). Starmedia was one of the first pioneer Latin portals (Malkin, 1999). Based in New York, StarMedia Network started with $80 million in private financing. The company's IPO in May 1999 raised $110 million. The company had over 750 employees and operations in Argentina, Brazil, Chile, Colombia, Mexico, Puerto Rico, Spain, Uruguay, Venezuela and the United States. Starmedia was mainly a portal with a few incursions in the ISP business. The traffic at Starmedia.com was estimated at 2.1 billion page views in the first quarter of 2000. StarMedia had a Pan-regional approach, targeting Spanish and Portuguese speakers worldwide. The company operated a network of sites in virtually all Latin American countries, including several in Brazil. The main

Table 1: Major players who targeted the US Hispanic population, the Latin American population, or both

STRATEGY	COMPANIES	DESCRIPTION
OPENING A SUBSIDIARY	YAHOO!	Yahoo! entered the market by opening a subsidiary.
ACQUISITIONS	STARMEDIA TERRA	Starmedia made a series of strategic acquisitions. Terra also acquired local companies in several countries
JOINT VENTURE	AOL	AOL formed a 50-50 joint venture with Venezuelan Cisneros group.
MERGERS	TERRA	Terra merged with U.S. Lycos.
PARTNERSHIPS	MICROSOFT TELMEX	Microsoft and Telmex joined efforts to launch T1MSN
NICHE	QUE PASA	Que Pasa was mainly focused on the U.S. Hispanic population.
GROWING OVERSEA CUSTOMERS	EL SITIO YUPI	El Sitio was entering the U.S. market Yupi was gradually targeting the Latin American population.

Table 2: Content vs. those emphasizing community features

COMPANIES	Emphasis on U.S. market	Emphasis on Latin America	Emphasis on content	Emphasis on community
AOL	X	X	X	
EL SITIO		X		X
QUE PASA	X		X	
STARMEDIA	X	X		X
T1MSN		X	X	
TERRA		X	X	
YAHOO!		X	X	
YUPI				

focus of Starmedia was the Latin American market, but it was also targeting the U.S. Hispanic market. Starmedia was one of the pioneers and offered community features both in Spanish and Portuguese. Starmedia specifically targeted users in major population capitals in Latin America and the U.S. The content was customized to every country.

Partnerships with advertisers and merchants was an important factor of Starmedia's business model (Fattah, 2000a). Most revenues at Starmedia came from advertisement. The site had about 150 advertisers, including Ford, Chrysler, General Motors, Intercontinental Hotels and Lufthansa (Mand, 1999). Starmedia acquired several local companies in 1999, including LatinRed, one of the largest Spanish-language online communities, OpenChile, a Chilean portal, Zeek!, a Portuguese site directory, and AdNet, a Mexican portal. Starmedia also owned several other media properties, such as Pidemasonline.com, launched in conjunction with Pepsi-Cola, Cade, Guia SP, and Paisas.com. Starmedia also operated StarMedia Mobile, its wireless division, and StarMedia broadband, its broadband services arm. Starmedia had strategic partnerships with several companies, including Netscape Communications, RealNetworks, Billboard, Dell, Reuters, eBay, NBC, Hearst Communications and Fininvest (Fattah 2000a).

StarMedia was recently faced with a major challenge to its position in the U.S. as Spain-based Terra Networks made a strategic move by acquiring the U.S. portal, Lycos.

Terra.com

Terra Networks S.A. was a publicly traded company and its major stockholder was Telefonica de Madrid, Spain, with portals and ISPs around Latin America. Terra's Web site, opened in 1997, was offering a balanced combination of customized content and connectivity features. Terra's Web site offered links to customized pages for every country it served. An audit conducted in the fourth quarter of 1999 estimated Terra's traffic at 1.2 billion page views.

Terra built a strong position in 1999, thanks to 2 million ISP customers in the region and to a $100 million IPO in late 1999 (Fattah, 2000a). Terra was expanding its market share in Latin America by acquiring Internet service providers in Brazil and Mexico (Ewing, 2000). Terra bought Infosel, its Mexico unit for $280 million.

Terra had just acquired Lycos in May, 2000 for $12.5 billion. Lycos was the fourth-largest portal in the U.S. and is a portal in 25 countries, through 65 sites in 13 languages. The combination Terra-Lycos would potentially reach 91 million users in 40 countries. (Disabatino, 2000). Terra was attracted to Lycos because of Latin America's proximity to the U.S. and the large Spanish-speaking U.S. population. The Lycos purchase would help Terra reach 30 million U.S. Hispanics (Fattah, 2000a). Terra-Lycos would be based in the U.S. and Bob Davis, former Lycos CEO would continue performing the same function.

Yupi.com

Yupi was a private company based on Miami Beach, Florida founded in 1996 by Colombian-American Carlos Cardona (Vidueira, 1999). Yupi started as a Spanish-language search engine on the AltaVista network (Robinson,

1999). Yupi was a leading search engine in Spanish offering community links and related content. Yupi's traffic was estimated at about 143 million page views in February 2000. Yupi featured special separate Websites focused on health, kids, and auctions.

Quepasa.com

The Hispanic portal QuePasa was initiated in 1998 and was based in Phoenix, AZ. QuePasa raised $48 million and surged from $12 to $19.75 a share on its first day of trading (Vidueira, 1999). It achieved 30 million visits at the end of 1999. Quepasa was targeting specifically the U.S. Hispanic population. The Web site provided two versions, one in English and one in Spanish. Content was focused on Hispanic pop starts and leaders in the U.S. and news generated in the U.S. Quepasa emphasized content over community options.

QuePasa.com launched in 2000 its own shopping pages targeting the U.S. Hispanic consumer market. The shopping site, available in both English and Spanish, featured merchandise from popular sites such as Amazon.com, eToys, Dell Computer, Barnes and Noble, Staples, JCPenney and other merchants in 13 product categories. QuePasa also entered a partnership with MapQuest to offer maps and door-to-door driving directions in both Spanish and English. This strategy was intended to drive traffic to the brick-and-mortar stores of QuePasa's online partners. QuePasa had also recently signed famous pop star Gloria Estefan as its spokesperson (Zoltak, 2000).

El Sitio

El Sitio, established in 1997, was based in Buenos Aires, Argentina. El Sitio was the first company from Argentina to go public on the Nasdaq. El Sitio started as a content provider, but gradually offered Internet features after acquiring several fiber network companies in Brazil, Argentina and Colombia (Fattah, 2000a). Nevertheless, the ISP unit was not considered the core function. El Sitio reached 300 million page views in the last quarter of 1999. El Sitio offered content in both Spanish and Portuguese. El Sitio focused on community aspects rather than content. El Sitio also bought DeCompras, a privately held Mexican online retailer for $44.7 million in stock and cash. El Sitio's increased its efforts to appeal to the U.S. Hispanic population. El Sitio signed on Sammy Sossa, a famous major league baseball player, as its spokesperson in the U.S. and developed a new site: Sammysossa.com targeting U.S. Hispanic sports fans.

T1MSN

The richest man in the world, Bill Gates, joined efforts with Carlos Slim, president and CEO of Latin America's largest telecommunications company, Telmex, to develop a Web portal in Latin America (Fineren, 2000). Telmex and Microsoft combined their expertise into a Spanish-language Internet portal aimed at Latin Americans. Telmex and Microsoft were equal partners in the venture and according to the agreement, Microsoft would offer Spanish-language content through its MSN Web service. In addition, MSN would give Spanish-speaking subscribers bundled software services: free e-mail through Hot Mail, instant messaging and Web publishing services. All 1.8 million Hot Mail registered users in Mexico were turned into users of T I MSN. The portal got a guaranteed captive audience because Spanish-language subscribers to Telmex's Prodigy and Microsoft's MSN.com were automatically forced into the portal. The site reached 2.3 million unique users only two months after launch (Fattah, 2000a). The portal also included online shopping and access to other Microsoft services (Rutledge, 2000).

AOL

Internet service providers such as America Online (Willoughby, 2000) were also beginning to target Hispanic Americans (Gonzales, 1999). AOL offered $575 million of stock to the public to feed its expansion in the Latin American Internet market (Goldsmith et. al., 2000). AOL took its first big step into the Latin American market by launching a Brazilian portal in partnership with the Cisneros Group, a Venezuelan media conglomerate (Fritsch, 1999). The Cisneros Group invested $100 million to fund a 50-50 joint venture with AOL to bring AOL to Latin America.

Yahoo!

Yahoo! was also offering local guides. For example, Yahoo! Argentina was designed specifically for users in Argentina and individuals with special interest in the country. Yahoo! also developed an agreement with Hispanic Television Network, a Hispanic television media company. Yahoo! would provide Internet broadcasting solutions for Hispanic Television Network through Yahoo! Broadcast. Yahoo also unveiled Camp Yahoo! in Spanish, a Spanish-language Internet education initiative.

THE FUTURE

The projected growth in Latin America initially attracted many investors, but the market was not accommodating all the companies looking for business. Despite the projected growth, pioneer companies had not posted a profit yet. The Latin American market was fragmented and overcrowded, and shares prices were dropping. Analysts expected that the numerous ISP players would consolidate to only a few major players via mergers, acquisitions and strategic partnerships, a trend that would gradually change the current landscape as foreign Internet competitors came to the Latin American market (Shetty, 2000). Many analysts predicted that troubled companies would become takeover targets (Druckerman, 2000a). Rumors about acquisitions were generated on a daily basis, followed by denials of the companies involved.

According to analysts, after the drop of the NASDAQ index in the U.S., the volume of investments in Latin American Internet companies was expected to dramatically decrease (Reuters, 2000). The plummeting NASDAQ index and the subsequent tightening of funds for Internet ventures were accelerating the pace of consolidation in the market. Many start-up ventures, including Yupi, had delayed their plans for initial public offerings.

Luis Mario Bilenky became president of StarMedia. Francisco Alberto Loureiro, formerly with AOL, became its chief operating officer (Petersen, 2000a). StarMedia posted losses in the first and 44 million for the second quarter of 2000 because of increased product development costs and marketing expenses. Star Media's shares dropped from a high of $70 in July 1999 to $15 in August 2000 (Petersen, 2000c). In the last quarter of 2000, StarMedia announced it was cutting 125 of its 850 positions, in a company-wide restructuring (Rewick 2000). This was called a proactive cost-cutting measure aimed at making the company profitable once more. There were some rumors that StarMedia would not rule out the possibility of a merger with larger U.S. Internet players. Terra had just established a stronghold in the U.S. Hispanic market after acquiring Lycos (Palatnik, 2000). El Sitio was hit by the collapse in the stock market and was facing major problems in its acquisition and expansion efforts (Fattah, 2000a).

QuePasa's stock was recently being traded at 33% below its first-day closing price. QuePasa.com laid off two-thirds of its staff as it recorded disappointing third-quarter results. Its shares fell 24%. QuePasa, Phoenix, said it was firing 38 of 58 employees in an effort to reduce spending, as it continues its search for a buyer. It also posted a third-quarter loss of $7.9 million, down from $8.3 million a year ago, and disclosed that at the end of September it had only $9.5 million in cash.

The chaotic situation implied that only a few companies would survive—the ones with the most resources to support the initial losses, and those patient enough to wait the years it would take to make a profit. Although industry forecasts indicated an expected growth, the future of the Spanish-speaking e-commerce market was still uncertain.

REFERENCES

Anonymous (1998). Blacks, Hispanics still own far fewer PCs than Whites: Study. *Jet*, August, 94(12), 39.

Anonymous. (2000a). El Sitio expands by acquiring Mexican online retailer. *New York Times*, March, C.4.

Anonymous. (2000b). AOL Latin America plans stock offering of up to $575 million. *The Wall Street Journal*, January, B8.

Anonymous. (2000c). Hypergrowth for e-commerce? *Futurist*, September-October, 34(5), 15.

Anonymous. (2000d). The wired Hispanic market. *Direct Marketing*, June, 63(2), 54-56.

Anonymous. (2000e). MasterCard continues tradition of innovation with first Spanish-language Web site by major payment card brand. *Business Wire*, December 19.

Azios, D. A. T. (2000). Hi-tech latinos. *Hispanic*, April, 13(4), 60.

Disabatino, J. (2000). US, Latin America blending e-commerce. *Computerworld*, May, 34(22), 45.

Dodd, P. and Graves, L. (1999). Globalization, overcoming challenges of geography and language. Vision report, February, *Jupiter Communications*. Retrieved on the World Wide Web: http://www.jup.com/sps/research/reportoverview.jsp?doc=sos99-14.

Drake, W. J. (1998). Toward sustainable competition in global telecommunications: From principle to practice. *International Lawyer*, August 23.

Druckerman, P. (2000a). Latin Web firms venture out to markets in Spain, US-Hispanics abroad offer quick route to retail revenue. *The Wall Street Journal*, April, A23.

Druckerman, P. (2000b). Latin American Web concerns struggle to stay in business. *The Wall Street Journal*, October 9.

Ebenkamp, B. (2000). Manana's opportunities. *Brandweek*, February, 41(9) 26.

Engler, N. (1999). Global e-commerce, how products and services help sites expand worldwide. *Information Week*, October 4. Retrieved on the World Wide Web: http://www.informationweek.com/755/global.htm.

Ewing, T. (2000). Deals & deal makers: Softbank aiming at online market in South America. *The Wall Street Journal*, January, C18.

Fattah, H. (2000a). Livin' e-vida. *Brandweek*, July, 41(27), IQ46-IQ54.

Fattah, H. (2000b). Latin crowd. *Mc Technology Marketing Intelligence*, August, 20(8), 36-44.

Fineren, D. (2000). Microsoft and Telmex plan a latin region Web portal. *New York Times*, March, C.4.

Fridman, S. (2000). *Global E-commerce Requires More Than A Foreign Language Website*, January. Retrieved on the World Wide Web: http://www.bizreport.com/news/2000/01/20000124-11.htm.

Fritsch, P. (1999). AOL takes major step in Latin America-US firm joins local group to launch Web site aimed at Brazilian users. *The Wall Street Journal*, November, A24.

Goldsmith, C., Boston, W. and Druckerman, P. (2000). You've got time Warner!—World looks much smaller from abroad-foreign media, Web firms see AOL deal sparking copycat acquisitions. *The Wall Street Journal*, January, B13.

Gonzales, E. J. (1999). Latinoamerica.com. *Hispanic*, March, 12(3), 34-38.

Gower, M. (2000). Helping emerging markets thrive in the digital age. *Business Mexico*, September, 10(9), 54.

Graves, L. and Nucete, V. (2000). No easy victories in Latin America's projected $8.3 billion online commerce market. *Concept Report, Jupiter Communications*, March 15.

Katz, I. (1999). La vida loca of a latin Web star. *Business Week*, November, (3653), 196.

Malkin, E. (1999). The Web's southern frontier. *Business Week*, December, (3661), 120.

Mand, A. (1999). Missing the target. *Brandweek*, February, 40(5), 65-68.

Mosquera, M. (1999). Lawmakers offer bills to spur e-commerce. *TechWeb News*, May. Retrieved on the World Wide Web: http://www.techweb.com/wire/story/TWB19990506S0024.

Oberndorf, S. (2000). Going worldwide via the Web. *Catalog Age*, February, 17(2), 41-42.

Oldham, C. (2000). Internet marketers search for way to reach latino audience on Web. *The Dallas Morning News*, November 29.

Palatnik, M. (2000). Nasdaq composite's drop speeds Latin American Internet M&As. *Dow Jones Newswires*, May 12.

Pereiera, P. (1999). E-business washes into Latin America. *Computer Reseller News*, December, (873), 5, 12.

Petersen, A. (2000a). Opening a portal: E-commerce apostles target Latin America, but it's a tough sell-limited use of the Internet, lack of venture capital stymie effort in Mexico-Big US players take aim. *The Wall Street Journal*, January, A1.

Petersen, A. (2000b). StarMedia lures executives, including one from AOL, to lead its operations. *The Wall Street Journal*, January, B23.

Petersen, A. (2000c). StarMedia net loss widened in quarter, but beat estimates. *The Wall Street Journal*, August 8.

Reuters (2000). *Internet en A. Latina no atraera grandes inversiones en 2001.* Feb. 7.

Rewick, J. (2000). Starmedia sets layoffs in effort to reach profitability by 2002. *The Wall Street Journal*, September 14.

Robinson, E. (1999). Salsa beat: Meet Latin America's Net Bets. *Fortune* 140(7), 346-348.

Rutledge, K. (2000). Increased interest speaks well for Spanish language Websites. *Discount Store News*, May, 39(9), 25-27.

Schmerken, I. (2000). Financial site serves up a Latin beat. *Wall Street & Technology*, February, 18(2), 52.

Shetty, V. (2000). Latin lessons. *Communications International (London)*, May, 27(5), 42-45.

Slover, P. (2000). Web companies cater to Hispanic market with Spanish-language site. *The Dallas Morning News*, September 28.

Trujillo, S. D. (1998). Opportunity in the new information economy: Technology, the great equalizer. *Vital Speeches of the Day*, June, 64(16), 490-492.

Vidueira, J. (1999). Rocketing to cyberspace. *Hispanic Magazine*, July-August.

Werner, H. M. (2000). International: Bank of America equity builds IT services co. for Latin America. *Venture Capital Journal*, June, 39-40.

Willoughby, J. (2000). Offerings in the offing: AOL ole? *Barrons*, July, 80 (31), 31.

Zbar, J. D. (1999). Powering up Internet en Español. *Advertising Age*, November, 70(49), S2.

Zoltak, J. (2000). The Web goes south. *Billboard*, June, 112(25), LM1-LM3.

Chapter VI

Inca Foods: Reaching New Customers Worldwide

J. Martín Santana, Jaime Serida, and Antonio Díaz
ESAN, Peru

This chapter describes the evolution of electronic commerce at Inca Foods, the largest supermarket chain in Peru. In 1997, it launched its virtual store as an additional way to improve customer service. The new service represented a challenge to the firm because Peru has a low Internet penetration rate and Peruvian people are used to shopping only in stores through face-to-face interactions.

However, an unanticipated consequence of going online has been the response Inca Foods has been getting from Peruvian communities overseas. Because of the difficult economic situation in Peru, many people have left the country in search for new opportunities. Most of these people regularly send money to support their families in Peru. Now, Inca Foods provides them with an alternative way to do that.

Inca Foods expects to achieve a high level of sales through this channel and is getting ready for it. This will help the firm to consolidate its leading position in the market, and it will constitute a new model for physical distribution of goods sold worldwide through the Web.

INTRODUCTION

In an increasingly global world, technology undoubtedly provides the underpinnings for integrating a gamut of players in the cross-border trade game. Information technologies, and particularly the Internet, put organizations before unforeseen challenges, creating both threats and opportunities.

This chapter aims at describing and examining the international expansion of Peru's largest supermarket chain through a virtual shop. What is noteworthy in this case is that orders unexpectedly started arriving from abroad. A study of these orders revealed Peruvian residents abroad had placed them who, instead of wiring money to their relatives residing in Peru, chose to send their financial aid by purchasing local goods and food from the supermarket's virtual shop.

This internationalization process has very peculiar characteristics, because instead of the company going global for selling and distributing its products around the world, as is the case in a typical Internet business, the company becomes international to sell worldwide, but keeps distribution in the local market for reasons that will be explained below. This peculiarity cuts the cost and complexity of international distribution logistics and so emerges as an interesting business opportunity for Latin American retail companies.

It is necessary to explain that the virtual shop's launching was due more to the company's commitment to permanent technological innovation than to the quest for short-term returns, even more so because Peruvian consumers are not used to remote purchasing and because of low Internet penetration in Peru (INEI, 2000). Likewise, the virtual shop was conceived as an additional marketing option that did not seek to replace the existing stores, so it can be considered as a typical case of *click-and-brick* organization.

BACKGROUND

The nature of a virtual organization allows for a competitiveness analysis approach, not only from the real or traditional value chain standpoint (Porter, 1985), but also from a new analysis perspective, mainly based on information, that has been recently named virtual value chain (Rayport & Sviokla, 1995). The first model considers information only as a support element within the process of creating value in organizations, but not as a source of value in itself. Company managers are obliged to explore the electronic market to find new business opportunities in which information is a value-generating source. Coordinating both value chains is what characterizes growth companies.

According to Rayport and Sviokla (1995), value generation through the use of information implies three phases: visibility, replication, and creation of new relationships with customers. Visibility, the first phase, implies the use of information technology to control business operations. The replication phase implies replacing virtual processes for existing ones to create a value chain in the electronic media. In the third and last phase, information is used to create new relations with customers.

As opposed to the real value chain, in the virtual one, value is extracted from information by sequentially executing five activities: collection, organization, selection, synthesis, and distribution. By combining these tasks of the virtual value chain with those of the real value chain, we obtain a matrix of value-generating opportunities in the electronic market.

An electronic market is that in which transactions are carried out electronically from beginning to end. Although e-business has been around for about 20 years, commerce over the Internet has experienced explosive growth during the last five years. Internet commerce can supplement a company's traditional business or become an entirely new business line. A commercial establishment that offers its products to a large number of customers visiting its shops located in different points of the city every day decides to enter e-business to market the same products and becomes a *click-and-brick* type of company. This means it has physical and virtual presence. On the contrary, a company conceived to carry out its operations exclusively on the Web is defined as a virtual company.

Many organizations currently bet on Web transactions, because they recognize their ease of use and low cost. The definition of operation mode, processes involved, players, and ways to generate income leads to identifying and classifying different business models.

Inca Foods, the supermarket analyzed in this chapter, is a *click-and-brick* company within the *business-to-consumer* scheme. This supermarket promotes its products through the Web and allows its customers to order and pay by the same medium, using the Web as an additional channel, Its presence on the Web provides it with an opportunity to increase demand for its products due to its ability to reach a numerous public anywhere at any time at a relatively reduced cost. Also, it can establish one-to-one relationships with its customers thanks to their repeated visits. These characteristics define a model called *e-shop*. According to Timmers (1998), this model has a low innovation level—since it is only replicating the activity it carries out in the physical world—and also a low function integration level, since it does not combine different activities.

We must keep in mind that any e-business model relies on available technological capacity making its execution viable. However, this relation does not work both ways. This means that technology itself does not define any business model, only makes it viable. Actually, technology only constitutes a criterion to be taken into account when deciding on a business model. However, whatever the business model to be chosen, the technology used must permit the following tasks: website development, reception of online orders, credit card or any other valid means of Webpayments, payment transactions, security and content development (Baker & Baker, 2000).

It should be noted that several factors influence the development of e-business. Among these, and particularly relevant for this study, is the national culture. In Latin America and, particularly, in Peru, catalog sales were never very popular. Peruvian consumers prefer a personal, face-to-face rapport with the salesperson. Since sales through the Internet are remote sales, there is evidently a great obstacle that companies must overcome in gearing their efforts towards e-business. Buyers mistrust having to share personal data they think are sensitive, while salespeople have to overcome their suspicions that the transactions will be refused.

A still non-fully studied issue is the "tax threat" that e-business represents for a developing country, such as Peru. As *business-to-consumer* trade grows, Peruvian consumers could prefer to buy online abroad instead of inside the country, thus weakening local businesses in favor of foreign ones, and, on the other hand, these purchasers would have to pay taxes at origin, decreasing tax collection in Peru (Barriga, 1999). This should make developing countries quantify this problem and pass laws to facilitate electronic transactions promoting the creation of companies using the Internet as their operation means.

Another topic related to the environment that must also be considered refers to the evolution of indicators for nationwide information technology infrastructure and growth. Organizations devoted to e-business must follow these figures closely to estimate market size and assess the technological infrastructure required to support the volume of transactions carried out. Recent research has shown that 20.5% of Lima households have access to Internet, while 42.2% of households that do not have access to Internet have a family member with access to the Web through other means (INEI, 2000). Other studies estimate that the Peruvian population with access to Internet is 560,000, a mere 2.24% of all inhabitants, even if an 18% penetration rate is foreseen for all Latin America in the next three years (Pyramid Research, 2000). Likewise, there are estimates showing that the value of transactions in Peru reached U.S.$500,000 in 2000, a figure that according to experts could be tripled in 2001 (Expreso, 2000). Low per capita income, about U.S.$2,065, definitely represents a strong barrier to e-business development in Peru. Therefore, it is necessary to seek innovative ways to develop this activity (INEI, 2000).

The most remarkable issue in this case is that the buyers and consumers are not always the same individuals, because in most cases the first ones make their transactions from overseas, an unusual feature for mass consumer products but not for gifts like flowers or books. This permits the supermarket to keep its own local distribution network to cater to orders coming from abroad without having to create a international logistics network.

A paradigm is broken when we show that daily use products sold at a supermarket can also be offered globally without the need of being transported outside the country of origin. Instead of having a global e-business that forces international distribution of products, this is worldwide e-business with local distribution.

MAIN THRUST OF THE CHAPTER

Inca Foods is the largest supermarket chain in Peru, with annual sales of U.S.$450 million. In 1983, it was just a small convenience store in the San Isidro quarter, in Lima, the main city in the country with a little more than seven million inhabitants. In just more than a decade, it found itself leading the self-service and supermarket segment.

The company's leaders summarize this success by referring to the achievement of a widespread organizational culture that permits it to assume its social responsibility vis-à-vis customers, workers, and the community. This organizational culture is based upon four corporate values: (1) Collaborating goes first; (2) Customers are our reason of being; (3) Permanent innovation; and (4) Superior performance. In this regard, Inca Foods' CIO points out:

> "Our corporate values have made the company assume a leadership position in the mass consumer goods industry. We pioneered IT in this industry: We introduced bar codes, call center service, EDI interconnection and recently service over the Internet."

Growth and Expansion

During the nineties, the supermarket segment in Peru was characterized by less stores and, at the same time, an increase in retailers' market share. The Appendix shows the most recent evolution trends among Inca Foods and its competitors in the supermarket industry.

In 1995, Inca Foods and its main competitor, the Marino supermarket chain, had covered income groups A and B of Lima's population. That same year, Inca Foods focused its growth strategies on segments C and D, which had shown a favorable evolution in the years before.[1] Inca Foods saw two points of interest:

- Growing in the C and D income groups is a clear strategy to prevent the likely entrance of large international operators such as Wal-Mart and Carrefour, which could enter the market with predatory prices.
- Actual prices in open stall markets and among street vendors are higher than in supermarkets despite the homemaker's perception in the opposite sense. This opens a window of opportunity for supermarkets.

At the end of 1999, Inca Foods had a million weekly customers, about 5000 employees and 21 stores. In 2000, Inca Foods opened its twenty-second store. This translates into 62% market share in the supermarket segment nationwide. When interviewed about possible investments in Latin America stemming from the recent merger between the European chains, *Carrefour* and *Promodes,* Inca Foods CEO answered that his company has been preparing to face new competitors for a long time.

Nationwide, supermarkets represent 17% of the retail market segment. Open stall markets and street vendors at all economic levels cover the largest percentage, with a smaller concentration in level A. There is a total of 300 open stall markets in Lima. Small convenience shops are another extremely important sales channels, with approximately 50 thousand shops in Lima, visited by people from almost all income groups.

Information Technology Use

Inca Foods has always been characterized by permanent technological innovation. In 1989, it was the first supermarket chain in the country to use bar codes on the goods it sold. The company assigned codes to national products and assumed those of imported ones, already coded using international standards. Additionally, each cash point and sales point installed *POS scanners* (bar code readers).

Likewise, each store is equipped with four workstations for the function of various information systems such as personnel, orders and procurement, product marking, and merchandise reception. These systems were developed by the corporation itself, as well as by third party services, mainly using a client-server architecture and the PowerBuilder language.

At each store, stations form a star-shaped network and are interconnected to corporate servers through dedicated telephone lines. Central databases and commercialization, sales, personnel, accounts payable, and finance systems reside in these servers.

From the start, Inca Foods saw the need to use information technology to optimize the processes involved in its complex logistics chain. Three kinds of companies make up the supply chain of Inca Foods supermarkets: producers, distributors, and retailers. Competition among this segment's retailers takes place mainly in Lima. On the other hand, producers and distributors can be grouped in two large categories of products: perishable (including dairy products) and non-perishable goods.

Nonperishable goods producers and distributors represent 70% of the volume sold by Inca Foods, and they are both local and multinational companies. As for perishable goods, the company buys directly from stockpiling centers such as the Wholesale Market and fishing terminals of Lima. Additionally, Inca Foods is supplied by a large number of small local vendors with sweets, bakery and dairy products, among others.

In 1994, Inca Foods got interconnected to Procter & Gamble IBM's VAN network, assuming a leadership role in changing traditional supply patterns. Standard forms were then defined for the "purchase order" and "response to purchase order" documents. That same year, EAN Peru was charged with defining EDI (Electronic Data Interchange) message standards from EDIFACT messages. At the same time, Inca Foods and other supermarket chains were promoting the application of bar codes based on international standards among their suppliers for using them on local products.

These technological developments permitted Inca Foods to take the next step and implement the Efficient Consumer Response (ECR) concept. Likewise, it currently aims at exploiting the enormous amount of information it has been able to gather with the launching some years ago of its IncaCard used by its customers when shopping at the supermarket. In this way, Inca Foods intends to achieve a personal relation with its customers through implementation of the Customer Relationship Management (CRM) philosophy.

Launching of the Virtual Supermarket

In 1994, Inca Foods implemented a system to respond to telephone orders from its customers. Three years later, in 1997, the corporation started to develop e-business through the Internet. In this regard, the CIO points out:

> The presence of the Internet reflects the corporation's interest in reaching customers in all ways possible: Store, telephone, Internet, and other means that could be developed.

The development of virtual supermarket, the first in Lima, can be divided in two stages. First, the project was led by the information technology area with little participation of other areas in the organization. Development had an IT approach more than a business one, which was reflected in an excess of functionality that overloaded service and made the system slow. As for communication, concepts related to e-business were disseminated to involve more areas in the project. Second, the development started to include other corporate divisions more actively, among them marketing and procurement, in terms of defining business processes and product presentation as well as the services that could be provided. Likewise, the most important customers were asked to send in their comments and suggestions.

Logistics support, one of the success factors of the system, is not completely decentralized. Four stores have been charged with responding to both telephone and Internet orders. Prices and rates or transportation fees are communicated by telephone and are published on the Web page.

Aspects such as including advertising and additional information are being negotiated with suppliers. Some questions currently being evaluated are the following: What product brands should be included in standard shopper carts? What should be the order in posting publicity or product photographs? What additional information should be included in the Web page?

By launching the e-shop, Inca Foods is combining its activities in the physical and virtual worlds, permitting it to identify new business opportunities and to generate value through appropriate use of information. As explained by Rayport and Sviokla (1995), Inca Foods can now generate new ways of relating to its clients. To do so, studies were commissioned to estimate acceptance of its virtual supermarket in the city of Lima. However, what happened later, surpassed all expectations.

Internet Buyers

Market research had revealed that Inca Foods could reach 130,000 potential consumers among Lima Internet surfers. However, in a little while and unexpectedly, Inca Foods discovered a new potential market, Peruvians abroad who wanted to shop for their relatives in Peru. In fact, a little after the Inca Foods website was launched, communications were received from Peruvians abroad, who were interested in shopping for their relatives residing in Peru.

For some years now, Peru has undergone a severe economic crisis that keeps more than 50% of its population in poverty. Some estimates, not official but quite accurate, show that more than two million Peruvians live outside the country. They have migrated in search of better living conditions and periodically send money to help sustain their relatives in Peru.

With the progress of telecommunications and the Internet revolution, expatriates were able to contact their relatives in Peru through the Web. Immigrant communities in different parts of the world no longer had to wait to receive country newspapers to get information about what happened in Peru, but they were now able to get almost instant information about the most recent events. A short while later, national portals were created that became a convergence point for Peruvians abroad, where they found political, economic and sports news, as well as entertainment, horoscope, publicity, and even the possibility of chatting with their relatives and friends. These portals created a very peculiar environment, where those who migrated felt somewhat at home.

This way, probably in one of those chat sessions or in surfing hours trying to learn new things about the country, the Inca Foods website was spotted at the end of 1999, and the idea of cooperating through food bought at the supermarket through an electronic transaction came up, instead of sending cash and paying a commission so it would reach Peru, resulting in an easier, wiser, and cheaper way of helping their relatives.

Differently from Wal-Mart, with stores in almost every city of the United States and in different countries like Germany, Argentina, Brazil, Canada, China, and the United Kingdom and, from the French supermarket Carrefour, with stores in twenty different countries, Inca Foods is only present in Peru. This makes it possible for the virtual store of Wal-Mart to reach a large public and close commercial transactions with customers anywhere in the world with a U.S. PO Box. Evidently, the virtual supermarket of Inca Foods still has a long way to go to reach such a capability, besides having to overcome exogenous problems stemming from the environment in which it operates. It is convenient to be aware that Tesco, the United Kingdom supermarket leader, tops the list of global online groceries sales with over U.S.$580 million yearly, within its chain of stores in the British Island.

Ahold Group from The Netherlands got the second place in online sales after its acquisition of Peapod, the largest virtual store of food and mass consumer products of the United States in April 2000. Now, Ahold Group has several supermarket chains in Latin America, as Bompreço in Brazil, Disco in Argentina and Uruguay, and Santa Isabel in Chile, Peru and Paraguay. Most of them, except Santa Isabel in Peru, practice e-business operations within each of the aforementioned countries.

However, it must be noted that Wal-Mart, Carrefour, Tesco and Inca Foods share a common problem: distribution logistics. The American supermarket has solved it by limiting distribution to the U.S. territory and protectorates. The French supermarket makes online sales only from its French stores to be delivered in France, while the British supermarket only sells inside its country. The Peruvian supermarket restricts delivery to the city of Lima, using its own distribution units, and, eventually, upon special request by some customers, it can take the order elsewhere inside the country charging a higher transportation fee. If compared, distribution costs are much smaller for Inca Foods.

Meanwhile in Lima, the Inca Foods CIO became aware of the potential this market meant for the organization, but was equally aware that an appropriate legal framework was necessary to acknowledge commercial transactions exclusively carried out through the Internet, if the company wanted to serve these unexpected customers.

The Inca Foods' virtual supermarket had been created to cater exclusively to the Lima market. Even with this restriction, the process to be followed to ensure transaction security was quite cumbersome. On this subject, the CIO says:

> The main aspect concerning Internet consumers is to count with a safe e-business mechanism. This will permit us to attract more Internet users and increase their confidence when they do their online shopping."

Operation Modalities in the Virtual Supermarket

The virtual supermarket started operating by implementing the SSL (Secure Sockets Layer) security protocol for credit card transactions. Peruvian commercial regulations are a limiting factor to e-business development because they require cardholders to sign a voucher at receipt of products bought with a credit card.

For telephone orders, operators interact with customers and validate their order at each occurrence. With some Internet orders, an operator needs to make some additional phone calls to validate them. This means an inconvenience to customers and occasionally sales are frustrated. However, the shop's officials point out this verification is necessary.

How to overcome these inconveniencies? That was the concern of Inca Foods' virtual supermarket officials. They wanted to increase the still small online sales. They decided to tackle the issue in two ways:

- To locate the main server of the virtual supermarket in the U.S., so that the transaction could be carried out under U.S. commercial transaction standards, which do not require the voucher signature.
- To implement SET (Secure Electronic Transaction), a security protocol not requiring voucher signing for payment with credit cards.[2] However, SET requires implementing electronic certificates in the stores', banks,' and customers' terminals, which are not being used by all banks and countries.

Additionally, a payment system was used at the Inca Foods, virtual supermarket consisting of debiting from a savings account in a local bank affiliate. To do so, customers were taken from said bank's Web page to approve the transaction. This debit does not require voucher signing and is restricted only to said bank's customers and, therefore, to residents in Peru.

Some months elapsed since the business opportunity created by Peruvians abroad was identified, and the regulations permitting e-business with local companies using servers located within Peru for local shopping.

Currently, Inca Foods offers customers five ways of payment for their purchases at its virtual supermarket. This has permitted it to continue serving local customers through the aforementioned modalities and add services to foreign customers. Payment modalities and conditions for each of them are the following:

1. Cash: Cash must be indicated as the chosen way of payment when customers want to pay at merchandise delivery. The order will be confirmed by telephone or email before it is sent.
2. Credit Card (with voucher signing): Visa, MasterCard or Diners Club must be indicated as the chosen way of payment at merchandise delivery. At this moment, customers have to sign the voucher for their purchase. The order is verified by telephone or email before it is sent.
3. Moneycash: This payment modality is only valid for Banco Money customers that hold the Moneycash card. Customers have to indicate Moneycash as way of payment. In this case, payment is completely electronic and Banco Money controls and approves or refuses the validity of the transaction and informs Inca Foods if the transaction may take place. Customers must enter their account access password and choose the account to debit.
4. SET (Visa): SET (with electronic wallet) must be indicated as way of payment when customers have a SET certificate and electronic wallet installed in their PCs. In this case, payment is entirely electronic and Visa controls and approves or refuses the transaction's validity with the customer's card and informs Inca Foods whether the transaction may take place. Customers must enter their electronic wallet access password and choose the card to be used.
5. MOSET (Visa): MOSET (without electronic wallet) must be indicated as the way of payment when customers are not available to sign a voucher for the corresponding consumption because they are not at the delivery site. This modality does not require entering an access password; only the card number to be used and its expiration date must be indicated. In this case, transactions from customers with free mail accounts are not accepted and the procedure is the following:
    *   At the end of the order, customers will receive an email indicating confirmation of received order.
    *   They will instantly receive another email informing them about the situation of their transaction with said card, that can be APPROVED or REFUSED. In case of approval, customers have to respond to this email by indicating the required data and confirming their acceptance of the operation.
    *   Customers will receive final confirmation email 24 hours after their response. Their orders are processed within 48 hours.

The Virtual Supermarket Goes International

The CIO considered that now that they had been able to solve the security problem, he was ready to launch Inca Foods in the virtual world. He now had to face the problem of reaching prospective customers in the best way possible among Peruvians residing abroad who were still not aware of the virtual supermarket.

To do so, he assessed the possibility of putting banners in Peruvian portals. After analyzing several of them, he decided Tierra Peruana was the most appropriate. Tierra Peruana is the portal of an important telephone group established in Peru. He also chose El Observador, a portal developed by the most prestigious newspaper in the country. His research led him to conclude that these were the two most visited portals by Peruvians abroad.

There is still a lot of debate around the effectiveness of advertising through banners. The recent e-branding concept creates and strengthens a brand by using all the resources offered by the Internet. Many advertisers think that a banner is equal to buying a TV spot to show a 30-second still graphic advertisement. To overcome this problem, they suggest using e-branding, a concept that makes the most of the main advantage offered by the Internet—interactivity (Callahan, 2000).

The CIO knew that Christmas time was the best chance to announce Inca Foods on the Web. Hence, publicity contracts signed with both portals established that banner exhibition would start in December. The advertising negotiation scheme was agreed with Tierra Peruana on the basis of hits to its different pages, while in the case of El Observador, a period of 30 days was hired. Table 1 shows the results of the campaign in Tierra Peruana banners and Table 2 shows those for El Observador from potential consumers worldwide.

Although the launching was short-lived, the information obtained was very useful for the company, since it permitted it to estimate the effectiveness of publicity through banners for the year 2000 Christmas campaign.

Table 1: Tierra Peruana Portal (from 12/03/2000 to 12/31/2000)

Page	Hits	Clickthrus	Yield
Opinión	42,568	228	0.4%
Fernando Lama[1]	17,616	561	3.8%
Mauricio Pre[2]	37,414	792	2.12%
News	132,870	1,596	1.20%
Sports	260,688	2,340	0.90%
Total	**491,156**	**5,517**	**1.12%**

[1] Peruvian TV interview and entertainment anchorman

[2] Peruvian writer, political analyst and interviewer who has a TV program in the USA

Table 2: El Observador Portal (from 12/17/2000 to 01/16/2001)

Origin	Hits	Clickthrus	Yield
United States	607,042	4,365	0.72%
Argentina	16,574	485	2.93%
Spain	15,689	113	0.72%
Japan	13,243	105	0.79%
Chile	6,453	83	1.29%
Italy	4,322	27	0.62%
Brazil	3,658	11	0.30%
Venezuela	1,862	4	0.21%
Peru	43,495	735	1.69%
Total	**712,338**	**5,928**	**0.83%**

Results

Although it was too soon for forecasting, since there were not enough data available, the supermarket gathered the information it had collected at the Inca Foods server in months prior to banner launching to visualize visit evolution and sales in the last months.

Inca Foods prepared summaries with information regarding visits to the virtual shop's Web page and transactions carried out at the virtual supermarket from September to November 2000, after which the portal promotion was launched. Tables 3, 4, 5, and 6 show results for said months. The increasing trend is maintained in January 2001.

Although break-even has not yet been reached at the e-shop, results so far seem encouraging and have generated lots of expectations at Inca Foods about the future of its sales abroad. Most Peruvian communities are in some of the main cities of Argentina, Brazil, Chile, Spain, United States, Japan, Italy, and Venezuela. But not only are Peruvians interested in visiting and buying at the virtual supermarket; foreigners linked with Peruvians in one way or another are also a target audience. Marketing executives at Inca Foods are currently trying to identify additional advertising means to reach the enormous number of potential customers. Meanwhile, they expect to accumulate more results to define effective yield in their advertising campaign.

On the other hand, and to facilitate purchasing for Inca Foods website visitors, besides having classified goods in different product lines and permitting consumers to define a list of repeat purchases, the virtual supermarket now offers the possibility of buying vouchers for consumption. These are coupons on behalf of the person chosen by the purchaser that stand for a money value redeemable against a purchase. Thus, customers save connection time abroad and their beneficiaries in Peru get the necessary flexibility to choose products they really want to acquire when they go to the supermarket.

Table 3: September 2000

Description	Total	Daily Average
Number of visitors	7,192	240
Number of visits	13,912	464
Number of pages seen	126,632	4,221
Number of orders	262	9
Billed orders	192	6
Amount purchased (in US$)	14,813.90	493.80

Table 4: October 2000

Description	Total	Daily Average
Number of visitors	7,224	241
Number of visits	17,278	576
Number of pages seen	136,286	4,543
Number of orders	280	9
Billed orders	206	7
Amount purchased (in US$)	16,763.00	558.77

Table 5: November 2000

Description	Total	Daily Average
Number of visitors	9,488	316
Number of visits	21,980	733
Number of pages seen	157,350	5,245
Number of orders	300	10
Billed orders	227	8
Amount purchased (in US$)	17,357.14	578.57

Table 6: December 2000[1]

Description	Total	Daily Average
Number of visitors	11,248	375
Number of visits	31,952	1,065
Number of pages seen	203,226	6,774
Number of orders	330	11
Billed orders	294	10
Amount purchased (in US$)	22,062.86	735.43

[1] Includes banner advertising.

The innovative idea of providing customers with consumption vouchers at e-shop does not benefit only the customers. It also saves on delivery costs and, on the other hand, lures customers to its stores, contributing to increase retail market share.

Always committed to satisfying its customers and firmly persuaded of the need for permanent innovation, Inca Foods, the largest supermarket chain in Peru, is currently planning to use new IT applications to make the most of the opportunities opened by the international reach of its shop.

FUTURE TRENDS

It is interesting to see a supermarket in a country where buying habits in this type of establishment and Internet penetration are still reduced making an innovative proposal such as launching an e-shop. Although it is clear that this initiative fulfills one of its corporate values and not seeking a way to increase profits, this circumstance cannot be sustained in the long term. Evidently, maintaining technological infrastructure, assigning personnel, advertising, and executing the processes involved with e-business demand an economic effort that sooner or later will have to be paid by some of the company's divisions.

Critical Mass

Inca Foods, executives were aware of the risk they were incurring, but they bet that, sooner rather than later, critical mass would be reached to achieve an appropriate cost-benefit ratio (approximately 10% of potential market). Business-to-consumer transactions are increasing worldwide. Consumers around the world go online to be able to experience this new buying experience. Peru is not an exception to this trend. As consumers' purchasing power and living conditions improve, they recognize the advantages of saved time and efforts through e-business. Data collected at Inca Foods show that—though still small in dollar amounts and volumes—Internet transactions in the country are climbing.

The greater growth projection for local transactions expanded suddenly due to the interest shown by Peruvian foreign residents in helping their relatives residing in Peru. This assistance translates into food purchases driven by the expatriates' sense of solidarity, longing, and generosity. Although its study is beyond the scope of this chapter, its reality cannot be underestimated. On the contrary, it should be duly studied to explore the possibility of generating business opportunities. Although undetermined, the substantial amount of money remittances to developing countries by relatives of local residents is by no means negligible and should be borne in mind. Perhaps, unintentionally, foreign remittances sent as family aid will allow reaching the critical mass that will turn the Inca Foods e-shop into a profitable venture.

Conditions of an Electronic Purchase

It cannot be denied that there are different factors affecting the realization or not of an electronic purchase. One of them refers to the products' characteristics and the sensorial experiences they generate (sight, hearing, touch, taste and smell). Some consumers may shy back at the idea of buying fresh vegetables through the Web. However, as long as the company is well known for its reputation of selling quality products and complete customer satisfaction, this refusal can be defeated (De Kare-Silver, 1999).

Product characteristics are intimately related with another key factor in an electronic purchase, i.e., familiarity. Consumer confidence increases with repeat purchases of known brands. The third and last factor refers to consumer attributes or their motivations to purchase electronically and their attitude in this situation (De Kare-Silver, 1999).

When Inca Foods launched consumption vouchers specifically devoted to buyers abroad willing to contribute to their family expenses in Lima, it sought to overcome the factors that could inhibit electronic purchase of daily consumption products. Considering Peruvian consumers and eventual coupon beneficiaries are social buyers, enjoying the opportunity of visiting an agreeable environment as Inca Foods stores are, a compromise is reached by which payers buy through the Internet and consumers spend pleasurable moments at a store. Here there is another great chance to promote the virtual supermarket growth.

Security and Reliability

Security has always been a concern for those willing to buy over the Internet. The use of passwords was thought to be able to guarantee a secure operation. Nevertheless, the use of passwords does not ensure the transaction's confidentiality nor information integrity, or eventual ulterior transaction repudiation. Now, in Peru, there is a discussion about the benefits of Public Key Infrastructure (PKI) and the need about a Certification Authority (CA) in order to promote e-business. A digital certificate can guarantee operation confidentiality and non-repudiation, information integrity, and authentication of transaction participants (Camp, 2000). Likewise, today a digital certificate is a proven technology with accepted standards and broadly disseminated in different applications.

Its characteristics make the certificate a sufficiently secure means to carry out commercial transactions on the Internet. Commercial establishments, banks, and card issuers trust them and assume the risk of an unlikely violation of security codes. Now, consumers need encouragement to shop on the Web and to realize that a credit card transaction in the virtual world does not entail a greater risk than one in the physical world. It must be noted that current trends show that e-business over the Internet will be inevitable in the following years.

Once the problem of sensitive data exchange in a Web commercial transaction is overcome, uncertainty of satisfactory end result is still to be resolved through the delivery of the goods acquired by consumers at their total satisfaction. Music, software, and texts are among a few items that can be readily delivered digitally in an almost immediate manner. Most other products, including those offered by supermarkets, need to be physically delivered. The great challenge of companies devoted to trading this kind of goods is to achieve and maintain an image of seriousness and honesty in their commercial dealings. Inca Foods' corporate philosophy has turned it into a supermarket that enjoys its clients' full trust. This reputation among Peruvian consumers, earned over almost 20 years, makes customers abroad who are aware of it increase their purchases at the Inca Foods virtual shop.

Advertising

Advertising through banners is still a mystery. It is necessary to consider that driving visitors to a site is one thing, converting them into customers is quite another. A NPD Group report points out that almost three-quarters of online consumers have abandoned a purchase (Saunders, 2001). What is clear is that a little more than 2% of the virtual supermarket visitors buy from it, matching Forrester Research estimations. The yield of banners hired at portals will have to be thoroughly analyzed in coming months.

The use of alternative advertising means to reach Peruvian expatriates and their relatives in Peru should not be discarded either. The goal is to let these two groups know that Inca Foods is an effective means to convey, in the case of buyers, and receive, in the case of consumers, the desired aid.

An eventual strategic alliance with the largest credit card companies like VISA, MasterCard, Diners Club, and American Express, should be evaluated in order to identify Peruvian people abroad who are credit card holders as a first step. Then, it could be possible to develop an advertising campaign offering the Inca Foods virtual supermarket services.

Virtual or Real?

Inca Foods was born to the real world and still carries out most of its operations in its *brick-and-mortar* stores, even if it also offers its products over the Web. It entered the virtual world as a concrete demonstration of its commitment to corporate values. Figures reveal the public has accepted the initiative and that interesting perspectives exist abroad. However, the same data show that a large percentage of sales by volume still comes from physical transactions. Among other factors, this can be due to the still low penetration rate the Internet has in Peru and to the short life of its e-shop.

Perhaps in some months, today's reduced sales volumes over the Internet may grow to become a significant percentage of Inca Foods' total income. Anyway, the nature of the products it sells and the warmth and elegant ambiance of its stores operate against the likelihood of their closing. Inca Foods will go on as a typical *click-and-brick* business. This characteristic will permit customer satisfaction within and outside the country, while at the same time increasing the firm's revenues.

A New Paradigm

If there were ever doubts about the possibility of a supermarket selling food and mass consumer products abroad through an e-shop, Inca Foods' experience has demonstrated the opposite. Its success leads to meditate about the actual and potential e-business opportunities for retailers – as supermarkets—in less developed countries.

Perhaps new terms should be coined to define this new modality of e-business. If global-out was the name given to what Amazon.com does because of its global delivery of books from a Seattle server, global-in could be the name for Inca Foods' scheme of global offerings and local distribution within a country.

Although Inca Foods does not have any plan to abandon its physical supermarket for now, the click-and-brick scheme allows it to develop a new distribution channel. This new distribution channel will help overseas and wealthier buyers to support the needs of local Peruvian consumers. Who otherwise would not be reached because the poor supermarket penetration.

CONCLUSION

When Inca Foods executives launched its e-shop, they did so with the firm purpose of offering an additional service to itscustomers. They never thought they would arouse the interest of people living outside their community. Also demonstrated was the possibility of selling products that are hard to sell electronically in a market where Internet penetration is still incipient. E-business breaks barriers and facilitates commercial exchange.

The fact that the virtual supermarket did not initially target foreign markets was not a reason for Inca Foods, marketing managers to discard the idea of satisfying this segment. On the contrary, it led them to create ingenuous modalities such as consumption vouchers to facilitate buying from the e-shop. Likewise, it led them to make an effort to identify Internet habits in the Peruvian communities abroad and to effectively reach them through advertising.

Even if it still needs to demonstrate that it can make a profit, the e-shop shows favorable acceptance from consumers and cost-effective distribution logistics. When costs are necessary, it has been shown that they are not higher than those the virtual shop had at birth, and also that they are way below those of large world-class supermarket chains.

According its forecasts, during the year 2001, Inca Foods expects to sell between US$4 million to US$9 million among the Peruvians living in the United States. It should be noted that food, beverages, and mass consumer products are projected to amount to 18% of online retail sales around the world by 2005 (Bakos, 2001). Given that Inca Foods e-sales are around 2% of its total sales, it would be reasonable to expect a great growth in the coming months.

The Inca Foods virtual supermarket is a corporate initiative that could be adopted by other supermarkets operating under economic, social, and cultural conditions similar to those of Peru.

ACKNOWLEDGMENT

The authors would like to express their gratefulness to the executives of Inca Foods supermarket for the information provided and their collaboration in this case.

ENDNOTES

[1] The number of homemakers in Lima is about 1,500,000: level A represents 4%, levels B and C, 56% and level D represents 40%.

[2] At the end of 1999, a SET pilot project was implemented by Visa International with the participation of five banks (Banco del Pacífico, Banco

del Amazonas, Banco Money, Banco Internacional, and Banco de los Andes), four companies (Inca Foods, Teléfonos del Sur, El Observador, and Soy Perú) and 250 customers.

REFERENCES

Accenture. (2001). *Beyond the Blur: Correcting the Vision of Internet Brands*. Retrieved on the World Wide Web: http://a456.g.akamai.net/7/456/1701/714743995ec965/www.accenture.com/xdoc/en/services/sba/sba_ideas_ebrand.pdf.

Amor, D. (2000). *The E-business (R)evolution: Living and Working in an Interconnected World*. Upper Saddle River, NJ: Prentice Hall, Inc.

Baker, S. and Baker, K. (2000). The 7th Annual Software Conference: E-commerce; whatever business you're in, you need to know something about e-commerce. Here are some tips. *Journal of Business Strategy*, 21(1), 13-17.

Bakos, Y. (2001). The emerging landscape for retail e-commerce. *Journal of Economic Perspectives*, 15(1), 69-80.

Barriga Cifuentes, A. (1999). Reflexiones sobre el comercio electrónico en América Latina. *Administración y Economía UC*n (39), 16-19.

Callahan S. (2000). E-branding vs. banners. *Millonario*, 4(23), 16.

Camp, L. J. (2000). *Trust and Risk in Internet Commerce*. Cambridge, MA: The MIT Press.

Carrefour. (2001). *Carrefour*. Retrieved on the World Wide Web: http://www.carrefour.com.

De Kare-Silver, M. (1999). *E-Shock: The Electronic Shopping Revolution: Strategies for Retailers and Manufacturers*. New York: American Management Association Publications.

Expreso. (2000). Comercio electrónico en el Perú cerraría con U.S.$500000 en ventas. Expreso. Lima, *Economía*, 4.

INEI (2000). Tecnologías de información y comunicaciones en los hogares de Lima Metropolitana. Lima: Instituto Nacional de Estadística e Informática.

OSIPTEL. (2000). Seminario Taller Internacional e-Security: Agenda pendiente. CD-ROM OSIPTEL. Lima.

Porter, M. E. (1985). *Competitive Advantage: Creating and Sustaining Superior Performance*. New York: The Free Press.

Pyramid Research. (2000). *Pyramid Research*. Retrieved on the World Wide Web: http://www.pyramidresearch.com/home.asp.

Rayport, J. F. and Sviokla, J. (1995). Exploiting the virtual value chain. *Harvard Business Review*, 73(6), 75-85.

Saunders, C. (2001). *Internet.com*. Retrieved on the World Wide Web: http://www.internetnews.com/IAR/article/0,,12_760471,00.html.

Tesco.com (2001). Retrieved on the World Wide Web: http://www.tesco.com.

Timmers, P. (1998). Business models for electronic markets. *Electronic Markets*, 8(2), 3-8.

Walmart.com. (2001). Wal-Mart Stores, Inc., Retrieved on the World Wide Web: http://www.walmart.com.

APPENDIX:
INCA FOODS AND SUPERMARKET EVOLUTION IN PERU

1942: To secure its family income through business, a young married couple opens a small convenience shop at the corner of a block in a new residential quarter in the city of Lima, San Isidro.

1950: The shop is entirely remodeled. Home delivery by bicycle starts. Credit is made available to customers.

1980: The shop in San Isidro operates to capacity. The need for another shop becomes evident.

1983: Growth takes off. A store in the Miraflores quarter is chosen among nine options because of its premium location. Once the second shop was inaugurated, the objective was to gradually learn how to manage two shops at the same time, as well as to consolidate before opening other shops.

1985: In February, Inca Foods opens its third shop and in June, a fourth one.

1989: Inca Foods starts identifying all its merchandise with a bar code and installs bar code scanners at each cash point in its shops.

1990: The supermarket segment in Peru consists basically of six chains in Lima with about 89 shops. These chains represent only 15% of the retail market.

1992: Inca Foods Delivery starts. It is a home delivery service that quickly reached its objectives and served record numbers of registered customers and daily orders.

1993: Inca Foods becomes still more consolidated after having bought Americanos and Calidad, two supermarket chains. In May, the Marino supermarket chain enters Peru, as a Chilean investment in 85% of shares from Nena supermarkets. Marino located its shops at A and B income group quarters, although it has also gained the acceptance of C income-group customers.

1994: By participating at EAN Peru, Inca Foods starts collaborating in defining of EDI message standards. The first virtual supermarket in Peru is launched by Inca Foods.

1995: Inca Foods and Marino supermarkets cover income groups A and B. Inca Foods focuses its growth strategy on segments C and D, by relaunching the hypermarket concept with all the characteristics sought by C and D housewives.

1997: Many competitors' shops close after a long struggle. Only 47 supermarkets remain nationwide. Of them, Inca Foods owns 14, Marino 14, and PinTop five in Lima and another five in cities in the interior of the country.

1998: In 1998, sales in supermarkets showed that Inca Foods had sold U.S.$449 million at its 18 shops, Marino U.S.$206 million at 20 shops, and the others with nine shops sold U.S.$68.8 million. These amounts gave Inca Foods undoubted leadership in the supermarket segment in Peru with 62% of market share, followed by Marino with a distant 29%.

1999: Nationwide, supermarkets account for 17% of the retail market, while the supermarket penetration rate in other Latin American cities such as Mexico is 40 to 45%. Inca Foods and Marino have remained as the main players. A new competitor has appeared thanks to a popular hypermarket launched by a well-known Peruvian group.

2000: Inca Foods consolidates its leadership position in the supermarket segment in Lima and now has 22 shops. Likewise, it decides to push its virtual supermarket by launching it through banners in two Peruvian portals to stimulate the purchase of products over the Internet.

Chapter VII

Reality vs Plan: How Organizational E-Commerce Strategies Evolved

David Gordon and James E. Skibo
University of Dallas, USA

Part of efficient management is measuring actual performance against desired metrics. In turn, actual strategic outcomes can be measured against plan. The authors show that this is also true of organizations' e-commerce performance versus planned performance. While most organizations with successful e-commerce tend to take the view "There's no stopping us now!," the authors explore the interesting relationship between what the organizations had originally intended versus what operations actually dictated and how those changes affected their sites' performance. To add to the literature, the authors explore the ramifications of the results of a survey conducted among some of the leading organizations in today's business and the analysis of several dot.com enterprises. Along the journey, the authors discovered changes in organizations' "desired capability" occurred as the organizations encountered various challenges to their global e-commerce, such as currency fluctuation and logistical considerations involved with order fulfillment, from industrially powerful countries versus third world countries. The authors also explore various aspects of organizational change evidenced when organizations entered into e-commerce globally. The authors show that theoretical approaches quite often must change with the realities of business when organizations commence e-commerce operations.

Business and industry are faced with a plethora of change in the 2000s on a scale that has not been equaled in the last century. Most of this change is being brought about by the rapid evolution of technology and equally rapid expansion of the Internet into everyday business functionality. One would expect that this evolution, or some might term it "revolution," would have certain aspects that are evocative of organizational upheavals of the past. However, our research shows that disparate organizational structures are evolving at the speed of business and that those structures are influenced by operational performance.

Much has been written and researched regarding the evolution of the Internet and the revolution it is bringing to today's businesses. For our research, we concentrated our effort on an area that has not been previously researched or explored too widely, and that is the adaptation of organizational structure to the strategic c-commerce plans of an organization.

Many companies are rapidly discovering that it behooves them to have an e-commerce capability for their customers. The reasons for this are both economy and survival. Economic forces driving the decision are that many companies are discovering they quickly can globalize operations by establishing a presence on the Internet, transforming themselves, quite literally overnight, from a regional business into a business with a global reach and global implications for operations (Skibo, Hughes and Gordon, 2001a). From a survival standpoint, businesses also are realizing that, unless they take this step into e-commerce, they will fail to meet the activity and customer access of their competitors in a consumer-centric world. The message to organizations is clear, they must have an Internet presence.

The research encompassed in this chapter centered on the forms of organizations that have evolved, and are evolving, to support the organizations' ventures into e-commerce as they begin the new millennium. Further, how do the organizations' plans for operation change over time. The organizations were of many sizes and complexity; however, all were what can be termed "Fortune 500" organizations. The most interesting structure observed is one of widespread dispersion of departmental functions throughout the organization for the purpose of meeting the organizations' e-commerce goals. For example, in the typical organizational structure, one would expect to see the MIS Department fulfilling its traditional technological support role by supporting the Marketing Department's and Operations Department's entry into e-commerce. That is, the MIS Department's software and hardware experts would rally to the support of the Marketing Department and Operations Department by establishing whatever hardware and software requirements were necessary to run the organization's e-commerce.

In that modality, the MIS Department would not take an active role in the management of the e-commerce of the company; rather, its role would be defined as strictly supportive in nature. That is, because, in a traditional modality, the Marketing Department would operate quite autonomously from the MIS Department, as well as other departments within the company deemed as fulfilling support roles (Skibo and Gordon, 2000a). For example, the Finance and Accounting department would provide ancillary accounting support to include financial accounting services, billing, charge card processing, claims processing, prepayments, etc. (Skibo, Hughes and Gordon, 2001b). Likewise, the Logistics Department might provide a supportive role by assisting with inbound freight routing and selection of shipping agents and modalities to offer to the organization's customers. In this scenario, the central player however would still be the Marketing Department who handled the charter of "running the store" or, in this case, the e-commerce site. In this manner, which is one that defines the traditional business structure, each department in the company would have a clearly defined role to play in the success of the organization's store operation and management.

To ascertain what organizational structures were extant within organizations active in e-commerce, the authors interviewed and surveyed forty resale businesses in the United States. The survey was designed to seek differences in organizational structure that evolved from the time the organization first constructed its e-commerce site, until the current time when the organization has had the benefit of experience in operation of its site. Based on the results of this research, one can see a clear pattern of organizational upheaval and change occurring in all of the organizations surveyed. The survey instrument's questions and results are in the Appendix.

IN SEARCH OF THE LEADER

A common trait disclosed among the organizations surveyed was that most gathered organizational structural information from their competitors in order to facilitate their own organization's entrance into e-commerce. This "lead dog" approach placed the organization in a position of reliance in this new e-commerce market upon those who already had experience with the market's problems, use of technology, and overall organizational methodological modifications to solve a problem of entry into e-commerce (von Hippel, 1986).

While it was not the intent of the research to explore the use of the Leonard-Barton (1991) model, there was some expectation that the research would disclose at least limited use of the multidisciplinary teams described by

Leonard-Barton. It was expected that organizations would use multidisciplinary teams in an anthropological modality to determine those organizational structures used in the past by the organization, and competing organizations, that might have some viability in the solution finding for the organization's current problems it was facing with its entrance into e-commerce. However, the research disclosed virtually no use of this modality.

We did find at least two instances where companies placed a high-value on the functional deployment to be realized in their future e-commerce sites, and those organizations conducted rather extensive team visits with known and potential customers and found the outcomes of those visits extremely useful (McQuarrie, 1993). Interestingly, the fol-low-up survey two years later showed a significant change in value placement towards customer involvement in the respective organizations' e-commerce sites' continuing development, thus validating the utility of the McQuarrie (1993) model in this application.

While the organizations who initially utilized the approach described by von Hippel (1994) stated that they had achieved their initial startup goals, our research disclosed that after initialization of the organizations' e-commerce sites, the evolution into a different organizational structure than that used initially by the "lead dog" had already started to take place. The most common initial organizational structure used to initialize the e-commerce site (shown in Figure 1) utilized resources within the organization and was structured very much along traditional organizational boundaries. The structure closely follows the organization's plan for entry into e-commerce. That is, the Marketing Department was typically the driving force behind the initialization of the e-commerce site with a support and concurrence role played by the MIS Department. A somewhat secondary support role was played by the Finance and Accounting Department for the processing of financial instruments to execute sales on the e-commerce site. The role of communication in this model also followed traditional operational mo-dalities.

Operational authority for the organizations' new e-commerce sites was somewhat more difficult to define because most organizations surveyed for our research indicated some difficulty in establishing operational lines of authority. The organizations indicated that, in their traditional brick-and-mortar stores, lines of authority were clearly delineated and understood within the company. Marketing would identify key markets that could then be exploited for profit. Operations would construct and operate a store in that market. All other departments in the company, chiefly the MIS and the Finance and Accounting Departments, played a strictly supportive role in that

Figure 1: Organizational structure utilized for entry into e-commerce

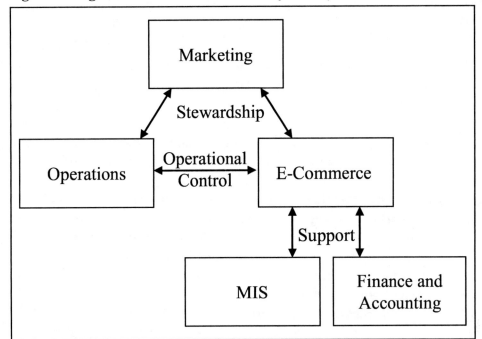

model. In this model, the MIS and Finance and Accounting Departments did not play a role of informing the Marketing or Operations Departments of where they could build a store; how that store could be built; how the store would look; how many customers could enter its doors; how many sales transactions could be achieved in any business day or hour of operation; or that the store would occasionally have to be closed for maintenance. The evolution of e-commerce changed that. The MIS Department was now cast in a new role, one that required them to provide input to the Marketing and Operations Departments for all of these issues (Skibo and Gordon, 2000a).

In large part, the new role evolved because of the e-commerce site's requirement for conceptualization and development. That demanded that innovators within the organization were required to solve complex problems, to overcome surprises, to develop "work-arounds" for barriers, and to bring together processes that required multidisciplinary talent from new and some-times somewhat unfamiliar resources within the company. Further, this effort required the organization to frequently amend its strategic vision for its e-commerce site's performance. This realm of change brought about fluidity in the organizational structure, fluidity in the planning process and fluidity in the financial results of the organization (Skibo, Hughes, and Gordon, 2001b).

The term "unfamiliar resources" is used because most large and complex organizations tend to focus on operational efficiency that translates quite often into the use of rigidly standardized procedures and processes, which tend to suppress and, one might argue, even punish originality of thought and action (March and Simon 1958; Quelsh et al., 1987). Additional difficulties faced the organizations because of the existence, in other operational modalities, of certain departments within the organizational structure possessing more power than others did. This condition, the research disclosed, existed because of a historical basis for the more powerful department having managed uncertainties for the organization previously (Pfeffer and Salancik, 1978; Nelson and Winter, 1982).

This rigid resistance to change and managerial preference for process and operational uniformity, combined with a likelihood of disparate power within the respective organizations' many departments, provided a rich basis for fragmentation into different "thought worlds" (Dougherty, 1992) which, one could argue, posed barriers to the integration and evolution of an entirely new process and environment such as e-commerce. This is also one of the reasons that many companies facing convergence in their industry (and the authors would argue that e-commerce represents convergence) must align their organizational and operational structures for e-commerce in order to survive in this brave new world (Gordon and Skibo, 1999).

How then do organizations overcome these barriers to development of their e-commerce site? As Dougherty (1997) suggests, it is necessary to link the internal and external customer needs with the organization's technological capabilities in order for a viable new product to emerge, which in this case, we submit is the e-commerce site. Our research shows that the organizations, after initially emulating those structures of the "lead dog" in the business, then moved forward towards a specific organizational structure in which power is somewhat evenly shared between widely disparate departments in the organizational structure. This even dispersal of power and authority over many agencies in the organization formed a new and unique structure (Figure 2). While this structure seems to have evolved to handle the day-to-day functioning of the respective organization's e-commerce site, there was still strong evidence of conflict with the organizations studied regarding which agency "owned" the e-commerce site.

Our research shows that the evolution to dispersed power among many organizational elements did not happen entirely without internal conflict and organizational self-discovery, or without the redefinition of functionality of the internal operating structures, procedures, and business models. Of the many companies reviewed, it is the authors' opinion that this evolution is still very much of a work-in-progress.

Figure 2: Dispersed e-commerce organizational structure

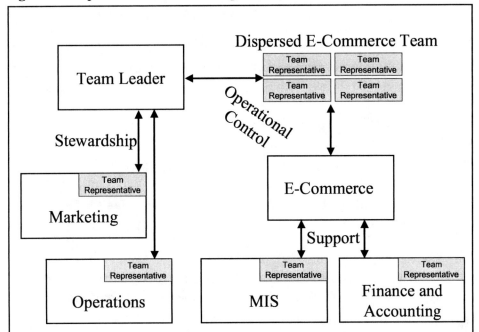

This equilibrium of power was largely because of the heavy reliance on the MIS Department by other departments within the organization. This reliance created a new and additional line of authority and power within the company. Operational control of the traditional brick-and-mortar stores rested squarely in the Operations Department and never within the MIS department. Leadership in the MIS Department now found itself in more than just a support role. Its new role placed it in a position where its advice for future decisions played a key role in the strategic development within the organization. However, most organizations surveyed for this research project indicated that overall responsibility for the site rested with the Marketing Department with the MIS Department fulfilling a support role. However, the shift of power, or at least perceived power, is clearly evidenced by the results of the survey taken.

The initial organizational structure that was most common in the organizations we studied was one where the Marketing Department was the driving force towards initialization of e-commerce within the organization. However, the MIS Department filled a somewhat central role by providing the mechanics of the Web site development software and hardware selections and ongoing maintenance of the hardware and software necessary to operate the e-commerce site.

While the above model is what one would have expected to evolve, our research shows the reality to be quite a different matter indeed. The structures evidenced in the research seem to indicate hands-on experimentation both within and across functionality within the organizations studied. Structures, rather than being very unmalleable, have displayed a remarkable fluidity over time. Souder (1987) showed that when technology and market are unfamiliar, the most successful structure is one that is task-dominant. In this structure, the task-dominant team takes the approach that everyone focuses on the entire developmental process rather than just one piece of it. The team members become functional specialists with continuous infrequent interactions and a freely flowing information exchange along multiple communication channels within the organization. In this environment, coordination mechanisms are loosely assigned among the team members rather than clearly assigned to certain individuals. This ensures there are no formal hand-off transfer points; thus it becomes a truly boundary-less structure.

The research confirms that this structure was indeed what the majority of organizations utilized for their startup of the e-commerce sites; that is, they used the existing structure that they were familiar with and in possession of to define and develop their e-commerce site. However, as the sites became operational, the organizations quickly learned that the traditional model was not serving them well, and they were unable to be very nimble in meeting changing demands of the marketplace, or were rather inflexible in being able to customize the site to meet their particular customers' needs. As the reality of the situation became evident to the organizations, the organizations realized somewhat quickly that an inability to meet these demands quickly and efficiently was affecting their perceived operational efficiency. The latter, of course, had implications for the bottom line of the organizations and was, therefore, unacceptable for the future operation of the respective organizations' e-commerce sites. This is very reflective of the disruption caused by segmentalism described by Kantor (1983) and the rigidity evidenced in highly complex organizational structures (Burns and Stalker, 1986).

While segmentalism breaks down highly complex problems and paths into smaller and smaller pieces that are perceived by management to be manageable, segmentalism also tends to rigidly compartmentalize functions, budgets, managerial expertise, and, in the case of technology, pathways to utilization of the technology possessed by the organization. Because of this, organizations wishing to construct their e-commerce sites were able to do so initially through a common will expressed throughout the organization that, therefore, made the construction of the e-commerce site something of a mandate for organizational survival as well as individual betterment. Once the luster of the initial e-commerce site waned, and the problems of day-to-day operation began to manifest themselves, the organization quickly realized that in order for the e-commerce site to survive and thrive, something would have to change and must do so rapidly.

What this meant for the traditional boundaries in the organization is that the MIS Department's expertise in constructing and technologically managing an e-commerce site were no match for the budgetary power that the Marketing and Operations Departments possessed. They possessed the financial power to have the site operate "their way." This created a tension in the organizations that one would argue took on the appearance of a classic power struggle within the organization. One has only to look at answers to questions the survey posed to the organization in order to see this. One survey question asked, "Who is the 'owner' of your organization's e-commerce site?" When the organization's e-commerce site was approximately one year old and this question was posed, the answer given by the MIS Department managers was that the MIS Department was the owner of the organization's site. When one posed the same question to the Marketing Department and Operations Department, each stated it were the owner of the e-commerce site because it was not any different than any brick-and-mortar store the company already operated. This difference in perception of ownership clearly set up the organization for internal conflict (Hardy, 1994), which had to be resolved before the business could move forward with the technological and operational innovation required for its e-commerce site.

The organizations studied tended to form multifunctional teams for the purpose of resolving the perceived internal conflicts and maintaining the viability of their nascent e-commerce sites. We believe that this was because the organizations' perceptions of value derived from the success of the e-commerce sites were highly relative to the means the organizations were willing to employ to ensure their sites' success. This means that organizations were willing to establish a variety of boundary-spanning roles to handle the many interfunctional communication requirements needed to ensure the organizations Web sites' success (Anacona and Caldwell, 1990). In other cases, we saw development of multi-team structures which were designed to leverage the organizations' technologies across what they perceived were multiple product offerings; for example, the organizations' brick-and-mortar stores and their e-commerce sites (Jelinek and Schoonhoven, 1990; Cusomano and Nobeoka, 1994). In all the organizations studied, the authors found a commonality of purpose among them; that is, they all desired every e-commerce site to be no less an offering for their customers than that presented by their traditional brick-and-mortar stores. This finding, in the authors' opinion, was a significant driver for the organizations to resolve any internal conflict. Following Clark and Fujimoto's model (1991), in virtually all instances, the organizations also placed a top-tier manager in a position that assured internal barriers could be quickly dealt with and had the necessary power to remove any internal barriers within the teams. The organizations also established reporting and coordination mechanisms (Adler, 1993) to insure that the time that they perceived was lost time, which occurred during the initial start-up phase utilizing traditional organizational structures, would not recur as the Web site's business elevated to significant levels within the organizations' overall business model.

The most typical change we saw occur in organizational structures was that of pooling of power between departments in the old organizational structure when one looks at the organizations' e-commerce business. This means that when one looks at the organizational structure now in place to manage e-commerce, one sees a fairly equal distribution of power and influence between departments typically associated with e-commerce business such as Marketing, Finance and Accounting, Operations, and MIS. However, when one looks at the organizational structures still in place in the organization for their traditional brick-and-mortar store operations, one finds virtually no change having taken place in those structures. This is an interesting phenomenon in the authors' opinion, because it denotes a willingness on the organizations' part to accept high-growth on their e-commerce sites and lesser growth in their traditional brick-and-mortar channels without perceiving the need for organizational change in order to achieve the same growth rate in its traditional brick-and-mortar operations.

In all cases, the organizations studied realized significant business volume on their e-commerce sites vs. projected business volume in their brick-and-mortar stores for the same period. We feel this denotes an expectation on the organizations' behalf that their e-commerce sites would represent something of a sales phenomenon for the organizations; however, the e-commerce sites had no connectivity with the organizations' traditional brick-and-mortar stores. One would expect that with double-digit sales growth being experienced on the e-commerce sites, the organizations would be quick to take an introspective view of their traditional brick-and-mortar business, with the view toward bringing some of the same growth experienced by their e-commerce sites into their more traditional market channel. However, the view that we found was quite the opposite; rather, the two were viewed as totally disparate operating entities with no similarities; and therefore, no ready base of comparison should be made between the sales and one channel in the sales and another. This is an area the authors feel is deserving of further research.

Organizational Lessons

There are several interesting organizational lessons to be learned from the methodologies that the organization's studied employed. In the traditional organizational structure, the Pfeffer and Salancik (1978) model suggests that new products such as the organization's e-commerce site would need to conform to top-down plans dictated by the organizations' hierarchy of management in order to achieve success. Using the same model, if the organization relied solely on the bottom-up method for the emergence of innovation in its e-commerce site, then innovations inherent in this new form of business would not build upon themselves in the future. In the organizations we studied, top managers utilized the "subtle influence" control methodology by framing their desire for technological innovation in the form of the organization's e-commerce site and then allowing the organization's internal innovators to develop the actual specifics of the site and its operation (Takeuchi and Nonaka, 1986). From this point, the organizations exercised the truly innovative approach by balancing the tension between determination and emergence. The organizations studied accomplished this by forming what we will call a pseudo-department (Figure 3) comprised of members from the task-dominant teams established to create the organizations' Web sites. This was endemic to all of the organizations included in our research for this project.

Figure 3: Organizational structure utilized after entry into e-commerce

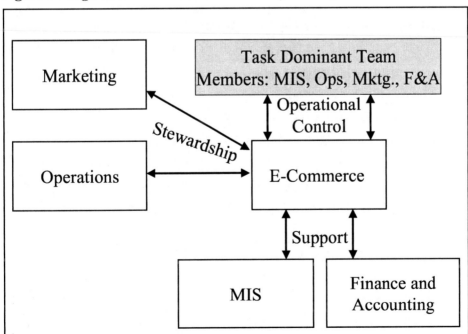

Large corporations, however, have the tendency to emphasize determination over emergence (Dougherty, 1997), and this has the effect of sublimating innovation in the organizations' e-commerce sites when such innovation emerges from the task-dominant teams created to establish the organizations' e-commerce. A servant-leadership role would, perhaps, be more beneficial to the evolution of the organizations' e-commerce sites, however, large and complex organizations are generally unwilling to adopt a servant-leadership role for high technology projects, especially when problems with the existing site or delays in the implementation are perceived by high management (Rosenbloom and Abernathy, 1982).

CONCLUSIONS

We think it is important to provide some measure of the efficacy of these organizational ecological patterns. While most of the patterns are still in their founding stage, we see some results that hold promise for the future as well as some cautionary notes for other organizations. Virtually all the organizations studied experienced significant problems due to rigid segmentalist structures existing in the organization, and an equally rigid approach to planning their e-commerce site. That topology of structures provided barriers to communication between the project management elements, yet all of the organizations studied were in the process of codifying these new structures. In essence, the organizations were digging themselves a new pit to fall into in the future. For that reason, we feel the organizations will face future challenges being built by their founding actions of today.

As stated previously in our research (Skibo and Gordon, 2000a), we are baffled by the organizations' inability to connect the viability and interest in their respective Internet sites with the level of business being conducted in their traditional brick-and-mortar stores. There are deep considerations to establishing financial plans for the future which, one would conjecture, have implications in the linkage of e-commerce performance to brick-and-mortar performance. Certainly if one is clearly outperforming the other, the measures of one should be considered as a performance baseline for the other. We feel that a hypothesis could be made for comparison of operational success in one closely related area with operational mediocrity in another. Yet, as obvious as this may seem, none of the organizations studied had considered this metric nor show signs of considering it in the future.

APPENDIX A

The following questions were posed in writing and during one-on-one interviews with the senior leadership of forty Fortune 500 companies in the United States. The basic questions in the survey instrument remained unchanged over a period of four years.

E-Commerce Survey						
	1997		1999		2000	
	Yes	No	Yes	No	Yes	No
1. When your organizations considered what organizational structure to utilize for management of your eCommerce site, did you consider the organizational structure of other companies who had established ongoing eCommerce sites?	39	1				
2. Did you adopt the structure of another organization?	27	13				
2a. If you answered "No" to the above question, would you consider adopting the other organization's structure if you were starting over again?	12	1				
3. Did you study what software/ hardware the other organization was using?	40	0				
4. Did you study what costs the other organization encountered in its startup phase?	38	2				
5. Did you involve your customers with development of your eCommerce site?	23	17				
5a. Did you conduct site visits with your customers?	2	0				

	1997		1999		2000	
	Yes	No	Yes	No	Yes	No
5b. How would you rank your customers' involvement with your eCommerce site development?						
5b1. Extremely important. "Vital" to the site's success	2		6		15	
5b2. Very important.	21		31		24	
5b3. Neither important nor unimportant.	0		0		0	
5b4. Useful but not important	2		0		0	
565. Not Important	15		0		0	

	1997		1999		2000	
	Yes	No	Yes	No	Yes	No
6. What organizational structure did you employ to develop your eCommerce site?						
6a. Traditional line and staff	30		0		0	
6b Team based	10		0		0	
Multidisciplinary teams:						
6c. Supervised by key Project Manager	1		0		0	
6d. Supervised by eCommerce committee	1		0		0	
Multi-functional teams:						
6e. Supervised by key Project manager	3		0		0	
6f. Supervised by eCommerce Committee	5		0		0	
Dispersed team.						
6g. Members report thru normal line and staff for non-eCommerce tasks, report to Project Manager for eCommerce tasks.	0		30		22	
6h. Members work in multiple departments and report to one autonomous Project Manager for eCommerce	0		8		1	
Non-team based.						
6i. Formed autonomous eCommerce department.	0		1		16	
6j. eCommerce handled as corrollary job function.	0		1		0	
6k. Other not descirbed above.					1	
7. There are clear lines of authority established for the control and operation of our organization's eCommerce site.						
Agree	4		19		35	
Disagree	31		21		15	
Neither Agree nor Disagree	5		0		0	

Respondants by Department:	MIS	Operations	Marketing	Logistics	Accounting	eCommerce	Other	Total
1997								
8. Is there one department in your company who you could say 'owns' the company's eCommerce site?								
8a. MIS respondents	37	1	2	-	-	-	-	40
8b Operations respondents	-	34	6	-	-	-	-	40
8c. Marketing respondents	-	-	40	-	-	-	-	40
8d. Logistics respondents	13	7	20	-	-	-	-	40
8e. Finance & Accounting respondents	15	15	10	-	-	-	-	40
8f. Ecommerce or Internet Dept.	-	-	-	-	-	-	-	-
Total	65	57	78	-	-	-	-	200
1999								
8. Is there one department in your company who you could say 'owns' the company's eCommerce site?								
8a. MIS respondents	31	5	4	-	-	-	-	40
8b Operations respondents	-	35	5	-	-	-	-	40
8c. Marketing respondents	-	1	39	-	-	-	-	40
8d. Logistics respondents	9	20	11	-	-	-	-	40
8e. Finance & Accounting respondents	8	25	7	-	-	-	-	40
8f. Ecommerce or Internet Dept.	-	-	-	-	-	-	-	-
Total	48	86	66	-	-	-	-	200
2000								
8. Is there one department in your company who you could say 'owns' the company's eCommerce site?								
8a. MIS respondents	34	-	1	-	-	5	-	40
8b Operations respondents	-	15	1	-	-	24	-	40
8c. Marketing respondents	-	1	16	-	-	23	-	40
8d. Logistics respondents	7	20	11	-	-	2	-	40
8e. Finance & Accounting respondents	2	15	-	-	-	23	-	40
8f. Ecommerce or Internet Dept.	-	-	-	-	-	40	-	40
Total	43	51	29	-	-	117	-	240

REFERENCES

Adler, P. (1993). The learning bureaucracy: New United Motor Manufacturing, Inc. *Research in Organization Behaviour*, 111-94.

Anacona, D. and Caldwell, D. (1990). Beyond boundary spanning: managing internal development in product development teams. *High Technology Management Research*, 1, 119-36.

Burns, T. and Stalker, G.M. (1966). *The Management of Innovation*, 2nd edn. London: Tavistock.

Clark, K. and Fujimoto, T. (1991). *Product Development Performance*. Boston, MA: Harvard Business School Press.

Cusumano, M. and Nobeoka, K. (1994). Multi-project management: strategy and organization in automobile product development. Paper presented at *ORSA-TIMS*, Boston, April.

Dougherty, D. (1992). Interpretative barriers to successful product innovation in large firms. *Organization Science*, 3, 179-202.

Dougherty, D. (1997). Organizing for innovation. *Handbook of Organization Studies*, 2nd edn. London: Sage.

Gordon, D. and Skibo, J. (1999). Convergence issues in the new millennium. *Business Issues for the New Millennium*, Corpus Christi, TX: SAM Publications.

Hardy, C. (1994). *Managing Strategic Action: Mobilizing Change*. London: Sage.

Jelinek, M. and Schoonhoven, C. (1990). *The Innovation Marathon: Lessons from High Technology Firms*. Oxford: Basil Blackwell.

Kantor, R.M. (1983). *The Changemasters*. New York: Simon and Shuster.

Leonard-Barton, D. (1991). Inanimate integrators: a block of wood speaks. *Design Management Journal*, 2, 61-67.

March, J. and Simon, H. (1958). *Organizations*. New York: John Wiley.

McQuarrie, E. (1993). *Customer Visits: Building a Better Market Focus*. Newbury Park, CA: Sage.

Nelson, R. and Winter, S. (1982). *An Evolutionary Theory of Economic Change*. Boston: Belkamp Press.

Pfeffer, J. and Salancik, G. (1978). *The External Control of Organizations: A Resource Dependence Perspective*. New York: Harper and Row.

Rosenbloom, R. and Abernathy, W. (1982). The climate for innovation in the industry. *Research Policy*, 11, 209-25.

Skibo, J. and Gordon, D. (2000a). Organizational structural encounters with technology: Achieving a dispersed modality. *Managing In A World Of Change: Learning At Warp Speed, Society for Advancement of Management*, Corpus Christi, Texas.

Skibo, J. and Gordon, D. (2000b). Organizational change: An exploration of e-commerce drivers. *Internet Commerce and Software Agents: Cases, Technologies and Opportunities.* Hershey, PA: Idea Group Publishing.

Skibo, J., Hughes, P. A., and Gordon, D. (2001a). E-commerce evolution: Management challenges at maturity. *Management in the Internet Age.* Corpus Christi, TX: SAM Publications.

Skibo, J., Hughes, P. A. and Gordon, D. (2001b). Organizational structural change: Financial impact of a new operating modality. *Proceedings: National Business and Economics Society,* Ohio State University, Columbus, Ohio.

Souder, W. (1987). *Managing New Product Innovations.* Lexington, MA: Lexington Press.

Takeuchi, H. and Nonaka, I. (1986). The new product development game. *Harvard Business Review,* 64, 137-46.

von Hippel, E. (1986). Lead users: A source of novel product concepts. *Management Science,* 32, 791-805.

von Hippel, E. (1994). Sticky information and the locus of problem solving: implications for innovation. *Management Science,* 40, 429-39.

Chapter VIII

Student Advantage Captures the College Market Through an Integration of Their On and Offline Businesses

Margaret T. O'Hara
East Carolina University, USA

Hugh J. Watson
University of Georgia, USA

This chapter describes how Student Advantage successfully transformed itself from a brick-and-mortar company to the leading online portal to the higher education community. The company has followed a business strategy that includes creating Web sites that appeal to college students and forming partnerships with businesses and universities. Through its activities, Student Advantage has assembled a wealth of information about college students, all organized around a common student identifier. This information is important to Student Advantage and to its partners who are willing to pay for the insights that Student Advantage can provide about the college market. Interestingly, Student Advantage only recently developed a strong in-house information technology capability. This capability is now allowing Student Advantage to implement a variety of e-marketing applications. Lessons learned from Student Advantage's experiences are discussed.

INTRODUCTION

In what many people call "the new economy," there are three kinds of businesses. There are the traditional "brick and mortar" companies that sell their products through physical retail outlets. Then there are the "pure plays" that operate only electronically and have no physical stores. And finally, there are the "bricks and clicks" that operate in both the electronic and physical worlds.

Each kind of company faces challenges. The brick and mortars are at potential risk, at least for lost sales opportunities, if they do not have electronic channels. The pure plays have the cost savings of not operating physical stores, but frequently experience serious order fulfillment problems that can lead to their demise. The bricks and clicks are normally the result of brick and mortar companies establishing a presence on the Internet, but they often have a difficult time adding an electronic business to their existing ones. There are several reasons for this:

- The need to change the mindsets of existing organizational personnel;
- The need to change organization structures and reward systems;
- The need to manage offline and online businesses in an integrated manner;
- The need to integrate disparate systems using a common customer identifier;
- The need to create a stable, scalable architecture; and
- The need to present a "single face" to the customer.

These are difficult challenges and not all companies have handled them well. One that has is Student Advantage. In 2000, The Data Warehousing Institute selected Student Advantage for inclusion in its study, "Harnessing Customer Information for Strategic Advantage: Technical Challenges and Business Solutions." The companies included in this study had demonstrated "best practices" in their use of customer information. Student Advantage was selected, in part, for its successful integration of its physical and electronic businesses. This chapter presents the Study Advantage case study and provides you with valuable insights about how to successfully create and operate bricks and clicks companies. It also describes how contemporary information technology can be used to support electronic marketing.

ABOUT STUDENT ADVANTAGE

In 1992, Student Advantage started as a traditional brick and mortar company. At that time, its only product was a card that college students used with participating merchants to obtain a discount on their purchases. Over the last five years, Student Advantage has successfully transformed itself and moved online with a variety of new products and services. It has become the leading media and commerce connection for students and the businesses and universities that serve them.

Student Advantage's mission is to help students save money, work smarter, and make more informed life decisions. In carrying out its mission, Student Advantage has developed relationships with universities and business partners. It helps universities provide services to their students at little or no cost. It helps business partners increase sales and better understand the college market. Information, in general, and information about the college market, in particular, is a large part of Student Advantage's business.

Student Advantage's position in the marketplace has been hard won. For its college student members, it has continued to be fresh and relevant with the products, services, and content provided. Equally important, Student Advantage has developed long-term relationships with universities and business partners built on trust and performance. This two-prong strategy has been the source of a sustainable competitive advantage.

Student Advantage's creative, constantly evolving business strategy—enabled by information technology—has allowed Student Advantage to:

- Develop an estimated membership base of nearly 2 million college students at the end of the fall 2000 semester, in over 125 local markets;
- Become the leading provider of online and offline content, products, and services for the college market;
- Develop proprietary business relationships with over 15,000 business partners; and
- Position itself for success in the networked economy.

In this case, the history and evolving business strategy of Student Advantage are described. Of importance is how the company has changed while still capitalizing on its previous strengths. Critical to the successful evolution have been the fundamental beliefs about how Student Advantage should responsibly handle its interactions with students, universities, and business partners. Next, Student Advantage's various products and services are described, followed by a description of the technology that makes it all possible. Several applications are described that illustrate how Student Advantage uses data and technology to understand and develop relationships with college students. The case concludes with a discussion of Student Advantage's business model, the lessons learned, and future directions.

COMPANY HISTORY

As a college student, Student Advantage founder Ray Sozzi wondered why no one had successfully organized the purchasing power of college students at a national level, as the American Association for Retired People (AARP) had done for senior citizens. After all, college students represent the most sought-after demographic group by marketers everywhere–first-time heads of household, destined to join the most educated, high-income segment of the economy. Faced with new decisions to be made every day–from simple to complex, from choosing a telecommunications provider to selecting soap–college students' good experiences stay with them, often for a lifetime.

For most businesses, recognizing the significance of the college market was easy; however, targeting marketing campaigns was more problematic. Although much generic information was known about the group, specifics were tough to come by. Businesses knew their average age–could even segment them into specific groups based on class year, and knew they lived predominantly in towns in which universities were located. However, college students are among the most transient population group; the typical college student moves twice every year. The college population has significant turnover, and students neither read the same publications nor watch similar television shows across their demographic group. Thus, the issue becomes, how does a firm really locate this easy-to-find population?

Following up on his idea, Sozzi started Student Advantage in 1992. The initial business model was to provide college students with a discount card that they could use with participating merchants. The idea was simple and inherently appealing on two fronts: (1) students did not have much money, and retailers felt good about cutting them a break, and (2) students were receptive to the discounts. For the next two years, Student Advantage systematically increased its reach to more college campuses and businesses. In the early years, the Student Advantage Membership Card was simply shown at the local retailer when a purchase was made. No data were captured beyond the initial membership application from the student.

In 1994, Student Advantage signed an agreement with American Express that made the Student Advantage Card available to student American Express cardholders. Continuing to go national, in 1996 Student Advantage struck an agreement with AT&T that resulted in the offering of an AT&T/Student Advantage Card that functioned both as a discount and a calling card. The agreement was a major turning point that extended AT&T's and Student

Advantage's presence in the college market, and almost overnight, Student Advantage increased its membership to 1.3 million students in 80 local college markets. As part of the relationship, Student Advantage also provided AT&T with information about the college market based on analyses of the Student Advantage student database.

Next, Student Advantage aggressively signed agreements with national, best of breed companies like Amtrak, Barnes and Noble, Greyhound, and Foot Locker that serve the college market but tend to not compete with one another. Once again, part of the agreement was to provide the participating companies with information about how college students use their products.

By 1996, the Internet had become important to interacting with customers and Student Advantage took its business to the Web. The initial motivation was to reduce the cost of servicing members by providing information on the Web rather than through the mail. This began the movement from an offline, bricks-and-mortar business to one with most of its activities online. This was a turning point for Student Advantage and created both challenges and opportunities. As with most dot.coms, the challenge was to grow market share by offering an increasing set of online products and services in order to create an electronic "community." To do this required in-house application development, the acquisition of competing companies, and the further development of relationships with business partners and universities.

On the university side, Student Advantage worked to become a trusted partner. For example, its acquisition of Campus Direct allowed students to access their grades online and to have a cash card that could be used on and off campus. The business model was to help universities better provide their students with an enhanced set of services but at little or no cost to the schools.

As a result of these efforts, Student Advantage's network of Web sites (e.g., studentadvantage.com, CollegeClub.com, uwire.com, FANSonly.com and estudentloan.com) offers a variety of products, services, and information –discounts on products, news from college campuses nationwide, entertainment, sports information, scholarship information, and help with term papers –all things that appeal to college students. In June 1999, Student Advantage went public and is traded on the Nasdaq as STAD. Student Advantage's corporate offices are located in Boston, Massachusetts. A series of acquisitions, most notably of FANSonly, a popular college sports destination, and CollegeClub.com, a leading integrated communications and media Internet company, has taken the size of the company's workforce to approximately 450 full-time employees.

THE COLLEGE MARKET BUSINESS STRATEGY

Student Advantage's objective is to enhance its position as the leading media and commerce connection for college students and the businesses and universities that serve them. It intends to increase the breadth and depth of its relationships with students by continuing to serve the needs of its three constituencies: students, businesses, and universities. The key elements of their strategy include:

- Strengthen the online destination for students. By extending its already comprehensive network of Web sites, Student Advantage through studentadvantage.com and CollegeClub.com, will offer students e-commerce services, content, and community, all targeted specifically to their demographic group. Toward this goal, Student Advantage is continuing to acquire or form strategic alliances with companies in the higher education space.

- Continue to build brand. Student Advantage's market leadership position has been driven by its membership program and by partnering with leading national and local sponsors and universities. To sustain this leadership position, Student Advantage will continue its aggressive brand-building activities.

- Aggressively grow membership. Student Advantage has implemented a variety of initiatives to increase its membership. It is currently promoting memberships through its Web site and has increased its e-commerce partners to increase traffic to the site. It has expanded its on-campus marketing services, added corporate sponsors, and begun to offer programs to high school students and college graduates.

- Enhance relationships with students, businesses, and universities. Concurrent with its aggressive marketing to students, Student Advantage is also offering new services to its corporate sponsors, such as visitor and membership data that will allow Student Advantage and its business partners to better target advertising, make recommendations to students, and provide for a more personalized and engaging experience for students. Student Advantage will also continue to offer universities an outsourcing solution for specific online services, such as providing transcripts and grade reporting online, and Web development and maintenance for university athletic departments and campus newspapers.

- Continue to pursue strategic alliances and acquisitions. Student Advantage has acquired and fully integrated ten businesses that have helped it expand and strengthen its online and offline offerings to students. Such acquisitions and alliances will continue.

A business strategy challenge that Student Advantage faced was what Todd Eichler, Senior Vice President, calls "the chicken and egg" problem. What comes first, develop the corporate partners or the student members? The corporate partners are needed to create the "deals" that attract students, while the students are needed to attract the corporate partners. The solution was to do both at the same time.

COMPETITORS

Currently, Student Advantage has no competitors that compete across the board with a comparable set of products and services. However, over the years, Student Advantage has faced many competitors who have focused on one of two areas. The first area is competitors who provide either online or offline student-focused products. This has included scores of young entrepreneurs offering discount coupon books and cards. Some of these competitors were hired by Student Advantage and their products were rebranded with the Student Advantage name. The second area is competitors who try to partner with universities and businesses to provide services to students. One of these was Collegiate Advantage who did events and promotions on campuses for companies. The competitive solution was to acquire Collegiate Advantage.

There have been numerous companies that have gone after specific niches in the college market. Some of them have been heavily funded by venture capitalists and were able to put much more money into their niches than Student Advantage. The founders (e.g., Ray Sozzi and Todd Eichler) internally funded Student Advantage until 1998. Competing against well-funded startups was one of Student Advantages major challenges. The disadvantage that these competitors faced was that they did not have the broad, synergistic set of products, services, and relationships that Student Advantage had developed. Many of these companies went out of business, while some of them (e.g., CollegeClub.com) were acquired by Student Advantage when it was felt that they could be made profitable within the Student Advantage business model.

Interestingly, the downturn of the dot.com world in 2001 reduced Student Advantage's competition. Venture capitalists became less willing to invest money in online businesses, including those that might compete with Student Advantage. This was a turning point for Student Advantage.

PRODUCTS AND SERVICES

Students can become a Student Advantage Member in several ways: (1) by paying an annual membership fee of $20; (2) by buying products or services from corporate sponsors, such as Barnes & Noble Bookstores and Wells Fargo, who "pay" for the students' memberships; and (3) through college or college-related programs where the sponsoring organizations purchase memberships in bulk for distribution free of charge to students. A Student Advantage Member has access to many products and services; see Figure 1 for examples of how students use their memberships.

Student Advantage's products, services, and structure are organized around three groups: Student Services, University Services, and Business Services. Each group's offerings are described below

Student Services

The Student Services group provides the leading online and offline resources for information, services and commerce for the student community, including exclusive discounts. The division's offerings are available throughout the United States, locally on college campuses, and on the Student Advantage

Figure 1: How students use Student Advantage

10:02a.m.	Tim (Student Advantage Member #3756831954), a UCLA junior, checks out the basketball scores at Student Advantage's FANSonly Network, FANSonly.com
12:20a.m.	Deb (Student Advantage Member #3556493274), an Ameri can University senior, gets a 15% discount on her spring break Amtrak tickets
2:05p.m.	Phil (Student Advantage Member #3017359284), a recent Seton Hall graduate, plans his dream "post graduation trip" to Europe at railconnection.com
4:55p.m.	Tom (Student Advantage Member #3788075344), a Carnegie Mellon senior, orders a bouquet from 1-800-FLOWERS.com for his girlfriend and saves 15%
6:37p.m.	Yolanda (Student Advantage Member #3869625124), a fresh-man at Penn State, checks her grades at Student Advantage's getgrades.com
7:33p.m.	Kerry (Student Advantage Member #3941304554), an Azusa Pacific junior, on a deadline for the upcoming newspaper, downloads an article from Student Advantage's U-WIRE, at u-wire.com
9:12p.m.	Peter (Student Advantage Member 3068676514), a Boston College sophomore, gets $3 off a regularly priced CD at Tower Records

Network, giving students the "advantage" in every aspect of their daily lives, in partnership with the universities they attend.

The Student Advantage Network of sites provides content, community, and e-commerce to address the needs of college students. The sites offer services and information targeted to college students, including discount purchasing, travel alternatives, college sporting news, career and job searches, lifestyle and extracurricular decisions, and financial aid information. The Web sites:

- enable access to approximately 500 college and university newspapers;
- offer an e-commerce marketplace; and
- include a searchable directory of sponsors that offer discounts for Student Advantage Members.

Business Services

The Business Services group serves the business-to-business market, offering experienced marketing information services, expertise in events and promotions, and database mining capabilities for national businesses that target students. Through this division, Student Advantage's business partners obtain critical information about this attractive demographic group.

Student Advantage reaches members through numerous channels: The Student Advantage Membership Program, the FANSonly Network, University Wire (U-Wire), Student Advantage Research, ScholarAid, Rail Connection, and Campus Direct. Other services include Student Advantage Cash and the SA Marketing Group.

Student Advantage provides a platform for businesses to market their products and services to a large, demographically attractive market. Student Advantage combines:

- access to the college student market;
- database marketing capabilities;
- a trusted brand;
- program usage tracking;
- quality online and offline content; and
- community interaction.

Student Advantage maintains contact with students throughout their college years and has established strong relationships with universities. In doing so, it benefits its sponsors by providing on-going targeted and continued access for advertising and marketing efforts. Additionally, sponsors also benefit from Student Advantage's experience, knowledge, and expertise in designing and implementing effective marketing techniques to reach college students.

University Services

The University Services group provides university-specific information services that are relevant to students' lives. The division's full range of capabilities creates tailored opportunities for each university by providing complete Internet content and data management, telephone grade reporting, networked news offices, sports information, and complementary school ID systems.

The Student Advantage Membership Program has been endorsed by more than 60 colleges, universities, and university organizations. The typical agreement is for schools to co-market the Student Advantage Membership Program to their students. This includes sending a letter to students explaining the program along with an application for membership, and receiving a percentage of the associated membership fees. Some universities have purchased Student Advantage Memberships in bulk, at varying discount levels depending on the number of memberships, and have distributed memberships to students free of charge.

Student Advantage has also entered contractual relationships with many schools whereby Student Advantage acts as a service provider to the school. Services provided include Athletic Department Web site operation and maintenance through FANSonly, school newspaper online publishing through U-Wire, grade and financial aid status reporting through the Campus Direct brand, and stored value card program operation and management through the Student Advantage Cash program.

THE EVOLUTION OF THE ENABLING TECHNOLOGY

Considering that Student Advantage in 1992 tracked no information about its cardholders, its transformation into an information-intensive business is remarkable. Before information technology provided Student Advantage with database capabilities, it was impossible to determine card usage electronically. Student Advantage would visit a campus, sell discount cards for $20 and leave campus with the sales revenues, but with no information about its customers. If Student Advantage wanted to know how much the cards were being used, it asked the retailers, and often got answers such as "Yeah, we saw a lot of cards this week."

Fortunately, Student Advantage recognized early in its history that keeping all the data it did collect in one place was critical, regardless of the data's source. Whether the data came from student memberships, sponsor reports, corporate partners, or its fulfillment vendor, the Student Advantage ID number was the control for everything. Pulling the data together was never the issue; using it effectively was something Student Advantage had to learn. However, by never creating islands of data, Student Advantage successfully avoided a major stumbling block to data integration.

Still, in 1994, its internal IT capabilities were extremely limited. Erik Geisler, the Director of Product Operations, was the only IT-skilled employee, and he was not trained for the emerging Internet world. The first real database project happened almost by accident. When American Express made the Student Advantage Card available to its college card holding members, it sent Student Advantage a tape containing member information, and Student Advantage sensed the opportunity to create a database of its student member information.

By 1994, when AT&T came on board, Student Advantage, with a very limited internal IT support staff, was able to access its customer data, and even provide valuable data back to AT&T. AERO (the fulfillment vendor) created an interface to a FoxPro database with some baseline query capabilities, and Student Advantage could, for the first time, respond to customer inquiries and verify current address information for those students who failed to receive a requested discount card.

When Amtrak and Student Advantage formed their business alliance, customer information became more critical, and Student Advantage was ready for the challenge. Amtrak asked Student Advantage to provide student customer information it could not generate itself. When college students bought train tickets using their Student Advantage Card, they did not supply their names and addresses, but Student Advantage had that data and could provide it to Amtrak. Because Student Advantage was not a threat to either Amtrak or AT&T's business, but rather a resource, both companies were willing to help Student Advantage learn what it needed to know about their databases.

Student Advantage's first online initiative was begun in 1996. Initially, the development and maintenance of the Web site was outsourced. The site only provided information about the Student Advantage discount program. The material presented was nothing more than "brochureware."

Student Advantage took an unusual next step to expand its Web site. The company went to Boston University and created the Student Studio—a program whereby BU sent students to Student Advantage to develop, manage, and run a portion of its Web site. It paid the students—who signed on for a single semester—through work-study programs, and in return, Student Advantage had a Web site for use by college students that was designed by college students. The program, which ran until summer 1999, was an outstanding success for both partners. Boston University could offer its students a real-world work experience, and Student Advantage received excellent support and a fertile proving ground for new hires. During the time of the Student Studio agreement, Student Advantage's Web site was voted one of the top five college Web sites in the world.

As the Web site was evolving, Student Advantage added the magnetic strip to its cards. Now, for the first time, it was able to collect reliable and accurate information about the card's usage at retail outlets. Although not all stores had the technology to read the cards, data began to flow in. As Student Advantage evolved, acquired more businesses, and formed more strategic alliances, its information processing needs grew.

In late 1998, Student Advantage started bringing in IT personnel. It hired a Vice President of Technology and seasoned Web developers. Once it filed to go public in 1999, it became a "dot.com" and needed to develop a sustainable IT infrastructure. Its Student Studio program was no longer adequate—especially during exam time when many of its student employees were unavailable. Working with firms such as US Web and Handshake Dynamics, it began to strengthen its online position and bring the database in-house and under tighter control.

Decisions that Student Advantage made during this transition from offline to online were critical to its successful migration. From the start, its online and offline customer database was integrated, and when it sent a mailer asking a college student to visit its Web site, it made sure that the student, once there, would not have to input any data that Student Advantage already had. Student Advantage already knew its students, and it was critical that the Web-savvy students realized this.

Although consultants are still used, Student Advantage has built a highly competent technology team. It currently is doing most of its projects in-house, sometimes using the technical expertise obtained through an acquisition.

Figure 2 shows how data flows in Student Advantage's current technical environment. Everything begins with a Student Advantage member taking an action. The student may go to an offline merchant, like a coffee shop, to make a purchase. If the merchant has a POS device, the student's magnetic card is swiped and the data related to the transaction is sent to Student Advantage's data warehouse. Some local merchants (as opposed to national chains) do not have the technology in place to read the student membership cards; consequently, data resulting from these transactions is lost.

A student may also go to studentadvantage.com and the details of this visit are recorded and sent to the data warehouse. While at Student Advantage's Web site, a student may link to a business partner's Web site, with the possible intention of making a purchase or obtaining information. The student may also go directly to a business partner's Web site, without first going to Student Advantage's. After authenticating that the student is a Student Advantage Member through a member I.D. number, the student is able to purchase at a discount. Data from students' visits to the business partners' Web sites is also sent to the data warehouse.

The data in the warehouse can then be analyzed using e-marketing tools. For example, the tools may be used to plan and execute a marketing campaign. If this is the case, the list of students to be included in the campaign, the campaign message, and the collateral materials are student to Student Advantage's SMTP server, where they are then sent to the targeted students.

Third-party software provides Student Advantage with its e-marketing capabilities. The software resides on Student Advantage's hardware. Figure 3 shows how this software supports closed-loop marketing. The starting point is the entering of data to the data warehouse from Student Advantage's internal systems. These sources include the student membership database, internal fulfillment databases, customer service applications, and general leads. Another source is from external systems. These tend to be ad hoc and might include a business partner that wants Student Advantage to market to its customers and make its data available. Student Advantage's internal systems usually have the same student keys (i.e., Student Advantage Member Number), but this is not the case with external systems. The software utilizes a cross-reference table in assigning a unique, universal key to each student and for use within the e-marketing software. The cross-reference table also makes it possible to go back to the source data using the universal key.

The e-marketing software then loads the data into its database. This is the basic extraction, transformation, and loading process associated with data warehousing. Once done, a process is used to import the data into the e-marketing campaign application. It is here that the market segment(s) are identified for the marketing campaigns. An outbound email server then sends the marketing message to the leads (i.e., students) that have been selected. The landing pad is used to buffer the responses to the campaign. When a student responds to the message, the landing pad gets the instructions for what to do. For example, the instructions might be to present a particular Web page, ask a set of questions, follow a particular workflow, and track everything that transpires. It has a "lights out" functionality that allows it to process responses around the clock.

Figure 2: The data flows in Student Advantage's technical environment

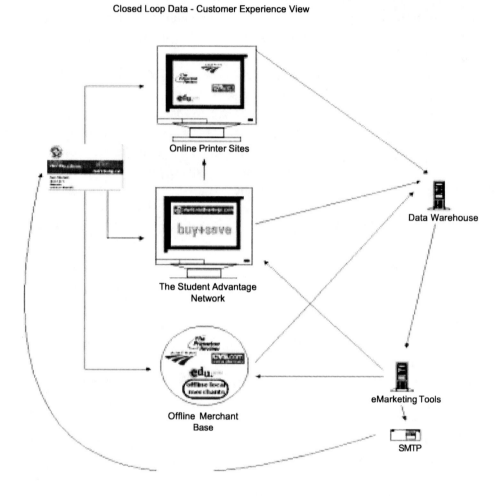

Closed Loop Data - Customer Experience View

The responses to the campaign are automatically entered into the e-marketing software. Also returned to the e-marketing system is data collected when students go to Student Advantage's or a partner's Web site in response to the campaign. When the campaign is for a business partner, information about the campaign outcomes is passed on to the partner. For example, the outcomes might be that these (listed) customers purchased these (particular) items on the partner's Web site.

Student Advantage uses Brio software to analyze the e-marketing data. A user can either view predefined reports, drilldown into existing reports, or generate new reports by writing queries to the database. The ability to create and track campaigns from beginning to end provides a closed-loop marketing capability.

APPLICATIONS

Student Advantage has used its college student data in a variety of ways over the years.

Early Applications

One of the earliest target marketing campaigns was done for Amtrak. To help Amtrak build ridership on its weakest routes, Student Advantage identified all its members who attended a university within 30 miles of an Amtrak station. They then drilled down within this group of students to locate those students whose home addresses were also within 30 miles of an Amtrak station. To this select group, Amtrak offered deep discounts (up to 50 percent) and companion tickets in a major "Home for the Holidays" campaign. The

Figure 3: Using Student Advantage's e-marketing system to provide closed loop marketing

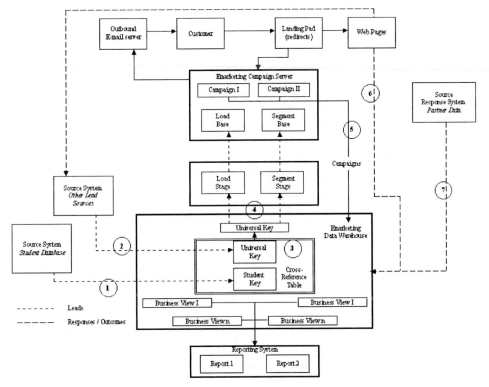

campaign was highly successful for Amtrak and Student Advantage, not only because it had the desired effect of increasing Amtrak's ridership, but also because it validated how useful Student Advantage's student database could be. It began to take information technology very seriously, and started analyzing the data from all its partners.

Another successful campaign was one of the first email campaigns. Emails advertising a Web site to purchase textbooks were sent to 60,000 students. Many responded by going to the site and buying a book. The site had so much traffic it had to shut down and a new server had to be installed. Those students buying books were also asked to participate in a survey and responses indicated a high level of trust in Student Advantage.

Recent Applications

The e-marketing system software is used for many recent applications. It is employed for ad hoc and predefined analyses of Student Advantage's data. Of primary importance are historical relationships: How did each student come to be a member of Student Advantage? Was the membership card purchased, or was it given to the student by a university? Is the card a renewal or a first-time membership? Is there a mailing address on file, or just an email address? In addition to the demographic profile, there is also a behavioral profile for each student. Has the student registered online, and shopped at one of the retailers? What has the student done lately? While the demographic profile is much more developed than the behavioral one, plans are underway to enhance this area.

Other applications analyze Web traffic and Web site performance. Most of this information is used for internal purposes, but a high level report is prepared quarterly and given to the financial community. The information is also used to report back the results of campaigns sponsored by Student Advantage's business partners.

Campaign planning and management are other applications that utilize the e-marketing system. A campaign might be designed to attract new members, generate business, and/or create traffic to a Web site. For example, an email campaign designed for Textbooks.com should result in increased Web traffic and textbook sales. Once a campaign is designed, the budget and market segmentations are determined, and the campaign collateral (e.g., the messages, surveys) is developed. The campaign is then tracked, with the results fed back, to provide closed-loop marketing.

The first test campaigns using the e-marketing system were developed in February 2000. One campaign had Student Advantage's on-campus student representatives offering incentives to other students to visit studentadvantagc.com. Here's how they did it. Using an on-campus "Wheel of Fortune" game, students either entered their email address, swiped their Student Advantage card, or signed up for a card, and then spun a "virtual" wheel to determine a prize. Within 36 hours of spinning the wheel, the students received an email message telling them what prize they had won and instructing them to visit the Student Advantage Web site to claim their prize. There was a 60 percent response rate to the email messages, and of that group, 14 percent went beyond the prize-claiming page to become registered members. While one goal of the promotion was to have current Student Advantage Members visit the Web site, 2,600 new students became Student Advantage Members, at an acquisition cost far less than previous campaigns.

ASSESSING STUDENT ADVANTAGE'S BUSINESS MODEL

Over the last decade, Student Advantage has evolved its business model from being an offline provider of a student discount card to being the leading online provider of content, products, and services for the higher education community and the businesses trying to reach the college market. This transformation has been achieved by a management team that has been willing to change organizational direction quickly, establish synergistic business relationships with business partners and universities, acquire other companies that complement the business strategy, and use information technology as the key enabler.

Like most dot.coms, creating market share is critical to long-term success. It is by this measure that Student Advantage has been especially successful. It has over 1.8 million college students as members – more than any other company that targets the college market. It also has established exclusive relationships with more than 15,000 business partners looking to attract college students. Student Advantage has also established an information technology infrastructure that allows it to develop and execute targeted marketing campaigns for itself and its business partners. Because of the data that Student Advantage has on college students and the ability to analyze that data, the company is well positioned to be the primary source of information on the most attractive demographic group in the country – college students.

An interesting problem that Student Advantage faces each year is the graduation of 20 percent of its members. There are ongoing discussions within Student Advantage about whether to try to retain these members by offering products and services designed specifically for them. An important complicating factor is that many of Student Advantage's business partners offer great deals to Student Advantage's members only because they are college students. Once they enter the workforce, it is hoped that they become lifetime "full value" customers. So, in addition to the question of whether Student Advantage should expand its focus to include college graduates, there is the issue of whether and how its business partners would be part of such an initiative.

FUTURE DIRECTIONS

Student Advantage plans to capture and use more student data in the future. These plans include:

- analyzing clickstream data more thoroughly and storing the findings with the member profiles. This will increase the ability to personalize interactions and messages with members;
- incorporating behavioral data from all of Student Advantage's business units. This will provide a more comprehensive view of members;
- installing tracking devices at a number of local and national business partners in order to better understand student behavior; and
- developing an application that will eliminate the need for business partners to send back information about member activity at their Web site. Instead, Student Advantage will track its members' activities on the Web site.

Student Advantage is also striving to become more involved in the transactions between students and merchants, and as a result, is increasing its revenue stream. This initiative is associated with Student Advantage placing devices for swiping student cards in merchants' stores (both national and "mom and pop") and the growth of stored value debit cards like the Student Advantage Cash card. These cards typically allow students to make purchases both on (e.g., school cafeteria) and off (e.g., coffee shop) campus. When cards are run through the devices at Student Advantage's participating merchants, Student Advantage is able to understand student spending patterns and can sell the insights gleaned to business partners. Student Advantage is also in a position to receive a share of each transaction, much like credit card companies do.

LESSONS LEARNED

Important lessons have been learned at Student Advantage, including:

- Integrate data from different systems whenever possible. Student Advantage began to implement a formal data strategy at the same time that it developed its Internet strategy. This enabled Student Advantage to create a data strategy that took all data sources into account from the beginning, including offline partner data, online data, e-marketing data, and customer service data. This approach eliminated inconsistencies in data across channels, thus better supporting data mining and creating the basis for providing a better customer experience.

- Partner data is valuable and sensitive. Much of Student Advantage's business model relies on obtaining student customer data from Student Advantage's network of business partners. Student Advantage had to present a strong business case for why its business partners should share its data. Student Advantage also has had to earn and maintain the trust of its student customers. Student Advantage spends a considerable amount of time researching and modifying its privacy policies. In addition, they are extremely careful in how it shares and uses student data.

- Give marketers access to the data. Initially, only employees with strong technical skills had access to Student Advantage's data. It was soon recognized, however, that most of the people who knew "what to do" with the data were non-technical. Student Advantage implemented simple data access tools that "put the power" back in the hands of the marketers.

- Do not over-collect data. Student Advantage has learned the hard way that just because data is available, it does not mean that it should be tracked. At first, Student Advantage was tracking every aspect of what its customers did. After running into performance and storage problems, Student Advantage focused on capturing only the "necessary" parts of these transactions. Prior to capturing any data, Student Advantage asks the question, "What will this data be used for?" in an effort to reduce extraneous data capture.

- Maintain a unique identifier across all channels. Student Advantage was able to eliminate any discrepancies or match problems by maintaining the Student Advantage Member Number across all membership-related channels. As the business grows, email addresses will be used as another identifier.

CONCLUSION

Ray Sozzi's original business model was to provide discount cards to college students who showed their Student Advantage Membership Card to participating merchants. This model changed as the Internet emerged and new business opportunities became apparent. The current business model focuses on college students and works closely with colleges and business partners, capitalizing on the information that Student Advantage has about the college market. A key part of Student Advantage's competitive position is the long-term relationships it had built with universities and business partners.

Like all dot.com companies, information technology is a vital, integral component of Student Advantage's business. Without it, there is no business. It is interesting to observe, however, that until recently, Student Advantage had little internal IT expertise and contracted out the required work. It even relied on Boston University students to maintain its Web site. What Student Advantage did have, however, was a strong management vision of how technology could be used. In the marketplace, it was able to acquire the technology and skills needed to implement the vision. For the long haul, Student Advantage recognized the need for in-house IT expertise to integrate, run, and manage an increasingly technologically complex environment and to provide leadership for future initiatives.

Student Advantage still has obstacles to overcome. It must continue to grow, evolve, and become profitable (targeted for Q4, 2001). It must continue to develop an internal IT staff and infrastructure that will allow the company to capitalize on its college student data.

Still, Student Advantage has done several things exceptionally well. It has successfully transformed from an offline to a predominately online business. Through internal development and acquisitions, it has expanded the scope and content of its Web site in order to become the major electronic community for college students. It is poised to take advantage of its large membership base, the relationships it has carefully developed with colleges and business partners, and the unique information that it can generate from its database.

ENDNOTE

The authors would especially like to thank Erik Geisler and Todd Eichler for the insights and information they provided.

Chapter IX

Turning E-Commerce Theory into Action in Ireland: Taming the Celtic Tiger

Ira Yermish and Dale A. Bondanza
St. Joseph's University, USA

INTRODUCTION

E-Europe is not a place or a group of countries but the philosophy of an emerging region within the scope of a technological revolution. E-Europe can be viewed from many perspectives including Euro currency makeup, European Union membership, or technological contributions to the region. Ireland, the "Celtic Tiger," presents an interesting opportunity of entrepreneurial activity. As Evans and Wurster (2000) have pointed out, the traditional value chains may be redefined. The availability of the Internet as an enabling communications technology has markedly changed the possibilities for countries far from the centers of economic power. On the other hand, the realities of the Internet have been obvious. Porter (2001) and Kanter (2001) have identified many of the realistic strategies for traditional and new businesses. Yet there will always be room for new ventures provided, of course, that entrepreneurs understand these issues and this challenging environment. Joshi and Yermish (2000) have summarized the challenges facing the entrepreneur in this kind of environment.

This case will examine a possible strategy for entrepreneurial consultants seeking to provide expertise to rising e-businesses. Readers of this case will be encouraged to explore the issues further, filling in the missing details and developing a full-fledged business plan for action for a pair of young entrepreneurs.

First, they will examine the demographics and technology issues facing Ireland. This will provide the appropriate background for the second section where they address the issues of the entrepreneur seeking to start an e-commerce consulting practice in Ireland. In the final section, they will suggest additional steps to be taken. Readers will be faced with evaluating these suggestions in light of the background information and any additional research that they may undertake.

SETTING THE STAGE

Colleen O'Conner and Sean Kelly are Irish citizens in their late twenties. Both of them just completed an MBA program in the United States after their undergraduate program in business in a university in Cork, Ireland. They have the entrepreneurial spirit and see opportunities to convert their new knowledge into a business venture. O'Conner and Kelly both have excellent communications skills and understand the basic technological details of the Internet. O'Conner seems very comfortable with the technological issues, while Kelly feels his greatest strength is in finance and planning. With this in mind, they felt that they would most enjoy developing a consulting practice targeted at helping businesses surmount the challenges of E-Commerce. Having done their studies well, they first set about researching the opportunities for success in their native Ireland.

BACKGROUND

How is the Republic of Ireland positioned to take advantage of this technological revolution and be a leader in e-Europe? Ireland is positioned socially, financially, and politically to take advantage of the shift in technology. Ireland is an island nation slightly larger then West Virginia. Forty percent of the population lives within 97 kilometers of the capital city of Dublin. Greater than forty percent of the population is under the age of 25. In 1997, the GDP of Ireland was IR£67 billion. Ireland exports US$60 billion, which is composed primarily of chemicals, data processing equipment, industrial machinery, and animal products. Sixty-seven percent of these exports go to other EU countries while eleven percent goes to the United States. Ireland imports US$43 billion, which is composed primarily of food, animal feed, data processing equipment, petroleum products, machinery, textiles, and clothing. Fifty five percent of these imports come from other EU countries while fifteen percent comes from the United States. Current unemployment rates are at 4%. Research indicated that this four percent would be unemployable in any vocation requiring third-level education (the American Bachelor's degree). Twenty-one percent of the population is between 0 and 14 years of age. Sixty-seven percent of the population is between 15 and 64 years of age. Twelve percent of the population is greater then 65 years of age. Sixty percent of the population that attends third level education is studying engineering, science, or business studies. As pointed out in a pamphlet from the Irish Industrial Development Agency, "The quality of Ireland's education is exceptionally high. The independent IMD World Competitiveness report ranks Ireland as one of the best in Europe for the quality of education which everyone receives."

Amarach ("tomorrow" in Gaelic) Consulting is Ireland's leading specialist in predictive market research, consumer trend analysis and business forecasting. It produces several reports tracking every aspect of Ireland's usage of the Internet and e-commerce issues and opportunities. Data from Henry and O'Neill (1999) in Figure 1 shows Internet growth in Ireland as a percentage of the total adult population.

Figure 1: Internet growth in Ireland

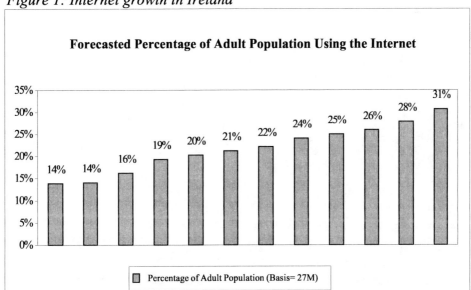

Its 6/2000 report indicates that Amarach's market predictions were almost exactly on target. A 2/2000 report indicated that 22% of the adult Irish population was online at that time. The June report indicated that the number of Irish online had grown sharply in the second quarter to reach 25% of Irish people who had access to the Internet. It is important to note that the use of the Internet implies access, primarily at home, work or school. Smaller percentages access the Internet from a friend's house or cyber cafe. The specific point of access is important to note within the context of the market that is being targeted for e-commerce. Obviously, if the consumer is the target audience, an increase in the number of access points at home is more important. B2B would naturally be looking for an increase in access points at work With an increase in the free Internet Service Provider market, there is a significant increase expected within Ireland.

Another perspective is the percentage of Internet users from home. The implication of the home usage chart is that future growth in Ireland will come from more uses in the home. This will include increasing the number of PCs or other access points to the Internet in the home. These opportunities will proliferate themselves in many ways, including non-traditional access points to the Internet.

Because the largest percentage of adult users is based primarily at home, the most immediate needs for e-commerce would be in the B2C marketplace. With "work" only 2% behind, however, there are more significant, longer-term possibilities within this market of B2B players.

A 3/2000 survey from Amarach indicated that sixty seven percent of people surveyed would prefer to access the Internet through their TV and the

Figure 2: Internet usage in four countries

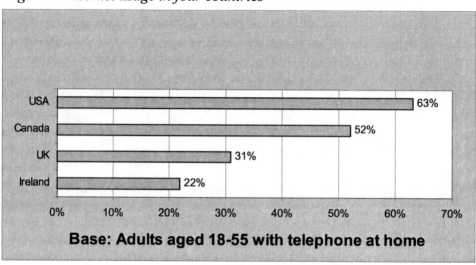

Base: Adults aged 18-55 with telephone at home

Figure 3: Home users as a percentage of all Internet users

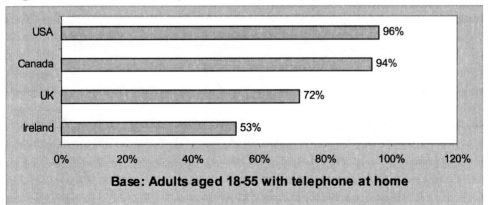

Figure 4: Internet usage in Ireland

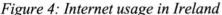

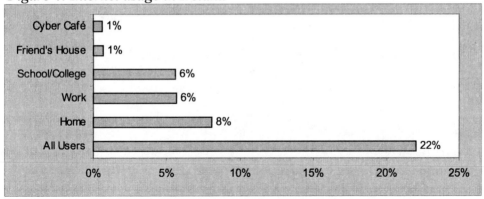

remaining thirty three percent said they would prefer mobile phone access if given only the two options.

Cellular phones are also an area that must be monitored with respect the opportunities in the e-commerce marketplace. Welcoming the announcement of the 1,000,000th customer, Stephen Brewer, Eircell Chief Executive, said in a press release, "This is a significant benchmark in the history of Eircell's growth and in the growth of mobile phone usage in Ireland. In 1995 only 3% of the Irish population had a mobile phone, this figure now stands (3/28/2000) at 43%- with over one million of these people having an Eircell phone." Forty-three percent of the population of Ireland is approximately 1.55 million potential customers for Wireless Access Protocol (WAP) e-commerce services.

The emergence of WebTV will also foster significant growth in the Irish consumer market in the coming years. Ninety seven percent of all Irish homes have a television with at least the three basic channels located within the country. Also, thirty percent of the population has some type of cable service and twenty two percent are reported to have a satellite dish. Since eighty-five percent of homes have the ability to access cable television, the cable modem market will also be another interesting development to watch and monitor.

An additional social issue that puts Ireland in a key position to leverage the emerging e-commerce trend is that it's the only English speaking country participating in the European Monetary Unit. Ireland will have the ability to trade and cross-market within the other European Union countries. Politically, the government is working closely with industry and academia to anticipate future skill needs. As stated in an Irish Industrial Development (IIDA) pamphlet, "A US$400 million program has been put in place which will double the number of computer science graduates and quadruple the number of software graduates within the next 5 years."

Culturally, the Irish are very customer satisfaction oriented. The Irish are easygoing, lighthearted, good-humored, polite, and cheerful. They are quick-witted and have the ability to laugh at themselves (Brigham Young University, 1999).

The largest negative factor affecting continued growth in the Celtic Tiger's economy relates to the skyrocketing cost of real estate and the potential for inflation to hit the eight percent mark in 2001. Wages are accelerating, spending is increasing and the government is lowering taxes. Government spending is also up. All of these factors in combination with Ireland giving up its monetary policy in favor of the Euro are causing this massive inflation. Basic economic textbooks would say that a government should increase interest rates, raise taxes, or cut spending. Pascal states that the Irish government is doing the opposite. Time will tell how these moves will affect the overall economy though it seems to be a simple matter of economics at this point. If interest rates or taxes are not raised soon Ireland could be facing inflation similar to the USA in the 1980s.

O'Conner and Kelly knew that developing an e-commerce consulting practice in a country such as Ireland offers unparalleled rewards but there are areas that must be considered before leaping into a business situation.

MARKET SUMMARY

Though the permutations of e-commerce operations are many (Business, Consumer and Government), it appears strategically advantageous in this environment to concentrate on the business-centered areas. Therefore, we suggest concentration in the B2B and B2C. Table 1 below, extracted from Mitchell (2000), represents the size of the potential e-commerce market within the next three years in Ireland.

Estimates by the International Data Group (IDG) have anticipated that in 2001 the entire e-commerce market within Western Europe will be US$30 billion. This research from IDG also indicates that Germany and the UK will be rivals for the spot of the largest Internet market in Western Europe. Germany is expected to drive one third of the e-commerce in 2001. American investors and technology companies fit naturally into the Irish culture. As Ireland is the only English speaking country participating within the Euro Currency market there are natural advantages to starting this enterprise in Ireland before extending it to other parts of Europe.

B2C is the first area to focus on. Ireland is not that dissimilar to the USA in its purchase patterns while online. The top five products most often purchased online in Ireland include: books, CDs, travel, videos, and software. The typical Irish purchaser is a male, aged 25 to 49 who is employed, owns a credit card, and uses the Internet from home. The ownership of a credit card is where the B2C market in Ireland hits the wall. The strategic guideline here is that the availability of credit distinguishes B2C consumers more clearly from their peers who do not have credit. For B2C e-commerce to become a true powerhouse, new means must be found of putting credit into young hands.

There is a strong need for more Irish companies to have online offerings, and they need to have a higher brand awareness of indigenous online brands to turn this around (Carpenter 2000). Again, significant market opportunities exist to get the smaller companies online.

Where will B2C growth come from within the Irish market? Clearly, the overall growth in people coming online will probably affect the e-commerce bottom line more than any other factor. The push here is to support access from home-based Internet users. Advances in WAP technology products will also stimulate growth within this sector.

Table 1: Size of potential e-commerce market within the next three years in Ireland

	B2C Purchases	B2B Purchases	Total
Usage in 2000	15% of Internet Users	19% of Businesses	€325M
Market Value in 2000	€75M	€250M	
Usage in 2003	32% of Internet Users	64% of Businesses	€5.3B
Market Value in 2003	€1.1B	€4.2B	
	14.7x increase	**16.8x increase**	

B2B is the largest area that we will look at within the scope of market opportunities. This is by far the largest area within the e-commerce sector with respect to the amount of money being spent online. Initial investment is a significant barrier to entry while return is not a short time frame. The rewards will be massive for those who capture the market with the proper branding as it's emerging. The Gartner Group says, "e-business is no longer just an issue of competitiveness–it's a matter of survival," and Kennedy (2000) states, "Global B2B e-commerce will hit US$2.7 trillion in 2004. While Internet trade between business partners will continue to flourish, e-marketplaces will fuel most of the growth, reaching 53% of all online business trade within 5 years."

A risk/opportunity to be cognizant of in the B2B arena is the diminishment of brand loyalty. Because information about products, including competitors, is available in a few keystrokes, the days of comparison on price will quickly evaporate. Competitive advantage will be based on customer satisfaction, the ability to provide value added services, as well as complementary product lines.

It is vital for any firm or consulting company to recognize that B2B business on the Web is still a business. A writer in the magazine B2B says: "You have to remember the basic rules when it comes to Internet technologies. It's got to make money or save money, and if you can't identify upfront how it's going to do that, in the majority of cases it's going to be a waste of money." The B2B business model is more sustainable than the B2C model because of the necessity for critical mass before becoming successful. A successful consulting company will assist its clients in overcoming these hurdles to add value to the top and bottom lines. Kafka (2000) remarks that "the key determinant in creating value in a B2B hub is increasing the number of participants, that is, creating liquidity."

O'Conner and Kelly wrapped up their marketing research by agreeing that the emphasis in this consulting company would be in the B2B area with consumer and government activities taking less emphasis. There should also be some effort dedicated to R&D of future e-commerce opportunities, including advanced technology investigation. They would focus on mid-sized companies given the likely presence of larger consulting firms handling the major business enterprises.

OPPORTUNITIES

O'Conner and Kelly continued to investigate the opportunities within the e-commerce market within Ireland.

As they discovered in their B2B research, the first issue that many Irish companies are having is getting started. There is confusion as to what products or services individual companies can or should offer via the Internet. Today, only 12% of Irish companies have e-commerce offerings. In a personal interview, John C. Moynihan, Director of Customer Marketing for Coca-Cola Greater Europe in London, acknowledged that they are attempting to get more into the e-commerce sector in Europe but are having many difficulties. The need created here for a consulting company is in the area of *strategic development and planning*. A team of e-commerce experts will guide management within Irish businesses to plan, target, acquire, implement, and measure the specific areas within B2B or B2C that are applicable to their environment.

Strategic development and planning does not stop once the Web services are up and running. Many companies go online only to find they do not keep their sites up to date and lose customers to lack of interest. The resulting service offering is to establish a Content Management Office. This office will continually monitor the Web site and confirm that the latest content/information pertaining to clients is visible to the outside world and that the e-commerce offerings are up to date and valid.

Another area that will be key to B2B will be the Web site's integration with back office systems, including legacy and ERP systems. Sales, inventory, and distribution systems must be integrated with the client's Web site so that misleading information is not portrayed to the public. This type of integration is often difficult when the back office systems are not up to date systems or are on alternative platforms including mid-range or mainframe computers. This consulting company will a specialize in solving these types of issues for clients.

Five focus areas: strategic development and planning, infrastructure, hosting, content management, and legacy/ERP integration services will be at the core of their offerings to clients. An additional aspect of service to clients will be continual education of clients on the latest forms of technology specific to their industry. Through the targeted service offerings above, including concentration in B2B and B2C e-commerce, this company can offer a significant value added for clients.

RESOURCE REQUIREMENTS

Next O'Conner and Kelly addressed the organizational issues of their venture. They weren't sure whether their venture should be a stand-alone business or a component of some larger general consulting enterprise. They did, however, come up with a preliminary organizational structure shown in Figure 5. It wasn't clear who would take which position or how they would fill the other positions and hire additional consultants.

O'Conner and Kelly agreed that Dublin is the appropriate site for their operations given the size of the city and the pace of business activity. They did understand that location might not be all that important given the growing ubiquity of communications technologies. They weren't sure how who should take which position in this organization, but they did know that the General Manager would be key in making the organization work. Would it make sense for one of them to assume this role, or would it make more sense to try to hire someone with more practical experience? This person would have to establish the other staff very quickly. These five people would then be responsible for coordinating the ongoing operations of the office, as well as retaining additional colleagues. Why is there no CIO? Because this is a technology consulting company and the GM is considered the strategic pivot point within the organization for technology decisions.

The GM may elect to initially establish a relationship (outsource) with a local office of Chartered Accounts within Dublin instead of hiring a Controller. All areas of financial responsibilities will fall under this person's area including A/R, A/P, treasury operations, tax, and general accounting.

RISKS & REWARDS

Are there risks in establishing a new e-commerce company during a time of rapid growth and inflationary instability? A large issue that would seem to be uncontrollable would be the inflationary pressures within Ireland. At a time when interest rates should be tightening, the government should be spending less and

Figure 5: Suggested organizational structure

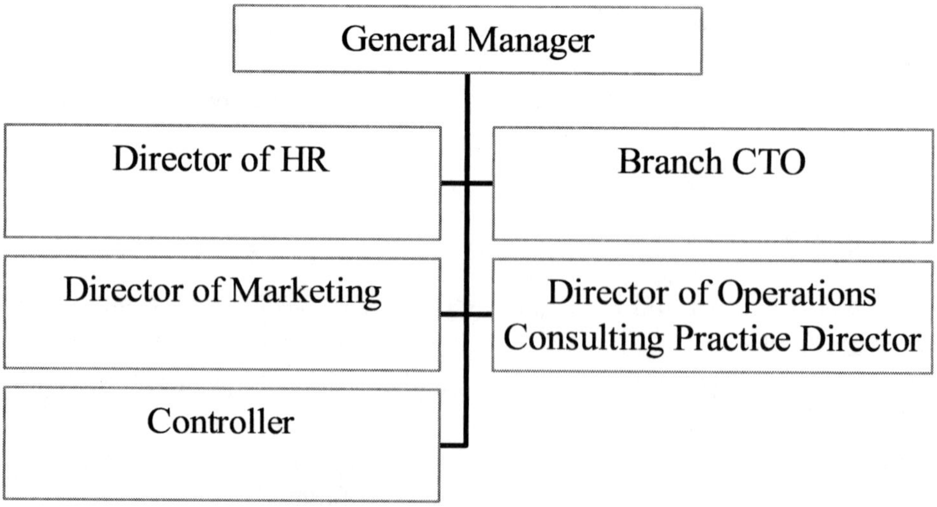

General Manager	
Director of HR	Branch CTO
Director of Marketing	Director of Operations Consulting Practice Director
Controller	

increasing taxes. The entrepreneurs felt that none of these factors would be a hindrance to their success.

Another risk within this market place is the talent shortage due to a significant increase in multinational investment in the country and a low unemployment rate. The solution to this issue is offering a superior product that is recognized within the IT industry and providing opportunities for people to be included in the future growth of the Irish economy.

A challenging issue within the Irish economy is the cost of real estate (largely impacted by inflationary pressures). In the past four years it has not been atypical of metropolitan area homes to increase in value by 400%.

Cultural issues that may impact the business include a lack of trust in the security of technology. Amarach Consulting measured three distinct groups, including "multi-techs, mobile techs, and anti-techs" (MacCarvill, 2000). Unfortunately, the anti-techs seem to make up about twenty-eight percent of the population. The fortunate part is that this group does not represent the target market that is sought within the scope of the client base.

NEXT STEPS

Having explored the organizational structure and the risks and rewards associated with the venture, O'Conner and Kelly considered their financing. They hoped that funding for this project could come from an already established consulting firm that has a desire to expand into the European market place. Additional funding should be sought from the IIDA and other Irish business incubators.

Pre-Implementation efforts include obtaining office space and recruiting the five top positions within the Irish market place. This should involve advertising in advance in many Dublin-based newspapers and recruiting agencies. Additional funding should be sought at this time to capitalize on the Irish desire to grow multinational influence within their borders. Another pre-implementation effort is partnering with an already established Irish consulting company in a strategically complementary aspect of IT and e-commerce. This partnership will provide insights not simply to the business atmosphere, but to the cultural and legal sensitivities not already outlined in this chapter. "In fact, in an e-business environment where partnerships are everything, relationship management becomes one of the key corporate competencies, and the IS executive who possesses these skills can ride them into new roles as GMs or COOs" (Field 2000).

Once the implementation of this plan was begun, O'Conner and Kelly knew it could be implemented quickly. Three months should be used to establish the office and hire the first wave of people to run the organization. Within six to nine months, the business should be up and operational including placement of consultants at client locations or on client projects working remotely.

O'Conner and Kelly knew that E-commerce is so much more then a technological revolution. It is a shift in thinking that is real, predictable, and appreciable. As they read in an April 2000, B2B article, Nicholas Negreponte, Director of MIT's Media Lab made an interesting comment about the future of business in an electronic world: "When you go out today to buy a car, you are actually buying a piece of metal with four wheels on it. Tomorrow when you buy a car you will be buying an entire transportation service [system]." We think that's a fundamental example of what this chapter has attempted to reveal. Price will not be the competition in the future. Other factors will influence people's decisions to buy, e.g., service, wrap-around features, and customer services.

The Celtic Tiger's influence on e-Europe will not be felt for a few years yet, however the time to capitalize on this European secret treasure chest is now. Ireland is not a market for "day traders" of technology but a safety position for a long-term success story. So many factors are influencing Ireland's ability to be a major player in the European e-conomy of the future that it's almost scary that the IT community isn't jumping up and down yelling and screaming: "Hey look here. Look at the open door to Europe. Look at all this free money!" The world of technology is moving so quickly that people don't have time to pick up their heads to look more then twelve months down the road. For those who do, and see the green of Ireland, they will also see the green of dollars before long. O'Conner and Kelly want to be there.

STUDY QUESTIONS

The authors of this chapter have suggested a strategy for a pair of entrepreneurs seeking to make their fortune in e-commerce using Ireland as a focus. This strategy is very much based upon standard theories of business strategy, organizational growth and information technology management. However, the world is changing so rapidly and the fundamental issues are so fluid that these theories may be called into question. The following questions should be used to open a dialogue into the theories, options and directions possible.

1.   What differences in strategy would be appropriate if the entrepreneurs described in this case were American seeking to enter a new market, or Irish, attempting to start a new local venture?

2.   Given the shakeout in the "dot-com" world, what advice would be appropriate for the consultants to give for their Irish clients?
3.   Using the dynamic resources of the Internet, what current social, political and economic issues are emerging that would change the strategies described in the case? What mechanisms should be incorporated in the theoretical consulting businesses practices to assure it of continued viability?
4.   What details are missing from the suggestions for business operations? How important is a comprehensive business plan in this environment?

REFERENCES

Amárach Consulting. (2000). About the future: Economic change. *Amárach*. Retrieved June 25, 2000 on the World Wide Web: http://www.amarach.com.

B2B Brief. (2000). *B2B*, April, 10.

Brigham Young University and eMSTAR, Inc. (1999). *Culturgram 2000–Ireland*, 153-156.

Business 2 Consumer. (2000). *B2B*, April, 24-25.

Business.com: Inside the Business of E-Business. (2000). *B2B*, May, 10.

Carpenter, P. (2000). *eBrands, Building an Internet Business at Breakneck Speed*. Boston, MA: Harvard Business School Press.

Case Studies. (2001). *VNU Business Publications*. Retrieved on the World Wide Web: http://www.room.vnu.co.uk/e_com/e_05_01.htm.

Codogno, L. (2000). Euro financial outlook. *Global Markets Group: Euro Economics & Interest Rate Research*. Bank of America, July.

Cross, L. (2000). *Overview of the Pfizer Tablet Plant at Ringaskiddy*. Cork Co., Ireland, August.

Dennehy, J. (2000). The pandora's box of e-business. *B2B*, May, 51.

E-Business is Here and Now. Open Up to it. (2000). Pamphlet, Enterprise Ireland, 1-2.

Eircell Press Release. (2000). *Eircell's Customer Base Exceeds 1 Million–An Increase of 66% in 1 Year*. Retrieved on the World Wide Web: http://www.eircell.ie/htm/oneir/company/word.

Ekoniak, J. (2000). Trends in the b-to-b space. *Upside*, August, 166-168.

The Electronic Commerce Association of Ireland. (2000). *EU E-Commerce Directive*. Retrieved on the World Wide Web: http://www.ecai.ie/.

Enterprise Ireland Press Release. (2000). *Irish E-Business Companies on US Partnership Trail in New York's Silicon Alley*, May. Retrieved on the World Wide Web: http://www.enterprise-ireland.com/english.asp.

Evans, P. and Wurster, T. S. (2000). *Blown to Bits*. Boston, MA: Harvard Business School Press.

E-Work Guide to Company Use. (2000). Pamphlet, Enterprise Ireland, 28.

Field, T. (2000). Special report-IS at the crossroads: A matter of life and death. *CIO*, June, 98-138.

The Future of E-Commerce UK Developments. (2000). *VNU Business Publications*. Retrieved on the World Wide Web: http://www.room.vnu.co.uk/e_com/e_04_e50.

Henry, M. and O'Neill, G. (1999). Facts and strategy for e-commerce in Ireland. *Eir-Commerce*, June, 1-11.

Ince, J. (2000). To B2B, or not to B2B. *Upside*, August, 130-160.

Internet Commerce to Top $30bn in Western Europe by 2001. (2000). *VNU Business Publications*. Retrieved on the World Wide Web: http://www.room.vnu.co.uk/e_com/e_05_50.htm.

"Ireland Becoming Europe's e-com Hub: Government Internet Policies Shaped to Appeal to the Major Players in Cyberspace," Backgrounders, http://www.ebizchronicle.com/backgrounders/january/ireland.

Ireland Industrial Development Agency. (1999). Achieve European competitive advantage in Ireland. Pamphlet, 1-10.

Ireland Industrial Development Agency. (2000). "e-commerce," Pamphlet, 1.

Irish E-Commerce to be Worth £3.4bn by 2002. (2000). *B2B*, May, 8.

ITS 2007: Opportunities for Ireland's High-Technology Internationally Traded Services (ITS) Sector to 2007. (2000). Pamphlet, Enterprise Ireland, 2-32.

James, M. (2000). Recruitment's e-volution. *Amárach*. Retrieved August 12, 2000 on the World Wide Web: http://www.amarach.com/.

Joshi, M. and Yermish, I. (2000). The digital economy: A golden opportunity for entrepreneurs? *New England Journal of Entrepreneurship*, 3(1), Spring, 15-22.

Kafka, S. (2000). Why all the buzz about B2B? *Upside*, August, 136-140.

Kanter, R. M. (2001). *Evolve! Succeeding in the Digital Culture of Tomorrow*. Boston, MA: Harvard Business School Press.

Kennedy, J. (2000). B2B exchanges-Chasing new vistas. *B2B*, April, 18-21.

MacCarvill, B. (2000). *New Report Shows Irish Youth Crazy for SMS*. Amárach. Retrieved June 25, 2000 on the World Wide Web: http://www.amarach.com/news/press7.

MacCarvill, B. (2000). *One in Four Now Use the Internet*. Amárach. Retrieved June 25, 2000 on the World Wide Web: http://www.amarach.com/news/press9.htm.

MacCarvill, B. (2000). *The Tech Divide-New Research from Amárach Consulting*. Amárach. Retrieved June 25, 2000 on the World Wide Web: http://www.amarach.com/news/press8.htm.

Molloy, C. (2000). E-procurement by Irish firms to grow 21% in 12 months. *B2B*, April, 4.

Morrison, S. (2000). *Technology Operations at Bank of America European HQ in London*, July.

Moynihan, J. (2000). *Customer Marketing and Overview of Coca-Cola Operations for Greater Europe*, August, .

Mr. Digital. (2000). *B2B*, April, 29.

The Numbers Page: 22% of Irish Adults Online-e-commerce Growth Low. (2000). *B2B*, April, 12.

Porter, M. E. (2001). Strategy and the Internet. *Harvard Business Review*, 79(3), March, 63-78.

Smith, I. (2000). Turn your business inside out. *B2B*, May, 36.

Taking Your Business Online. (2000). Pamphlet, Enterprise Ireland, 2-40.

War Stories of the Web: Why Businesses Fail Online. (2000). *B2B*, May, 22-24.

Wheatley, M. (2000). Mobile technology: High wireless act. *CIO*, July, 126-136.

Zachary, G. P. (2000). Euro limits options for Ireland as Dublin copes with inflation. *Wall Street Journal*, May.

Chapter X

ENI Company

Ook Lee
Hansung University, Korea

INTRODUCTION

ENI Company is an electronic commerce firm in South Korea. ENI Company provides English news items and English lessons to the subscribers through daily e-mail service that includes free English news-related question and answer sessions via e-mail. This case study deals with the struggle of this firm to establish and sustain its business in a less-developed national information infrastructure. Information on national information infrastructure and the Internet in South Korea is provided in order to facilitate understanding of the difficulty that ENI Company faces while conducting e-commerce in South Korea. The chronology of ENI Company evolution is described and the organizational structure of ENI Company is also presented. The marketing of ENI Company's products that is the biggest challenge for the firm is also discussed. This case is a good example of how to conduct an e-commerce in a county where national IT infrastructure is not ready for it.

BACKGROUND

Literature Survey

We can easily suggest that doing an e-commerce business in a developed country should be different from doing it in a less-developed country; here "development" refers mainly to the level of national IT infrastructure development. National IT infrastructure can be defined as the vision of broadband communications that are interoperable as though a single network, easily accessible and widely distributed to all groups within society bringing business, education, and government services directly to households and facilitating peer to peer communication throughout society(Kraemer, et al., 1996). But this idealistic vision is hard to achieve for countries with less economic resources. By conducting a literature survey on e-commerce in developing countries, the following factors in addition to having a well-developed national IT infrastructure, were found to be necessary for a country in order to provide a fertile ground for e-commerce.

1. **Active use of credit cards in the Internet**: countries such as Philippines, India, and China, where credit cards are not widely used, can not find a workable payment method for e-commerce (Asuncion, 1997; Bhatnagar, 1997; Liu, 1997; Rao, 1998). In a way, South Korea is similar to these countries even though credit cards are widely used since many consumers on the Internet are very much reluctant to give out their credit card number. In the cultural point of view, another reason can be the fact that Koreans love to use cash in most business transactions even for a large sum just like people in Hong Kong (Westland, et al., 1997). As for the payment method in e-commerce in Korea, many companies use money transfer through a bank account, i.e., the buyer sends money to the bank account of the seller and the seller will send the goods to the buyer. This kind of pay-first-get-the goods-later payment method is obviously an obstacle for e-commerce to grow since many consumers feel insecure. Thus it is clear that without the full trust between consumers and e-commerce companies, even a country with widespread credit card use can not facilitate the growth of e-commerce.

2. **Fixed fee option of the unlimited use of local telephone lines**: Unlike the U.S., the South Korean telephone company is a government-owned monopoly. Even though it is trying to upgrade the communication lines with fiber-optic cables, its business policy has not changed, i.e., there is no concept of separate billing for the unlimited local call option. In other words, if a person makes a local call to the Internet Service Provider and surfs the net for a long time, the person will get a very expensive phone bill. With this kind of environment, it is not easy to do e-commerce.

South Korean Internet Statistics

It is estimated that the number of Internet users in Korea is about 350,000 in 1996 as shown in Table 1(NCA, 1997).

In Figure 1 (NCA, 1997), we can see the rapid growth in the number of users of dedicated lines for their Internet use in Korea. The users are, in general, institutions which then provide Internet access to employees or students in the institution.

In Figure 2 (NCA, 1997), we can also sce the rapid growth in the number of owners of PPP/Shell accounts for their Internet use in Korea. The owners are normally individual subscribers of commercial Internet Service Providers.

Using a Web-based survey(NCA, 1997), National Computerization Agency(NCA) of Korea was able to collect important statistics on the demographics of the Internet users in Korea. The total number of respondents who visited the survey Web site and completed the questionnaire was 1725 and following is the result of the survey.

- SEX: male (1463), female (262).
- AGE: under 15 (26), 15-20 (459), 21-25 (453), 26-30 (457), 31-35 (173), 36-40 (75), 41-45 (55), 46-50 (18), over 50 (9).
- OCCUPATION: college student (952), worker-non computer or Internet industry (305), worker-computer industry (125), primary and secondary school student (73), researcher (67), worker-Internet industry (52), teacher and professor (40), government (28), business executive (8), miscellaneous (75).

Table 1: Number of Internet users in Korea

	Commercial ISP users	Non-Commercial ISP users
Institution	51,850	69,000
Individual	231,226	221
Total	283,076	69,221

Figure 1: Number of dedicated line users (Institutions) in Korea

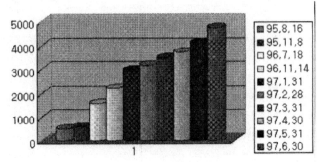

Figure 2: Number of owners of PPP/shell account in Korea

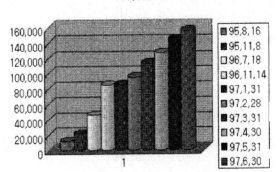

PPP/Shell

Legend:
- 95,8,16
- 95,11,8
- 96,7,18
- 96,11,14
- 97,1,31
- 97,2,28
- 97,3,31
- 97,4,30
- 97,5,31
- 97,6,30

- EDUCATION: primary school (39), middle school (34), high school (754), 2-year college (261), 4-year college (471), master's (145), doctoral (21).
- PURPOSE OF USING INTERNET: information collection (1301), research (135), entertainment (151), business (82), miscellaneous (56).
- YEARS USING INTERNET: less than 6 months (147), 6 months to one year (854), one-two years (410), two-three years (161), over 3 years (153).

The result shows that the Internet in Korea is a new medium used mainly by young college students and professionals for non-business-related activity; this also means that user population is not very active in utilizing e-commerce as of 1997.

NCA also reports that the total number of e-commerce Web sites in Korea is 140 where only 50 have all the mechanisms for automated shopping, i.e., the payment method using credit cards is workable for these sites as of March, 1998 (NCA, 1998). In the same report, NCA estimates the volume of e-commerce in 1998 to be around 9.4 billion won (7 million US dollar). Thus it is clear that e-commerce is in its infancy in Korea.

ENI Company Introduction

ENI Company (pseudonym is being used to protect the anonymity of the firm) is a South Korean firm that specializes delivering overseas news in English and its translation with lessons on English language to the subscribers via e-mail. The primary goal of this business is to educate the public in English reading comprehension as well as inform through up-to-date foreign current affair items. The business was formed in 1997 by a university professor who had extensive knowledge in world affairs. The business charges the subscribers a monthly fixed fee that was approximately US$10. The English news and its translation with lessons on English expressions are delivered everyday via e-mail to the subscribers. The subscribers can also ask questions regarding the content of the news item and its explanation and the firm answers them as soon as possible.

SETTING THE STAGE

Before we embark on presenting our case, we need to address following issues. Since our subject firm is an e-commerce firm in South Korea, it is bounded by the level of development of South Korean national IT infrastructure. Thus information on South Korean national IT infrastructure is given. Our subject firm also needs to conduct marketing in cyberspace and in order to facilitate understanding of the concept of cyberspace marketing, we introduce some background theories of cyberspace marketing.

Table 2: Size of domestic PC market

Year	1991	1992	1993	1994
Quantity	614	665	773	1200

Table 3: Telephone lines per 100 population (1993)

Korea	US	Japan	Germany	UK	France
38	53	47	46	47	53

Table 4: Subscribers of mobile communications

	1993	1994
Mobile Telephones	472	960

Table 5: Multimedia industry (1994)

Type	Sales (Billion Won)
Multimedia PC	94.5
CD-ROM drive	37.5
CD-ROM Title	38.0
Sound card	51.4
Image card	25.0
Tools	5.4
Total	251.8

South Korean National IT Infrastructure

South Korea embarked on building its national IT infrastructure in 1994 which was officially called "Korea Information Infrastructure (KII)" project (Jeong and King, 1996). The Korean government committed itself to promoting industries such as computer makers, telecommunication network builders and value-added service providers, multimedia firms, cable TV industries, and Internet-related companies. Major aspects of Korean national IT infrastructure are described in following tables (Jeong and King, 1996).

E-commerce firms in South Korea have to struggle in a national IT infrastructure which is not adequate for effective commercial activity yet. This case shows that despite this kind of hardship, it is possible to create and run an e-commerce firm even though it will be difficult to generate a big financial bonanza.

Cyberspace Marketing

As many firms throughout the world try to conduct business on the Internet, the importance of marketing in the Internet has become an important issue to IS scholars and practitioners alike (Copfer, 1998). Some businesses are interested in setting up a WWW site to expand their reach to customers in addition to the physical entity in real world, whereas others try to establish a presence in the Internet without having any physical entity in the real world. In both cases, firms need to conduct marketing in order to solve vexing questions such as who the customers are, how to advertise effectively, etc. (Mosley, 1998).

In this case study we define those consumers who are using the Internet and/or an online information provider such as America Online as consumers of cyberspace. Now that cyberspace is born and all these users of cyberspace are reachable by the Internet and they, therefore, have become attractive consumers to the companies that always try to get any individual consumer's attention. For example, a consumer spend their awake time in watching TV or listening to the radio; this is the reason that advertisements exist in those mediums. Thus, similarly, more and more people are spending their time surfing the Internet, which means that companies should advertise in this medium too, since the consumers' precious attention span is being used here just as with TV and radio.

Thus how to advertise effectively in cyberspace has become a very important issue. To advertise effectively, a business should choose the right kind of tool in order to reach enough customers with a reasonable amount of time and money. Many businesses now have Web pages which were made for variety of purposes. For example, big corporations created Web pages to promote corporate image, thus these Web sites are not for trading goods and services. On the other hand, some firms created Web sites for the purpose of selling goods and services such as books, computers, flowers, etc.. Among them, some exist only in Web sites, i.e., no physical entity exists, while others have physical entities with Web sites used for additional business from cyberspace consumers. Except for corporations which created Web sites for public relations purposes, all other Web sites are engaged in profit-making ventures, which consequently need sophisticated marketing strategies and tools (Hansen, 1998). Thus, Internet marketing can be defined as marketing strategies and tools that are designed to enhance product purchases on the Internet. In other words, Internet marketing is geared toward consumers of cyberspace.

These consumers of cyberspace have some distinctive characteristics compared to real-world consumers. The main differences are as follows. The consumers of cyberspace choose only the Web sites which are of interest to them, which means that unlike TV, radio or print advertisement, it is difficult to promote a product to unsuspecting mass customers. In other words, people who are interested in adult-related products will go to those Web sites without wandering into some other Web sites, such as those selling flowers. Thus, making people aware of the existence of particular Web sites even though they are not of interest to the consumer at the moment is not easy. There are some technological breakthroughs such as PUSH technology which does provide Web site information to the consumer who seems to have potential interest in the particular area (Burke, 1997).

But even in PUSH technology, one can only push things after the information regarding the customers' behavior is gathered. Thus, with millions newly signing-up to the Internet everyday, the PUSH technology has its limits. Nowadays, Internet advertising is often done in banner ads which take up small space on a Web page, are supposedly noticeable and, hopefully, actually being read. But banner ads can appear only in Web pages which a particular consumer reads, i.e., if the Web site is not visited by consumers, the ad becomes simply obsolete. There has to be a better way to market a product in the Internet in order to reach more people possibly in mass numbers.

Direct e-mail advertisement can be a good answer to solve the above stated problem in Internet marketing. One can not reach mass customers if only banner ads are used. Direct and bulk e-mailing literally means sending bulk or mass number of e-mails directly to unsuspecting users of cyberspace (Gustavson, 1997). The product that is advertised in a direct e-mail advertisement can be anything, which means that unlike PUSH technology which advertises only products considered to be of interest to consumers whose online browsing behavior is known, the direct e-mail advertisement can send promotional messages of any product to almost anybody who has an e-mail address. Thus, direct and bulk e-mailing is more or less similar to the direct marketing in real-world shopping. In direct marketing, shoppers are either called or sent a so-called junk-mail by the direct marketer.

Culnan (1993) investigated the consumer attitudes toward direct mail advertisement. In her paper, she claims that strategic uses of information technology based on personal information may raise privacy concerns among consumers if these applications do not reflect a common set of values. Her study addresses what differentiates consumers who object to certain uses of personal information from those who do not object. Data collected by questionnaire from young consumers are used to identify a research approach for investigating attitudes toward the secondary use of personalinformation for direct marketing. Secondary information use occurs when personal information collected for one purpose is subsequently used for a different purpose. While secondary information use is both widespread and legal, it may be viewed as an invasion of privacy when it occurs without the knowledge or consent of the consumer.

But in the case of direct e-mail advertisement, there is no prior knowledge or consent of the consumer, therefore there can be serious problems using direct e-mailing as a marketing tool. The setting for her study is the use of point-of-sale data from a supermarket frequent shopper program to generate direct mail solicitations. Control emerges as a clear theme in differentiating individuals with positive overall attitudes toward secondary information use from those with negative attitudes. Study participants with positive attitudes are less concerned about privacy (measured as control over personal information, i.e., some people don't like to try hard to keep every aspect of his/her life under tight control while some people like to be secretive about almost everything; like to be in total control over one's life), perceive shopping by mail as beneficial, and have coping strategies for dealing with unwanted mail.

Notice that this result happens when the use of secondary information was already consented. Thus, in direct e-mailing advertisement, even people who have a tendency to favor less control over his/her life and are more tolerant of junk surface mail, can react negatively to those direct e-mail ads since there was no consent of their address for information use, whatsoever. But people who have tendency to tolerate junk surface mail, might still react positively since those e-mails contain information about products that can be useful or cheaper for the consumer.

Some merits of direct e-mail advertisement are as following.

a) Unlike direct marketing which can cost heavily, the cost of bulk e-mailing is very low since sending e-mail letters to any number of people in the world does not cost a dime, at least for the use of the communication line, i.e., Internet communication is free. All the firm has to pay is a local phone bill and, if the firm does not own a server, to pay the Internet service provider which does not charge by the number of e-mail letters, but by the time spent online (sometimes, just a flat fee per a certain period time, say, a month).

b) E-mail can cause a very direct response from the consumer since unlike junk letters in real world marketing, people tend to read e-mails even though those are advertisement (Martin, 1998). Junk-mails can be thrown out without even considering what the content could be. But junk or spam e-mails are harder to delete away because people tend to read any e-mail before they delete it. Once they read it, the information which is contained in the ad e-mail can be very effective in terms of getting attention from the customer.

CASE DESCRIPTION

Chronology of ENI Company

1997 January: ENI Company was founded by a marketing professor who spent 10 years studying and working in US and Australia.

1997 February: With 108 subscribers, ENI started to send English news via e-mail.

1997 May: The number of subscribers: 220. ENI Company started an advertising campaign in the conventional media as well as cyberspace.

1998 May: The number of subscribers: 1,002. The amount of projected annual sales revenue: 120,000 dollars. The amount of projected annual net profit: 30,000 dollars.

Organization of ENI Company

The founder, who is also the CEO, wanted to minimize bureaucracy which he regarded as a major cost center. Thus the organization of ENI Company is very flat, with primary workers being teachers whose main tasks include translating English news items and answering questions from subscribers. Currently ENI Company has 10 teachers who work in an autonomous environment where each teacher has the authority to work, i.e., teachers

Figure 3: Organizational structure of ENI company

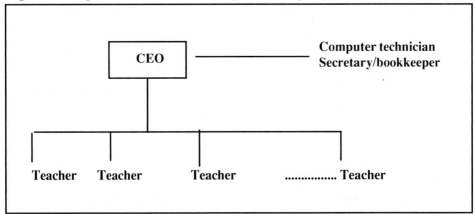

have no management interference on how they write English news items and how they answer questions from subscribers. They are given a PC and an e-mail account for their work. Thus translating English news from sources such as AP or Reuters which provide up-to-date news in the Internet, and sending the translated English news plus explanations on English expressions in the news via e-mail, and answering e-mail questions from subscribers, all fall into each teacher's responsibility. With the current 1,000 subscribers, each teacher deals with 100 subscribers personally. Other staff include a computer techni-cian and a secretary who also works as a bookkeeper. Figure 3 shows the organizational structure of ENI Company.

Marketing Strategy of ENI Company

The marketing strategy of ENI Company can be analyzed through marketing mix components as following.
1. **Product**: ENI Company tried to differentiate its products from its competitors by giving a personal touch. In other words, by answering questions from subscribers promptly and paying attention to each subscriber's needs in English learning, ENI Company was successful in attracting loyal followers.
2. **Price**: ENI Company tried to differentiate its price from its competitors by offering a fixed monthly fee regardless of the number of questions answered. Other services charged customers by the length of time they spent on their service, since other services were available on the online information providers unlike ENI Company which supplies via e-mail.
3. **Place**: ENI Company did not see a presence in the Web as a viable option due to the small number of Internet surfers. Instead, ENI Company

noticed that even though there were relatively small number of people surfing the Internet, many more people have e-mail accounts either from commercial Internet Service Providers or from non-commercial Internet Service Providers such as one's own schools and companies. Thus ENI Company decided to exist only in the e-mail form until there will be more Web surfers in Korea.

4. **Promotion**: ENI Company tried cyberspace advertising medium such as banner ads which failed due to the small number of Web surfers, and bulk e-mailing ads which failed due to the high telephone bill for modem-based mailing and the law against such bulk e-mailing ads for non-modem-based mailings. ENI Company relied more on conventional advertising medium such as magazine and newspaper ads.

In summary, Table 6 outlines the marketing strategy of ENI Company.

In CEO's Own Words

The CEO of ENI Company provided detailed information on the firm. Following conversations are taken from the interview with the CEO.

Q: When and how was ENI created?

A: "In the beginning of 1997 I created the firm since I thought that I could use my extensive knowledge on world affairs in helping Koreans understand foreign news and at the same time, teach them on English lessons using expressions used in the news items. The Koreans are very interested in improving their English skill, especially young students in high school or college since it is vital to acquire a good English skill in order to get into a good college and to land in a better job. My idea was that if ENI Company could provide attentive answers to questions regarding English promptly, many people would sign on to our service. It turned out to be true. But there was a serious difficulty in getting our company known to the general public."

Q: What are its short and long term objectives?

A: "In short term, our objective is to create a critical mass of loyal subscribers whose size should be at least 1,000 people, which we achieved in a year. In long term, our objective is to move to the Web eventually and be able

Table 6: Marketing strategy of ENI company

Product	Personal Touch
Price	Fixed Fee
Place	E-mail Form
Promotion	Conventional Medium

to serve multimedia English news and lessons when the IT infrastructure of Korea improves and the number of Internet users increases significantly."

Q: Who are ENI Company's competitors?

A: "There are several similar services in the online information providers such as "Chollian" which is similar to AOL in US. But they don't send out individual e-mails; they put English news and lessons in the directory of online information providers. Thus they can not give the personal touch as ENI Company does. ENI Company is the only one that provides daily e-mail English news service to the individual subscribers in Korea."

Q: What were the challenges ahead? And how has ENI addressed the challenges?

A: "The challenge was marketing, especially advertising. In order to get more subscribers, it was critical to do effective advertising campaign. We tried conventional advertising medium such as magazines, radio, and news-papers as well as cyberspace advertising medium such as banner ads in the Web page and direct e-mail ads. Besides conventional advertising medium whose effect was obvious, we thought that cyberspace ads could be effective too. At first, the banner ad in the Web page looked attractive but soon we realized that the number of people who browsed the Web pages in South Korea was still not big enough due to the low development of national IT infrastructure. We finally looked at mass mailing technique and it looked workable. We sent out direct e-mail ads and found out that modem-based bulk mailing used up so much telephone time that it was not financially feasible since there was no fixed fee option for local phone call in Korea. Non-modem-based bulk mailing through the Internet could not be used either since the Internet bulk mailing was already against the law in Korea. Thus we relied more on conventional medium such as magazine and newspaper ads."

Q: What were the critical events and outcomes in the evolution of ENI Company?

A: "The critical event happened after we installed the mass mailer and used it for sending advertisement mails for ENI Company. We didn't realize how big the telephone bill could be when the dial-up connection was used for a long time. In other words, during the peak hours the performance of the mass mailer got downgraded, which resulted in taking much longer time to finish sending out all mails. This meant a disaster for ENI Company since the increased revenue from the bigger number of subscribers thanks to the mass mail advertisement was wiped out because of astronomical amount of the local phone bill. This event forced us to give up advertising through the mass mailer."

CURRENT CHALLENGES/PROBLEMS FACING THE ORGANIZATION

Following matters can be considered to be current challenges/problems for ENI Company.

First, how to sustain an e-commerce venture in a less-developed national IT infrastructure is a big concern for ENI Company. Effective e-commerce activity requires well-developed national information technology infrastructure such as well-connected fiber optic computer networks that cover the entire country, and easy availability of computers and affordable cost of network use among ordinary citizens of the country.

Second, how to conduct marketing for the venture is another big concern for ENI Company. Not only is it very difficult to establish a functioning e-commerce firm but it is even more difficult to do marketing on the Internet. The product of an e-commerce firm is usually advertised in banner-style ads in the Web page, which is a common practice and is considered to be a working solution in developed countries. However, in countries such as South Korea, not many people are surfing the Internet, i.e., the number of people who can afford to surf the Internet for quite a long time are very limited due to the outdated billing practice of the government-owned monopolistic phone company. Thus, in this environment an e-commerce company which wants to sell a tangible product such as computer hardware components or software items has no choice but to create a Web page that sells those products and faces the problem of how to make its Web page noticeable to the small-number of Web surfers in Korea. Furthermore, those e-commerce companies who sell intangible goods face even more difficult challenge in advertising their products. The company which is the subject of this case sells English news and English lessons as products; they deliver these products to the individual's e-mail account. In short, any e-commerce company in Korea faces the same problem in marketing, which is how to advertise effectively in an environment where there are only small number of people who are surfing World Wide Web pages.

Third, how to establish a workable payment method is the biggest concern for ENI Company. This matter is a serious obstacle in the development of e-commerce even in developed countries such as the U.S. since consumers are worried that their credit card numbers might be stolen and might not get the ordered goods after paying with credit cards. In less developed countries such as South Korea, the consumers are, of course, very much worried when they order a product online or through the Internet, not because of the possibility that their credit card numbers might be stolen, but mostly because of the fact that the cash they have already paid might be robbed, i.e., the goods never arrive. The reason is rather simple. In a less-developed country like South Korea, not many people have credit cards and even for those with credit cards, tend to prefer cash when the price of the good is not very high. For this reason, most online payment is made as follows: First, the customer goes to the bank and does a wire-transfer of cash to the designated bank account of the seller which is an e-commerce firm. Second, the e-commerce firm's employee goes to the bank and checks if a certain customer's cash was transferred. Last, if the money-transfer is confirmed then the firm sends out the good that was ordered by the customer. With this kind of payment method, the consumers are naturally worried, since in actual incidents some firms took the money and ran away, i.e., no goods arrived.

Last, how to handle customer relations is also a concern for ENI Company. The subject of our case is a firm that claims to be attentive to the needs of the customers, i.e., it promises to answer all questions regarding English news items and lessons using those news items that are delivered to the subscribers. But in reality, it is very difficult to give satisfying answers to every question from the customer. Thus, quality control of customer service is a challenging puzzle to solve.

FURTHER READING

Kalakota, R. and Whinston, A. B. (1996). *Electronic Commerce: A Manager's Guide*. Addison-Wesley Publications.

Kalakota, R. and Whinston, A. B. (1996). *Frontiers of Electronic Commerce*. Addison-Wesley Publications.

Keen, P. G. W. and Ballance, C. (1997). *Online Profits: A Manager's Guide to Electronic Commerce*. Harvard Business School Press.

Meeker, M. and Stanley, M. (1997). *The Internet Advertising Report*. HarperCollins.

O'Keefe, S. (1996). *Publicity on the Internet: Creating Successful Publicity Campaigns on the Internet and the Commercial Online Services*. John Wiley & Sons.

Sterne, J. (1997). *What makes people click: Advertising on the Web*. Que Education & Training.

Whinston, A. B., Stahl, D. O. and Choi, S. Y. (1997). *The Economics of Electronic Commerce*. Macmillan Technical Publishing.

Wong, P. K. (1996). Implementing the NII vision: Singapore's experience and future challenges. *Information Infrastructure and Policy*, 5(2), 95-117.

Zeff, R. L., Aronson, B. and Zeff, R. (1997). *Advertising on the Internet*. John Wiley & Sons.

REFERENCES

Asuncion, R. M. (1997). Potentials of electronic markets in the Philippines. *Electronic Markets*, 7(2), 34-37.

Bhatnagar, S. (1997). Electronic commerce in India: The untapped potential. *Electronic Markets*, 7(2), 22-24.

Burke, R. (1997). Do you see what I see? The future of virtual shopping. *Journal of the Academy of Marketing Science*, 25(4), 352-360.

Copfer, R. (1998). Marketing in an online world. *American Salesman*, 43(3), 19-21.

Culnan, M. (1993). How did they get my name?: An exploratory investigation of consumer attitudes toward secondary information use. *MIS Quarterly*, 17(3), 341-361.

Gustavson, J. (1997). Netiquette and DM. *Marketing*, November, 102(42), 46.

Hansen, G. (1998). Smaller may be better for Web marketing. *Marketing News*, January, 32(2), 10-11.

Jeong, K.H. & King, J. (1996). National Information Infrastructure Initiatives in Korea: Vision and Policy Issues. *Information Infrastructure And Policy*, 5(2), 119-133.

Kraemer, K., Dedrick J., Jeong, K. H., King, J., Thierry, V., West, J. and Wong, P. K. (1996). National information infrastructure: A cross-country comparison. *Information Infrastructure And Policy*, 5(2), 81-93.

Liu, Z. (1997). China's information super highway: Its goal, architecture and problems. *Electronic Markets*, 7(4), 45-50.

Martin, J. (1998). You've got junk mail. *PC World*, 16(4), 45-46.

Mosley, J. (1998). Deck us all in online shopping. *Marketing News*, January, 32(2), 6.

NCA (National Computerization Agency of Korea). (1997). *A Study on the Technical Trend of the NIC(Network Information Center) and Internet Technologies*. Retrieved on the World Wide Web: http://ncalib.nca.or.kr/HTML/1997/97066/f97066.htm.

NCA (National Computerization Agency of Korea). (1998). *The White Paper on Informatization of 1998*. Retrieved on the World Wide Web: http://calsec.nca.or.kr/knowledgebase.htm.

Rao, M. (1998). Ad convention: Indian advertising agencies urged to harness Internet technologies. *Electronic Markets*, 8(1), 48-49.

Westland, J. C., Kwok, M., Shu, J., Kwok, T. and Ho, H. (1997). Electronic cash in Hong Kong. *Electronic Markets*, 7(2), 3-6.

Chapter XI

SAFECO®: Leveraging the Web in a Knowledge-Based Service Industry

Debabroto Chatterjee and Leonard M. Jessup
Washington State University, USA

The Internet and World Wide Web present significant business opportunities and threats, particularly for business organizations that are knowledge-based and/or that offer primarily information-based services. For these types of firms, the Web offers opportunities that range from exchanging information with partner organizations, the delivery of existing services to customers, and the creation of new services. The potential threats include choosing the wrong strategies for adopting We7b technologies, poor implementation of Web technologies, entering late into the realm of electronic commerce and thus losing market share, or worse, ignoring the use of the Web altogether and potentially being replaced by more nimble rivals.

The majority of large organizations in a variety of industries have slowly, cautiously begun deploying Web technologies. This is perhaps not surprising considering the implementation challenges and risks posed by this new technological innovation. It is not yet clear how large organizations, particularly those that are knowledge-based and provide primarily information-based services, should strategize about, adopt, and implement Web technologies. The purpose of this study is to understand how SAFECO, a large corporation in the insurance and financial services industry, is strategizing for and implementing technologies to exploit the Web. SAFECO was recently ranked as one of the leading innovative users of the Web technology in its industry. This further legitimizes the selection of the company as an appropriate case study site.

> When I am at Disneyland, I can come in through Main Street, where I have access to all the lands that are available, or I can come in on the monorail and get off at Tomorrow Land. When I am in Tomorrow Land it is distinctly different from Adventure Land but it is clear to me that I am still in Disneyland. There is a continuity of experience there. That's the general philosophical vision that we have for our corporate Web presence.
>
> *Rod Sargent, Director of Marketing, SAFECO*

BACKGROUND

In November 1998, George Johnson, senior vice president of marketing and operations for SAFECO, reflected on the progress the company had made during the last four years in adopting Web technology:

> The Web-based marketing and distribution initiative is a fundamental component of our strategy today. As far as what Web-based electronic commerce can do for us, it can drive up sales (by driving more prospects to our agents) and thereby drive up our revenue, and it can drive down unit costs by reducing manual interventions in our work flows. It can automate a lot of the work processes back and forth between our consumers and between our agents.

While much progress had been made in assimilating this new technology into the business activities and strategies of the firm, he recognized that a great deal still needed to be done to take full advantage of the Web's technological capabilities.

The Company

SAFECO's origin can be traced back to 1923, when Hawthorne Dent founded Dent's General Insurance Company of America in Seattle. Though it started out as a fire insurance company, today SAFECO and its subsidiaries provide a wide range of insurance and investment products sold through independent agents. Its diverse product lines include property and casualty insurance, life and health insurance, pension and annuity products, mutual funds, and real estate. The company also provides commercial financing and leasing services. It has been ranked among the top 20 "diversified financial" companies in the U.S. by *Fortune* magazine.

One of the major and critical strengths of this company is its large and loyal force of independent agents. These agents form the company's channel of distribution, and SAFECO is committed to continually enhancing its relationship with them. The following excerpts from the Message to Our Shareholders (1997 Annual Report) captures the extent of the importance the company attaches to this relationship:

> We envision SAFECO as an insurance and financial franchise unequaled in its ability to provide value and service through its independent partners. Our mission is to be the premier company distributing insurance and financial products through independent agents.

Considered one of the leading users (among independent agent insurance companies) of information technology, SAFECO proactively seeks ways to improve agents' customer service through technological and other means.

The company's business philosophy rests on a tripartite cornerstone: 1) "products of the highest quality," 2) "a strong commitment to the best customer service," and 3) "a powerful sense of responsibility to our customers, our stockholders and the many communities that we call home."

In 1997 SAFECO acquired American States Financial Corp., boosting its property/casualty business by nearly 50%. After the acquisition of American States, the management team of SAFECO felt the need for reexamining the brand identity of both SAFECO and American States. Interbrand Schechter, an internationally renowned company, was hired to conduct a brand audit of both SAFECO and American States. Such an audit was conducted, examining different aspects of the two organizations from employee, agent, and customer perspectives. The results indicated that SAFECO had extremely strong brand name recognition and it was recommended that all of SAFECO's subsidiaries and enterprises should use the same brand name. As a result, the old practice of creating unique brands for each company is giving way to a new strategy of building national brand awareness for SAFECO.

In 1998 the company contracted with the Seattle Mariners Organization to name their new baseball park SAFECO Field™. In 1999, the company announced plans to sell its real estate holdings.

The Industry

The modern insurance industry is characterized by contrasting emphases and ownerships. This hybrid nature is reflected in the diverse product lines offered by mutual (policyholder-owned) and stock (investor-owned) companies. These companies sell personal and commercial insurance for almost everything – from health and life to property and casualty. They also offer financial services that range from asset management to commercial leasing and lending.

Over the last ten years, sales have stagnated in the two major sectors of the insurance industry—life/health and property/casualty. The lack of growth can be attributed to a variety of factors. For instance, the emergence of wealth-maintenance products (such as annuities and mutual funds), designed to provide a comfortable retirement, have lured away customers from traditional life insurance products. As health-related expenses have skyrocketed, many insurance companies have abandoned selling health insurance. The property/casualty sector is also changing rapidly, especially on the commercial side, where large customers are turning to self-insurance and other risk-management alternative measures. This is in addition to the regular underwriting losses suffered due to the unpredictable acts of nature and frequently of human beings. As a result, property/casualty insurers depend on their investments to pull them into the profit column.

In addition to intra-industry competition, especially heavily concentrated in the life/health and property/casualty sectors, insurance companies are facing increasing competition from banks that are broadening their range of services. Much of this can be attributed to deregulation that has allowed a greater percentage of the total sales of a bank to be contributed by insurance subsidiaries. The 1998 mega-merger of Citicorp and Travelers Group is an example of huge corporate conglomerates that are likely to emerge to cash in on the new business opportunities created by changes in the law.

Though insurance companies, brokers, and agents added only about $197 billion (about 2.4%) to the gross domestic product in 1996, the U.S. economy relies on the insurance industry: Its significant investments in stocks, bonds, real estate and other assets provide considerable liquidity to the financial markets.

The advent of the Internet and the WWW has had a major impact on the insurance industry. It is transforming the traditional ways of selling insurance. New e-commerce business models are emerging in this industry, characterized by direct sales, increased personalization and customization of product offerings. For instance, Internet companies like termquest.com and e-insure.com are enabling potential customers to identify appropriate policies, compare them and even buy them online. Other Internet-based companies like Ebix.com, an on-line portal, are using a "reverse auction" model to sell personal lines of insurance. It allows prospects to quote a price that they are willing to pay for insurance coverage and then enables firms to offer bids in response to those quotes. Even traditional insurance companies (like Allstate and State Farm) that operate primarily in the physical market place are also setting up shop in the virtual market space to reach out to existing and potential customers (refer to Appendix 1 for competitor-related information).

While industry analysts and experts agree that face-to-face contact is still a critical part of the insurance buying process, the convenience of shopping over the Internet medium is becoming an attractive proposition to many. Moreover, with the availability of Internet-based information intermediaries that help potential customers make insurance decisions, the role and the value of traditional agents are under scrutiny. While the threat to independent agents is real, many companies continue to value and support their existence.

Despite the huge growth over the last few years, the use of the Internet to facilitate sales of insurance policies is still in its infancy. Jean Gora, manager of research for the Life Office Management Association in Atlanta, GA, points out that "business to consumer e-commerce is only one of the many ways insurers will be using the Internet in the years to come." In other words, more and more companies will be using the Internet to sell insurance to not only individual customers but also to business organizations.[5]

SETTING THE STAGE

To trace the evolution of Web application development at SAFECO, one has to begin in 1995, when the first Web project was launched. This was an intranet (refer to Appendix 2 for a primer on the Intranet platform) pilot project with which SAFECO hoped to explore Internet (refer to Appendix 2 for a primer on the Internet platform) and Web technologies. In the same year, the content development and hosting of the corporate Web site (*www.SAFECO.com*) were outsourced. While working on the intranet pilot, the technical staff grew in confidence, and soon a project was launched to build and host the Web site in-house; it has been maintained in-house since 1997.

Intranet Platform

It was an intranet pilot project that launched SAFECO's foray into Web technologies. Rod Sargent, director of marketing, commented on the evolution of the intranet.

The intranet was created by the IS community in a maverick way. They created the intranet to be able to communicate with each other. Though its growth has been kind of chaotic, this loose frontier approach allowed people to create that Web culture.

During the last four years, significant progress has been made in building an intranet environment that will enhance both operational efficiency and effectiveness (refer to Appendix 3 for sample screen shots of the intranet environment). For instance, a Grand Prix project resulted in the creation of an intranet site that allows SAFECO field staff to introduce the latest products to agents while also providing sales training and support. In addition, the site keeps track of how much new business the agents are submitting, information used to decide what marketing territory needs an extra little boost to sell more products. The intranet is envisioned ultimately to become the desktop of the company.

Internet Platform

The Internet-based public site serves as a corporate brochure, providing a variety of information relating to the company and its products and services. It primarily caters to the information needs of three types of browsers: a) existing and potential shareholders, b) existing and potential customers, and c) existing and potential independent agents (refer to Appendix 4 for sample screen shots of the SAFECO site on the Internet). For instance, it provides a historical overview of the company including how it evolved and grew over the years. There is also a range of performance related information, such as annual financial highlights, quarterly earnings, and stock quotes. There are also product and service details on the site, such as the types of insurance and investment products offered and the claim services provided. An interactive agent locator feature on the Web site enables browsers to locate agents using different search criteria—state, city, area code, zip code, and name.

Rod Sargent uses an interesting analogy to articulate the philosophical vision driving the corporate Web presence. He explained:

> When I am at Disneyland, I can come in through Main Street, where I have access to all the lands that are available, or I can come in on the monorail and get off at Tomorrow Land. When I am in Tomorrow Land it is very distinctly different from Adventure Land but it is clear to me that I am still in Disneyland. There is a continuity of experience there. That's the general philosophical vision that we have for our corporate Web presence. I need to allow each of the subsidiaries the opportunity to do affinity-type branding.

Conceptually, that meant developing a look and feel that was continuous throughout yet allowed each subsidiary to be unique and to arrange their content in a way that makes sense to their respective customers. Basically, the goal was to create a one-company image and a one-company experience for a company with many different faces. The underlying rationale here is that a customer who is interested in knowing about the range and array of products and services does not care which subsidiary offers one or more of them. In addition to the concept of a "one-company experience," there is the belief that the corporate site needs to be a much more image-focused site, while the business sites should be more service-focused.

Numerous Web application projects are in the works to realize these visions and goals. For instance, a recently developed application offers a variety of value-added services to retirement services customers. They will be able to a) check account balances, b) view unit values, yields, and existing premium allocations, c) change existing premium allocations, and d) order statements (refer to Appendix 4 for sample screen shots of the SAFECO site on the Internet).

Extranet Platform

The SAFECO extranet environment (refer to Appendix 5 for sample screen shots of the SAFECO extranet) is known by the acronym SAFESITE™ (SAFECO Architecture for Enabling Secure Internal Transaction Execution). It is a secure Web-enabled public (i.e. Internet-based) network that enables the company to provide value-added services to its agents and customers.

Some of the objectives driving the SAFESITE project are best captured in the words of Steve Schuler and Randy Balsiger (senior systems analysts in the Web Group of the Network Services Department), who have been heavily involved in this project:

> Our extranets are beginning to deliver some of our internal systems out to the agent population and replace technology that has been out there in various forms. We have a very large 3270 private network that agents dial into today. This is a replacement for that. There are some client-server applications out there for agents to use. This is again a vehicle for replacing those. It is time to rewrite some of those legacy applications and it is time to bring them together in terms of the desktop concept of "I am doing these six applications and they look different. Why don't they look alike?"

In addition to providing a user-friendly and uniform interface to a variety of legacy applications, the extranets enable secure exchange of sensitive information (like medical information) between SAFECO and its agents. The agents' concern about this matter formerly had made them reluctant to be on the public side of the Internet.

Numerous related extranet projects are in the works, most of them aimed at helping the independent agents serve SAFECO customers better. One such project is aimed at developing an automated Agent Pending Report. The deliverable of this project will allow agents to track the pending status of an application on a daily basis. Currently, they are given a report once a week. By the time the report actually gets out to the agent in the field, it is almost two weeks old. In that time a policy could have been issued or dropped without their knowledge. The result was continuous calling in to the in-house sales support staff for updates. Giving Agents daily access to this information, therefore, yields a two-fold benefit: agents will have more timely information, and the sales support unit will have additional time to work on other more important and higher priority issues.

Another project will result in the Electronic Forms and Applications system. The purpose of this project is to automate the applications submission process. The project will be completed over five phases, during which four different versions of the software will be developed. The first version will be a CD deliverable; i.e., the different application forms will be made available on a CD. The second version will be an extranet deliverable, allowing agents to access the forms via the Web interface. The advantage of the extranet deliverable version is that information can be updated at any time as compared to CDs, which would be mailed out once a quarter. Agents can thus have quicker access to any new forms (relating to new products) that have been added or to any changes that have been made to existing forms. The third version of the software will result in Web-based intelligent forms that will prompt agents to fill out sub-forms based on how they fill out applications: This way they won't have to rely on memory and risk neglecting some vital area in the paperwork. The version four deliverable will automatically complete the application and submit it for the agent.

To further help the agents, extranet-based systems are being built that will allow customers direct access to relevant information (like account balance, total coverage amount, etc.) and enable them make changes to existing policies and/or investment portfolios. In the process, these systems will not only reduce transactional costs, but also save time for both the agent and the customer. Recently, SAFECO rolled out a Web-based extranet application called SAFECOM® that enables 250 of the company's largest commercial customers to enter and analyze workers' compensation claims.

SAFECO's Web-based initiatives thus far have been successful. Indeed, *PC Week Online* recently ranked SAFECO as number five in their fast-track 100 rankings of innovative financial services sites and in the top three for insurance sites. This ranking reflects the hard work and success that SAFECO has had thus far in moving forward with leading-edge E-Commerce initiatives.

CURRENT WEB IMPLEMENTATION CHALLENGES FACING SAFECO

The company must cope with a variety of challenges to effectively assimilate Web technology into its business activities and strategies. One major challenge has been to make business sense of this technological innovation. Some of the questions that are being asked and addressed are: a) What are the key functionalities of this technology? and b) How best can we use it to serve the company's strategic objectives? Recognizing the need to consider the perspectives of both the business and IT managers, the E-Business Advisory (EBA) group was formed. Sargent, who chairs this group, explained:

> We created the EBA group to be able to integrate Web projects into our normal planning process. We are integrating it into the culture. Web technology is a reality and is here to stay. We are trying to integrate it into our main stream of business activities and strategies.

Johnson sees the EBA group performing two specific roles:

> One is to set the overall strategic tone for the company and the second is to act as a clearinghouse for all the different ideas that are generated in the different operating units in the different SAFECO companies.

While the EBA group comprises 14 senior business executives, each representing a specific business area, a similar group comprising IS executives from each of the business areas was also formed. These groups meet separately and jointly to discuss and approve, among other things, potential Web initiatives. Similar cross-functional teams also are being formed to serve as steering committees for managing the various Web projects. While these cross-functional teams have worked relatively smoothly and effectively, Johnson admits that it didn't come easily.

Building sophisticated Web applications also requires a certain level of technical expertise and this has presented SAFECO with a number of additional technical challenges. Schuler and Balsiger describe some of these challenges:

> The Web systems that we are seeing now are highly componentized and distributed and that presents a management challenge. In our environment now where we have this Web-based system with a great looking front-end, we are trying to tie it to the back-end mainframe environments and the rest of our emerging corporate distributed network as well. There are 10 or 15 different techniques of getting access to data, where there used to be two or three. The

complexity of the way you go get the data has just skyrocketed. And we really didn't do that in a distributed environment to this degree. We don't have change control processes that work across multiple services or multiple areas or problem resolution methodologies in these complex areas. For instance, if there are eight services involved and the function fails, which service went bad and how do you fix it? And if you fix this service during that time, how many applications are you impacting? Just a number of procedural and mechanical issues that we have learned to deal with extremely well in a mainframe environment, a little bit better in a distributed environments, but in the Web environment we are just all over the map. So, we have a lot of policies and procedures and infrastructure to build to do this right.

SAFECO's challenge of working its way up the Web technology learning curve is also reflected in the views expressed by other Web developers. Rudy Erb, one such Web developer, offers further illustration:

Web (applications) that interact with SQL haven't been developed here before. And so that's been probably one of our biggest technological challenges. Getting up to speed with the latest technologies, how they interact with each other and how to pass variables from one Web page to the next and how to execute stored procedures from your scripting code. Even little things like why is this tag working on IE and not Netscape are some of the daily little challenges that we have to deal with.

Schuler, who wrote the reverse proxy for securing SAFESITE, the company extranet, considers security to be a critical implementation issue. Many of the other developers concur on this and consider writing 'security' programs to be a major technical challenge. Considering that SAFECO deals with information (health and investment related) of a very confidential nature, SAFECO employees have to be extremely alert and sensitive to data integrity and privacy issues (refer to Appendix 6 for a primer on Internet security issues). Every effort needs to be made to build a very secure computing environment to collect, store, and display client information; especially, since the company offers clients the option of submitting and retrieving information online.

In addition to building Web sites, the company will also have to maintain them. Susie Barrett, SAFECO's Webmaster, draws attention to this issue:

Keeping a Web site alive, new, and fresh is a big challenge, not just for SAFECO, but for any company. There has to be a draw that gets people to come to your site, then there has to be something there for them to keep them coming back. Once we build a reliance on a site, we have to deal with the whole issue of production readiness and recoverability. Once people start relying on our Web site for business use, we have to make sure that the site is there for them whenever they might need it. What happens if the Web server goes down? What happens if only parts of it go down? These are the types of issues we're currently dealing with.

Beyond the technical challenges associated with Web application development, there is also the managerial challenge of coordinating the design and development work. This gets revealed in a developer's explanation of how building Web systems is different than building traditional mainframe applications:

Normally, when you are developing an application, it is within your group and you have all these people (within your group) going through the walk-through process. With the Web, there are also some centralized areas that are working on pieces of it. Some groups located at the home office are working on the html pieces, some groups are working on the graphics pieces and we have to pass that information to them, and so we are not doing all of the development here. So we are working with different groups to help us build this and so coordination becomes crucial.

Because each of these centralized groups receives a number of projects from different business areas, they are likely to prioritize them in the order most suitable to them. This could lead to delays in completing certain projects. As a result, constant follow-up is necessary to keep track of the status of a project. One project manager commented that because of his good relations with a particular centralized group, he was able to get the work done a lot faster.

Some Internet-based Web applications are subject to external approval processes which can take anywhere from three days to three months to complete, yet another potential project slow-down.

The company is also helping its agents and customers get up to speed on the technology. Since Web applications are being designed to provide value-added services to customers, it is imperative that agents be trained to use them. In addition to offering training sessions, the company is engaged in building agent Web sites. Sargent provides the rationale for building turnkey Web sites for the agents:

We don't want agents to become Web programmers and we don't want them to hire a high school kid who knows how to program a

Web site but does not understand the business. Also, they will get the value of our marketing expertise, our legal expertise, and we can make sure the content is accurate. They can use part of our agent incentive money to pay for the Web site. So we are fiving them incentives to use that bonus money in the right way.

Future Plans

The company plans to continue to roll out the Web-based systems described above and to continue to exploit new Web-based technologies as they evolve. In addition, the company remains firmly committed to using the Web technology to enhance business relationships with its customers and agents. This strong commitment reverberates in the following proclamation by Sargent:

Our fundamental strategic driving force in this company is the independent distribution system. We have made a really contrary statement. While other insurance companies have said that they will sell products multi-modally (directly through our call centers and also through our agents), we have said something quite to the contrary. We are committed to our agents and are committed to help agents use the new technology.

DISCUSSION QUESTIONS

1. Describe the e-business model of the company.
2. Visit SAFECO's Web site and evaluate it using the following design guideline criteria: a) usefulness, b) ease of navigation, c) elegance of organization and design, and d) interactivity.
3. Considering SAFECO's overall strategic objectives, is it making optimal use of the Web? Explain your position with examples and recommendations.
4. What is your understanding of Rod Sargent's Disneyland analogy to articulate the philosophical vision driving SAFECO's Web presence? Has this vision been realized yet? Refer to the corporate Web site features to back up your argument.
5. Describe the Web implementation challenges being faced by the company. To what extent are the challenges technological and/or organizational in nature?

ENDNOTES

1 This case study is not designed to highlight either good or bad management practices; rather, this case study is designed to highlight important strategic and implementation issues with Web usage within this context.

2 http://www.SAFECO.com/1bfrm.htm

3 The News, Vol. XXXVIII, Sept./Oct. 1998

4 http://www.hoovers.com/features/industry/insurance.html

5 National Underwriter, Dec. 20, 1999

6 National Underwriter, Jan. 12, 1998

7 PC Week Online, December 13, 1999

8 PC Week Online 1999 rankings available at http://www.zdnet.com/pcweek/stories/news/0,4153,2405179,00.html.

APPENDIX 1: COMPETITOR INFORMATION

Name	Op. Environment	Products	URL	Other
The All State Corporation	Physical and Virtual	Auto, property, casualty, and life	http://www.allstate.com	
GEICO Corporation	Physical and Virtual	Auto insurance, Cycle-Gard motorcycle insurance, emergency road service, and GEICO Overseas Insurance	http://www.geico.com	It has traditionally provided auto and other insurance to preferred low-risk demographic groups (such as government and military employees) but has also begun to target nonstandard (high-risk) drivers.
Berkshire Hathaway Inc.	Physical and Virtual	Auto insurance, fire insurance, property insurance, casualty insurance, life insurance, financial services, shoes, and furniture products.	http://www.berkshirehathaway.com	In addition to offering insurance and other financial products and services, Buffett and his partner, Charles Munger, invest in what they know: low-tech companies like Borsheim's Jewelry Company, See's Candy, a variety of shoe and furniture companies, and publishing (encyclopedias and newspapers). Berkshire Hathaway is also moving into the power sector, planning to buy a stake in MidAmerican Energy.
American Financial Group Inc.		Auto, property, casualty, life, and annuities.	http://www.amfnl.com	The company has shed its commercial lines to concentrate on property/casualty and life and annuities businesses, though it continues to invest in noncore companies such as Chiquita and Provident Financial Group (49%).

CIGNA Corporation		Life, Accident, Health, Disability, and Financial Services	http://www.cigna.com	Having sold its property/casualty business in 1999, the firm is now concentrated on employee benefits. In addition to expanding its product lines to meet clients' needs, CIGNA plans to expand into serving more small and mid-sized businesses.
e-insure.com	Virtual	Auto, home, health, life, business, and speciality insurance products	http://www.einsure.com/	
4Insurance.com	Virtual	Auto, home, health, and life insurance	http://4insurance.com/	4Insurance is a free, no obligation service that helps you save time and money by conducting an insurance auction for your business.
INSWEB.com	Virtual	Auto insurance	https://secure1.insweb.com/	InsWeb is a free on-line service that makes it easy for you to shop for and compare quotes from many of the nation's leading insurance companies.
Insurance Online.Com	Virtual	Automobile, homeowners, business & life insurance	http://www.insure.net/	On-line marketplace for insurance information, products and services
Insurance Shopping Network Inc.	Virtual	Auto, home, health, and life insurance	http://www.800insureme.com/	On-line marketplace for insurance information, products and services

APPENDIX 2: A PRIMER ON WEB PLATFORMS

	Internet	Intranet	Extranet
Definition	Global computing network that supports a variety of communication and information management services like e-mail, FTP, Telnet, Usenet, and World Wide Web (WWW).	Web-based secure network that supports intraorganizational activities like information dissemination, interactive communication and transaction processing.	Web-based secure network that supports interorganizational activities like information dissemination, interactive communication, and transaction processing. There are three types of extranets – the private network, the public network, and the virtual private network.
Commonality	Use of TCP/IP Network, Web server hardware and software, and Web clients.		
Differences	1. Web-based public network. 2. Open to public.	1. Web-based private network. 2. Use of firewalls to secure the network from public access.	
Benefits	1. Access to a global market. 2. Reduced communication costs. 3. Lower transaction costs. 4. Reduced marketing costs. 5. High quality customer support service.	1. Richer and more responsive information environment. 2. Reduced information distribution costs. 3. Facilitates collaborative work. 4. Enhances employee productivity.	1. Responsive customer support services. 2. Reduced information distribution costs. 3. Facilitates collaborative work.
Applications	Car rental companies like Alamo and Hertz provide on-line reservation services via their Web sites.	By posting the complex assembly instructions of CyberSURFR modems on the intranet, Motorola was able to considerably reduce the time normally required by the engineers to prepare and disseminate the step-by-step instructions for assembly, testing, packing, and shipping.	Prudential HealthCare has designed an extranet application that provides a variety of customer support services. Customers at their own convenience can access the extranet to change their primary-care physicians, check the status of claims, and request ID cards — among other services.

APPENDIX 3: SAMPLE SCREEN SHOTS OF INTRANET PAGES

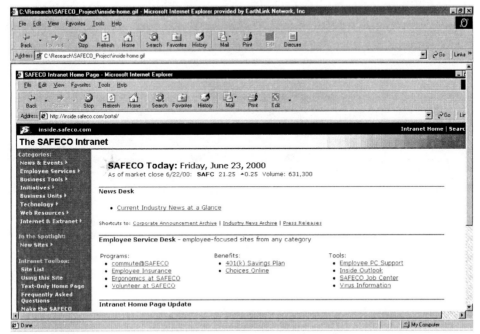

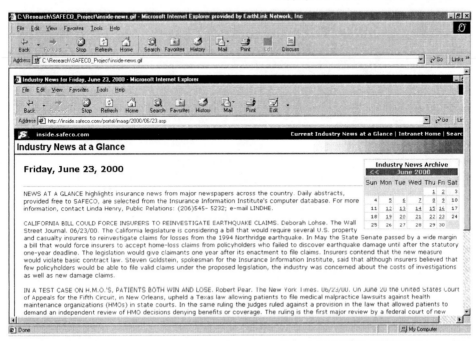

APPENDIX 4 : SAMPLE SCREEN SHOTS OF INTERNET PAGES

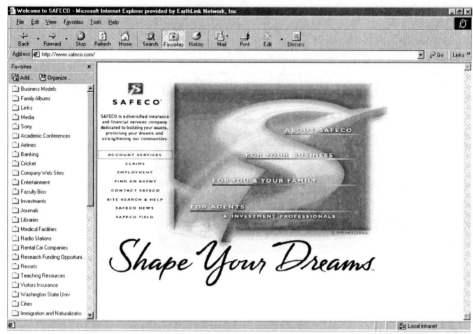

Copyright © 2000, SAFECO Corporation.

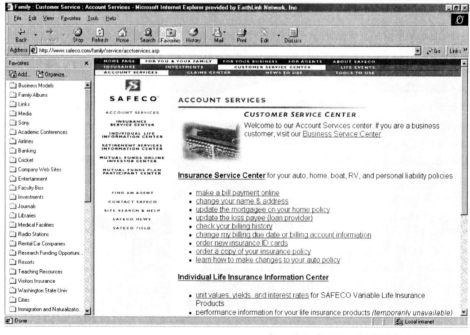

Copyright © 2000, SAFECO Corporation.

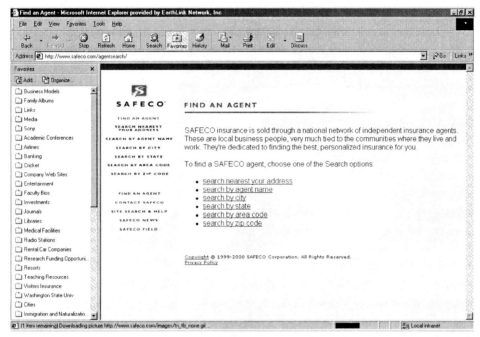

APPENDIX 5: SAMPLE SCREEN SHOTS OF EXTRANET PAGES

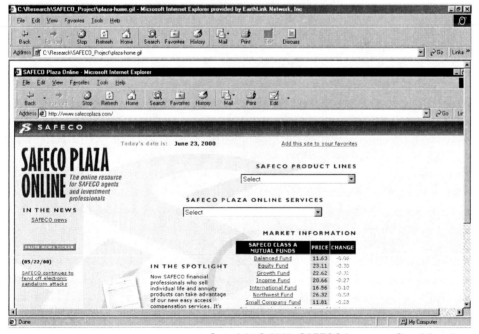

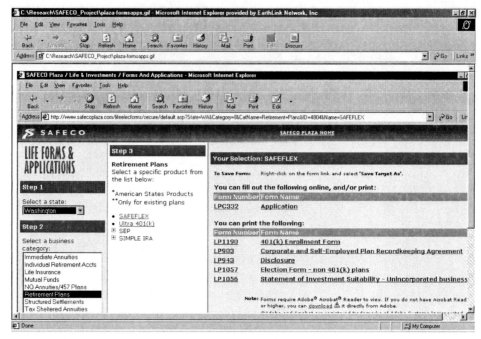

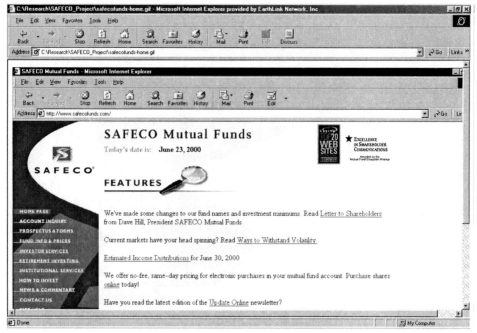

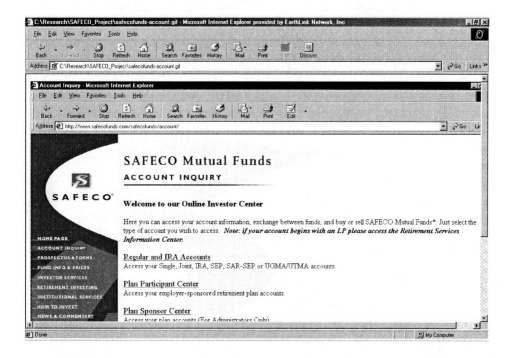

APPENDIX 6: A PRIMER ON INTERNET SECURITY ISSUES

Types of Security Issues	Methods of Security	Brief Description of Security Methods	Examples
Access Control and Authentication (Insuring that only authorized person can access the data/information)	User ID & Password	Assigning User ID and Password is a common way of restricting access to authorized personnel.	Most operating systems like UNIX, Windows NT, Linux, SunOS, and Solaris have password and user authentication systems in place. Secure Computing's SafeWord™ authentication product.
	Biometrics	A scientific technique that uses unique human attributes like fingerprint, retina scan, or voice print to identify a person.	Identicator Technology BioLogon 2.0 Server Application. Identicator Technology BioLogon 2.0 Client Application.
	Smart Cards	A smart card has an embedded chip that contains the necessary information to identify and authenticate the card holder.	The M.O.S.T. Card from CardLogix Inc.
	Digital Certificates	This technique combines authentication with identification. A digital certificate is actually a password-protected and encrypted data file that includes a) the name and other identification information of the holder, b) a public key, c) name of the issuer, and d) validity period of the certificate.	X.509 digital certificates issued by ID.Safe, a certification authority.

Types of Security Issues	Methods of Security	Brief Description of Security Methods	Examples
	Packet Filter Firewalls	These are the most basic firewall devices and work in the lower layers of the network protocol stack. They are often called screening routers. Screening routers can look at information related to the hard-wired address of a computer, its IP address (Network layer), and even the types of connections (Transport layer) and then provide filtering based on that information. A screening router may be a stand-alone routing device or a computer that contains two network interface cards (dual-homed system). Administrators program the device with a set of rules that define how packet filtering is done.	The Cisco 800 Series router. The Cisco 1417-ADSL router.
	Gateway Servers	These devices filter traffic based on the application they request. These servers limit access to specific applications such as Telnet, FTP, and HTTP. In contrast to the packet filtering technique, this firewall operates at the application layer of the network protocol stack.	Sidewinder™ 4.1, a network access control gateway solution for the enterprise.
	Proxy Servers	These servers operate at a higher level in the protocol stack to provide more opportunities for monitoring and controlling access between networks. Using proxies reduces the threat from hackers who monitor network traffic to glean information about computers on internal networks. The proxy hides the addresses of all internal computers. Traditionally, using proxies has reduced performance and transparency of access to other networks. However, current firewall products solve some of these problems.	Microsoft Proxy Server 2.0.
Integrity (Insuring that files or messages have not been altered in transit)	Public-key Encryption	Also known as an asymmetric encryption technique, this method requires the use of a pair of public and private keys to encrypt and decrypt data/information. While this method eliminates the problem of sharing a secret key, it is much slower than private-key encryption.	Secure Sockets Layer (SSL) system from Netscape communications and the Secure HyperText Transfer Protocol (S-HTTP) from CommerceNet are two protocols that provide secure information transfer through the Internet. Both these protocols allow the client and server computers to manage encryption and decryption activities.
	Private-key Encryption	Also known as a symmetric encryption technique, this method allows the use of a single numeric key to encode and decode data.	

Chapter XII

E*Trade Securities, Inc., Pioneer Online Trader, Struggles to Stay on Top

Adam T. Elegant and Ramiro Montealegre
University of Colorado, Boulder, USA

E*Trade revolutionized the securities brokerage industry by "creating" Internet trading. E*Trade's original strategy was to deliver cost savings to customers while amortizing fixed costs over a greater number of accounts. In 1997, several competitors established Internet sites and E*Trade was dethroned as the price leader. Its management team introduced a strategic initiative to transform the company into a financial, one-stop shop for investors. The initiative included expanding its information technology, improving its marketing and advertising program, and developing new strategic alliances.

By early 1999, E*Trade had established a popular Web site offering the convenience and control of automated stock, options, and mutual fund order placement at low commission rates. E*Trade's success pleased management but was challenged by fierce competition and emerging ethical and operational problems.

BACKGROUND

The Securities Brokerage Industry

Before the securities industry deregulation on May 1, 1975, full-service brokerages charging fixed commissions were the only firms in the industry (Glasgall, 1999). A full-service broker is a stockbroker who gives personal attention and advice to clients and charges a flat fee or percentage of the transaction. Such a broker acts as an agent, providing advice and buying or selling securities for the client. The client interacts with the broker face to face or over the telephone. Full-service brokers provide a wide array of services, including investment strategizing, estate planning, and insurance advice, and they usually attempt to influence their clients' investment decisions.

After deregulation, most full-service brokers began to target households with assets ranging from $100,000 into the millions. In addition, given that commissions were no longer fixed, discount brokerage firms began to appear that targeted price-sensitive, self-directed investors who did not require the level of service and high-priced advice offered by full-service firms. Discount brokerage firms made profit from margin balances and per-trade commissions; technology also enabled them to employ less-skilled labor. Fidelity and Charles Schwab, two of the dominant discounted brokerage firms in the mid-1990s, led the charge by introducing lower-cost investment services without advice at significantly lower commissions. Discount brokerage customers typically had assets ranging from $5,000 to $250,000. To execute trades, they could visit a branch office or they could call an "800" number to speak with a "live order taker," who would place their trade orders but was prohibited from giving any investment advice. Over time, discount brokers added touch-tone trading, which offered further commission reductions to investors who would key-in their trade orders.

By 1995, with the continued expansion of the Internet, technology offered another alternative with more convenience, lower costs, and easy access to investment information: online trading. Most online trading firms were offering customers numerous ways to access their accounts and place trades, including individual company Web sites, direct dial-up connections, online services (America Online, CompuServe, and Microsoft Network), interactive television, touch-tone telephone service, a broker on the telephone (as a situational alternative to online trading, for an additional fee), and 3Com Palm Pilots (available through selected online trading firms). With online trading, investors paid lower commissions—ranging from $10 to $30. They had full control over their investment decisions, with no one to blame but themselves—investors could enter trade orders any time of the day or night (Piper Jaffray, 1998d). Online brokerage accounts could be opened with as little as $1,000. While these firms first targeted frequent traders by offering low commissions, online trading evolved to support the needs of almost any individual investor.

History of the Company

E*Trade was a pioneer in online trading, a phenomenon that was rapidly changing the face of investing for both individuals and the firms that served them. The firm's growth mirrored that of the online trading industry as a whole. Trade*Plus, the company that would later become E*Trade, was founded as a service bureau in 1982 by Bill Porter, a physicist and inventor with more than a dozen patents to his credit. The company provided online quote and trading services to Fidelity, Charles Schwab, and Quick & Reilly. Using primitive information technology, Porter placed the first online trade on July 11, 1983. He imagined that someday everyone would own computers and "invest through them with unprecedented efficiency and control."[1] He spent most of the 1980s refining and adding to his vision without introducing his plan to the world.

In 1992, Porter founded E*Trade Securities, Inc. and began providing back-office, online processing services to discount brokerage firms and offering all-electronic investing through America Online and CompuServe. The minimum balance required by E*Trade to open an account was $1,000 ($2,000 for a margin account), well below industry standards at that time, and only a short, user-friendly application was required to set up an account. E*Trade began offering online trading through its company Web site in February 1996, and the demand flourished. To transact securities, a customer had only to log on to E*Trade via the Internet, a dial-up connection, or an online service such as America Online. However, for the first four years, E*Trade's trade processing, settlement, and custody of trades were provided by Herzog Heine Geduld, a third-party clearing and trading company.

In mid-1996, Porter handed E*Trade's reins over to Christos Cotsakos, a veteran of Federal Express and A.C. Nielsen. He immediately initiated in-house clearing activities to enable E*Trade to keep 100% of the revenue associated with its customers' margin and money market accounts (Piper Jaffray, 1997). This action proved crucial to the company's immediate success, since online investors, on average, carry margin balances three times those of traditional investors (CNN, 1998). On August 16, 1996, lead underwriter Robertson Stephens took E*Trade public at $10.50 per share. With the news spreading about E*Trade's capabilities, individual investors took notice. In 1992, E*Trade was processing barely 100 trades per day (Byron, 1997). By the end of 1996, that number had grown to almost 10,000 per day.

One of the keys to E*Trade's success was its stable and experienced management, consisting of technology, operations, finance, and marketing professionals who had a passion for the business. Figure 1 and Exhibit 1 present E*Trade's organizational chart and brief biographies of E*Trade's key leaders, respectively.

By 1997, the company had 650 employees and only three offices (located in Atlanta, Georgia; Sacramento, California; and Palo Alto, California). Thus, low overhead enabled it to offer low commissions that traditional brokerage firms could not afford to match.

With relation to information technology, E*Trade's computer system, fine-tuned over 15 years, permitted 85% of its transactions to be executed without human intervention (Piper Jaffray, 1997). Once a trade order was entered, E*Trade's computer system in Palo Alto took over. The computer system queried the prices available on at least four market makers, searching for the best executable price. Trades were usually executed in seconds, trading results were available shortly thereafter, and the customer's account balances were updated immediately.

SETTING THE STAGE

In 1997, E*Trade began to recognize that having low prices was not sufficient to compete with the discount brokerage firms that were moving into online trading. It needed to provide investors with a more comprehensive online service, including better research, charting, quotes, and stock screening. E*Trade began designing a new Web site, called "Destination E*Trade," which it hoped would become a financial portal, a one-stop shop for investors, customers, and non-customers. Breaking away from its competitors, E*Trade planned to open up 90 to 95% of its Web site to non-customers (Lipton, 1998). This first portal Web site within the online brokerage industry was originally slated for a launch date of January 1998.

CASE DESCRIPTION

The objective of E*Trade's expansion was to offer its customers the tools to handle all of their investment needs at one convenient, comprehensive, and secure online location. E*Trade CEO Christos Cotsakos reflected,

We are committed to offering independent investors the most comprehensive selection of financial services available in the online industry....
Our strategy is to be a financial full-service online provider (E*Trade,
1998b).

Figure 1: E*Trade organizational chart

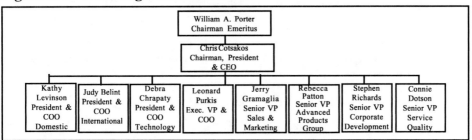

Exhibit 1: E*Trade's management

Christos M. Cotsakos, Chairman, President, Chief Executive Officer, and a Director of E*Trade Group, Inc.

Before taking the reins at E*Trade, he was a senior executive at Federal Express, as well as AC Nielsen, Inc. He also serves on the boards of several leading-edge technology companies. He received a B.A. from William Paterson College, and an M.B.A. from Pepperdine University, and is currently pursuing a Ph.D. in economics at the University of London. Christos Cotsakos is also a decorated Vietnam War veteran.

Kathy Levinson, President and Chief Operating Officer.

Kathy Levinson came to E*Trade from Charles Schwab, where she served in a number of senior executive positions. She earned a B.A. in economics from Stanford University and a master's of human resources and organization development from the University of San Francisco, and completed the program for management development at Harvard.

Judy Balint, President and Chief Operating Officer, E*Trade's International Division.

Judy Balint is responsible for building E*Trade's global financial network. Before joining E*Trade, she spent a number of years living and working abroad. She received a B.A. in journalism from the University of Wisconsin and an M.B.A. in international business from the Monterey Institute of International Studies in Monterey, California.

Debra Chrapaty, President and Chief Operating Officer, E*Trade Technologies, and Chief Information Officer of E*Trade group.

Debra Chrapaty invents proprietary technology solutions for E*Trade. She came to E*Trade from the National Basketball Association, where she was vice president and chief technology officer. She has a bachelor in business administration and economics from Temple University and an M.B.A. in information systems from New York University. She often works around the clock and sleeps on a cot next to her desk. In 1998, she was named the chief information officer of the year by *InformationWeek*.

Leonard C. Purkis, Executive Vice President, Finance and Administration, and Chief Financial Officer.

Len Purkis is responsible for building and managing E*Trade's financial architecture. Before joining E*Trade, he was chief financial officer for Iomega Corporation and senior vice president of finance for General Electric Capital Fleet Services. He is a graduate of the Institute of Chartered Accountants in England and Wales.

Jerry Gramaglia, Senior Vice President, Sales, Marketing, and Communication.

Jerry Gramaglia is charged with creating innovative ways to build and expand global brands. Before joining E*Trade, he was vice president of Sprint's $3 billion consumer division and held senior management posts at Pepsico, Procter & Gamble, and Nestle. He earned B.A. in economics from Denison University.

Rebecca L. Patton, Senior Vice President, Advanced Products Group.

Rebecca Patton is responsible for designing E*Trade's new product strategies. Before joining E*Trade in September 1995, Ms. Patton served in a variety of management positions at Apple Computer. Ms. Patton received a B.A. in economics from Duke University and an M.B.A. from Stanford University.

Stephen C. Richards, Senior Vice President, Corporate Development and New Ventures.

Stephen Richards's mission is to increase E*Trade's leadership position through strategic alliances, partnerships, mergers, and acquisitions. He previously served as E*Trade's senior vice president of finance and chief financial officer. Before joining E*Trade, he was managing director and CFO of correspondent clearing at Bear Stearns & Company. He has a B.A. in statistics and economics from University of California at Davis and an M.B.A. in finance from University of California at Los Angeles.

Connie Dotson, Senior Vice President, Service Quality.

Connie Dotson makes sure that everyone in E*Trade's customer service, operations, and trading areas provides end-to-end quality service. Before joining E*Trade in 1996, she served as senior vice president of operations for U.S. Computer Services/CableData, Inc.

Three general principles guided the firm's service expansion: (1) attract new investors and fortify existing customer loyalty, (2) develop multiple revenue streams to protect against an extended market correction, and (3) increase customers' switching costs in order to prevent them from jumping to another online brokerage firm. E*Trade embarked on a strategic initiative that began by restructuring the company into three business groups—technology, international operations, and brokerage. Debra Chrapaty, who was the chief information officer of E*Trade, was promoted to president and chief technology officer of the newly formed technology division. Fully half of E*Trade's 650 employees reported to Chrapaty. She controlled a budget of more than $130 million—a whopping 39% of E*Trade's $335.7 million revenue for the year ended September 30, 1998 (Dalton, 1998). The strategic initiative followed by E*Trade, however, included not only the expansion of technology but also a significant improvement of its marketing and advertising program. The initiative also included the development of new strategic alliances to increase its national and international reach.

Information Technology

Although technology had fueled the growth of the securities brokerage industry, some observers estimated that in 1995 the percentage of mishandled trades was as high as 45%. Many early entrants into the online trading segment were plagued by technological glitches, and as the existing problems were rectified, new problems appeared when online trading firms expanded their services. Industry-wide concerns related to technology included the following:

1. *System Outages* – Online trading firms were continuously refining their systems to eliminate crippling glitches, such as lost e-mails, system overload, and system crashes, and to create backup systems and contingency plans. Many of these outages were caused by software and hardware upgrades that were intended to increase capacity.

2. *Web-Based Transaction Glitches* – Trade orders could get lost after the customer had entered them, but well before the order reached the online brokerage. The problem could occur between the customer and his/her Internet service provider (ISP), between the ISP and the Internet backbone, or inside the Internet backbone itself. Although the Internet was a self-healing network and traffic was automatically routed around glitches, the rerouting process could take anywhere from seconds to 20 minutes. As Web traffic increased, the number of routing glitches was expected to increase. Many investors did not understand the technological side of online trading, and often misunderstood who was at fault when trades went awry (Olmstead, 1998a).

3. *Removal of Human Intervention* – As an online investor explained, "I electronically entered a limit order to buy Zenith at $15, while the stock was trading around $16. The stock then rose to $22. While [I was] working, not paying attention to the market, negative news sent Zenith plummeting toward $5. When the stock fell, my order executed at $15, on the way down, and cost me thousands of dollars." The electronic system did what it was told: it executed the order at $15. A full-service brokerage firm might have called the customer, told him about the negative news, and suggested that he cancel the order or sell immediately after the purchase to cut his losses. By the time this investor realized that he owned the stock, it was trading at $6.

4. *Poor Customer Service* – Almost every online firm had been accused of poor customer service. Most customer service issues were handled via e-mail. However, often the responses did not provide a detailed response to every concern voiced by the customer. In particular, many customers felt slighted by the "canned" answers that firms used for frequently asked questions. Account holders who used telephone customer service commonly complained about extended hold times.

Chrapaty was well aware that in order to expand the firm's online investment services, she had to do more at E*Trade than simply implement technology. The expansion had to be done while continuing to support the level of online services—which meant paying special attention to accommodate the volatility of online trading marketplace, where trading volumes may soar and fall wildly. The rapid growth of the company also had to be supported—E*Trade was adding 2,000 customers a day to a base of 550,000 and the number of trades made daily, which averaged around 15,000 in July 1997, was running about 40,000 to 50,000 by the same time in 1998 (Dalton, 1998).

In August 1997, Chrapaty established daily 5:30 a.m. meetings—one hour before the opening of the stock markets in the United States—including all employees reporting to her. "Everyone needed to understand the changes and how they tentacle into their organizations," she explained (Dalton, 1998). These meetings, which Chrapaty referred to as change-management sessions, had an immediate impact—system errors dropped 75% during the next quarter. But that was the beginning. Over the next 12 months, she restructured the company's trading system and Web site. In 1998, $75 million was spent to upgrade these systems (Pettit, 1998). Much of this money was spent on the Destination E*Trade Web site and on E*Trade's proprietary information technology architecture. This technology enabled more than one million visitors to use the Web site simultaneously and allowed up to 150,000 customers to place orders simultaneously (E*Trade, 1998h). E*Trade's original computer system had used a common gateway interface (CGI) to link the servers of its Web pages to its databases (Stirland, 1998). The system was mainly coded in the computer language C++. The new system was based on BEA System's Tuxedo Architecture, which manages a distributed, component-based computing environment, and includes load balancing, distributed transaction processing, and security. Other elements of the new architecture include a Cisco Systems Local Director and several Netscape Version 2.0 Enterprise Servers. The BEA Tuxedo system manages transactions, while the Netscape servers manage user sessions.

Marketing and Advertising

E*Trade complemented its technology development efforts by further investigating who traded online and what attracted them. It was found that the original online investors tended to be active traders who jumped in and out of positions rapidly, looking to make a quick profit. They were especially concerned about commission rates and reliability of execution. Over time, however, the situation changed as investors began to give careful consideration to the types of services offered by each online brokerage firm. With the stabilization of commission rates, price became only one factor in investor choice. The breadth of products, services, and amenities became the critical deciding factors. The types of services required by online investors included electronic bill payment, free real-time quotes, low margin rates, quality of research reports, access to IPOs, and excellent customer service.

While there are many ways to describe online investors (see, for example, Exhibit 2 for typical demographics of online investors), three distinctive categories can be identified (Piper Jaffray, 1998a).

Straddlers – Customers who occasionally invested online but still preferred traditional investment channels, such as branch offices and the telephone. These people were still hesitant about trading online and preferred conducting business with companies with established reputations.

Active Investors – Investors who used online trading only after conducting their own, self-directed research. These people were comfortable investing online. Their main needs were information and tools that would help them make better investment decisions.

Retail Traders – A new class of investors created by the low cost and speed of execution associated with online trading. These were short-term investors looking to take advantage of quick profits in the market. Retail traders, also known as "day traders," cared only about fast, cheap, and efficient execution of their orders.

Table 1 shows the key services required by each segment of the market and examples of the companies that met their needs.

Exhibit 2: Demographics of typical online investors

(According to Forrester Research, Inc.)
• 75.7% of online investors are male. • Age ranges between 25 and 44, mean is 39. • Mean annual income is $69,000. • Mean net worth is $144,177. • 70% use a PC at work. • 44% have completed college. • Average investor places 7.86 trades per year. • Online investors make 47% more trades than traditional investors. Source: Pettit, 1998

Table 1: Online services required by type of customer

Type of Customer	Straddlers	Active Investors	Retail Traders
Commission Level	$20-$30	$10-$20	Less than $10
Key Needs	Service & Reputation	Information & Tools	Price & Execution
Marquee Firms	Schwab & Fidelity	E*Trade & DLJ Direct	Datek & Ameritrade
The Firm's Key Attributes	Channels & Distribution	Partnerships & Brand	Execution & Technology

Source: Piper Jaffray, 1998a

E*Trade understood from its inception that establishing brand identity was critical in the online investment industry—customers are hesitant to deposit money with a firm they have never heard of. Accordingly, the company has been an industry leader in marketing and advertising expenditures, and its campaigns can be described as aggressive, savvy, and eye-catching. In 1996, E*Trade was advertising in the *Wall Street Journal, Individual Investor, Smart Money*, and *Forbes*, but in 1997 it decided to increase its marketing and advertising program. E*Trade kicked off its first major campaign by spending $3.2 million on advertising during the NCAA basketball tournament. Since 1997, E*Trade has consistently spent four to five times more money on advertising per active account than its competitor Schwab (Piper Jaffray, 1997). By the end of 1997, E*Trade had spent $20+ million in advertising campaigns. The first half of 1998 was quiet, but E*Trade broke the calm by announcing a $100 million advertising campaign to coincide with the launch of its Destination E*Trade Web site.

While Cotsakos felt that this level of expenditure was necessary to transform E*Trade into "one of the blue-chip Internet companies for the 21st century" (Buckman, 1998), some analysts estimated that advertising had pushed E*Trade's account acquisition costs past $400 per account in 1998. The company began looking for cheaper ways to acquire accounts: direct mail, Web site sponsorships, and E*Mobile—a purple and green, 38-foot recreational vehicle that was to spend 200 days per year traveling to sporting events, college campuses, and trade shows. E*Mobile had nine demonstration suites on board and was projected to attract 15,000 visitors annually (Piper Jaffray, 1998a).

Strategic Alliances

To further increase its customer base and diversify its revenue steam, another key ingredient of E*Trade's expansion was seeking partnerships and alliances. Cotsakos explained,

> E*Trade has made a significant commitment to identify and ally with innovative organizations who are leaders in their fields, and who share our vision of providing the consumer with the convenience and control of Internet-based solutions (E*Trade, 1998b).

E*Trade established alliances and business agreements with leading technology, content, and distribution partners to provide relevant, insightful, and proprietary value-added investing and research information to its customers. Exhibit 3 provides a list of selected alliance partners.

At the same time, E*Trade began to pursue international licensing and partnership programs to reach new markets and to provide new capabilities to its users. E*Trade sought to buy stakes in companies that advanced online trading and kept its brand name in the forefront to reinforce and leverage the E*Trade brand franchise worldwide. The following is a summary of E*Trade's international expansion efforts:

Canada - E*Trade signed its first international license in January 1997. The license created an E*Trade franchise in Canada, where it became the first online firm to offer a broad mutual fund center.

Australia - On April 22, 1998, E*Trade launched service in Australia after signing an agreement with Australia's Nova Pacific. Nova Pacific has since adopted the E*Trade name and also plans to launch online trading in New Zealand. As of October 1998, E*Trade had more than 3,000 active accounts in Australia (Olmstead, 1998b) and as of December 31, 1998, after nine months of operation, E*Trade Australia was handling 1% of the daily transaction volume on the Australian Securities Exchange.

Japan - On June 4, 1998, E*Trade initiated two joint venture agreements with Japan's Softbank Corporation. One agreement established the E*Trade brand name in Japan, a key target of E*Trade's international expansion. Japan opened its securities industry to foreign companies, and Japanese citizens have an estimated $10 trillion in individual savings.

Korea - An agreement with Softbank helped in establishing E*Trade Korea. Korea's government has changed its stance and is now allowing foreign investment, especially in technology. As of July 1998, Korea had over 2.5 million Internet users (E*Trade, 1998d).

United Kingdom - On June 11, 1998, E*Trade signed a joint venture agreement with Electronic Share Information, LTD., a leading financial services provider in the United Kingdom. The venture, called E*Trade U.K., will give E*Trade access to Electronic Share Information's 170,000 customers (E*Trade, 1998a).

France - On December 3, 1998, E*Trade announced a licensing agreement with CPR, a premier French investment and asset management bank. The new company, CPR E*Trade, had the exclusive right to use the E*Trade brand, technology, and services in France. As of December 1998, there were 1.5 million Internet users in France.

In addition to the countries mentioned above, E*Trade initiated service or was in the process of developing the E*Trade brand in Germany, Poland, Russia, and Israel (E*Trade, 1998a). Although international revenue accounted for only about 3% of its total revenue in 1998, E*Trade estimated that that percentage would increase to 30% by 2003 (Olmstead, 1998b). E*Trade also envisioned enabling investors in one country to trade stocks in several other countries, but this would require major changes in international legislation.

*Exhibit 3: E*Trade's Partnerships, Alliances, and Acquisitions*

The following is a list of selected alliance partners (in alphabetical order):

America Onlline (AOL)- E*Trade has provided online investing services to AOL users since 1992. As of January 1999, more than 14 million AOL members have access to E*Trade from the AOL Personal Finance Channel. In 1998, E*Trade agreed to pay America Online $25 million for two years of "premier placement" on the AOL service (Kane, 1998).

BancBoston Robertson Stephens - E*Trade's exclusive alliance with BancBoston Robertson Stephens provides Professional Edge subscribers with access to proprietary research and recommendations formerly available only to the largest investors and institutions.

BancOne - BancOne customers are able to manage their investments using E*Trade's online securities transaction, information, and portfolio management services. E*Trade customers, in turn, have online access to a range of integrated financial services, including checking and savings accounts, loans, and credit and debit cards.

Barclays Global Fund Advisors - Barclays has teamed up with E*Trade to offer a selection of index, enhanced index, and fund products that will be offered exclusively through E*Trade.

Bridgeway Capital Management - E*Trade is the exclusive no-transaction-fee outlet for the Bridgeway family of mutual funds. As a result of this agreement, no other brokerage firm will offer Bridgeway funds without charging transaction fees.

CNNfn - E*Trade has a significant branded presence on CNNfn, including the site's new Broker Center. That presence will be promoted on CNN, the cable network.

CompuServe - CompuServe users have had access to E*Trade online investing services since 1992. More than 5 million users have direct access to E*Trade from the CompuServe Personal Finance Center.

CUSO Financial Services - CUSO Financial Services credit union customers have the option of directing their own investments through E*Trade.

Critical Path - On July 14, 1998, E*Trade entered into an agreement to provide venture capital to Critical Path. Critical Path is an industry leader in providing outsourced e-mail services and infrastructure for Web portals such as Destination E*Trade. In addition, Critical Path became the exclusive host for E*Trade's Web-based e-mail system. E*Trade hopes that an increasing number of account holders will access their trade confirmations via secure e-mail, thus reducing E*Trade's enormous postage expenses.

Data Broadcasting Corporation - Data Broadcasting Corporation, a leading online investment information service, provides millions of investors access to E*Trade from its online trading center at *http://www.dbc.com.*

Digital Island - E*Trade's investment in Digital Island, the first global IP applications network, allows it to leverage Digital Island's distributed star network to distribute E*Trade products around the globe.

E*Offering - E*Trade plans to invest in E*Offering, a full-service investment bank on the Internet. The deal will help provide E*Trade customers with greater access to subscribed public offerings. E*Trade will own 28% of E*Offering.

First USA - E*Trade has joined with First USA to offer Platinum and Classic Visa credit cards to E*Trade customers at competitive interest rates and no annual fees.

InsWeb - E*Trade assists customers with their personal insurance needs, allowing consumers to comparison shop for insurance on the E*Trade Web site.

Microsoft Corporation - E*Trade's strategic partnership with Microsoft gives users of the popular Microsoft Investor service and MS Money application direct access to E*Trade's online investing services.

Novo/Ironlight - E*Trade has contracted with Novo/Ironlight to create and deploy its multilingual Web sites in several international markets. The Web sites will be culturally specific while building and maintaining the E*Trade brand and quality standards.

Omega Research, Inc. - E*Trade is the exclusive online investing sponsor of all of Omega Research's sales seminars.

OptionsLink - E*Trade's acquisition of the OptionsLink division of Hambrecht & Quist allows it to offer a Web-based and custom interactive voice response order entry system for employee stock option and stock purchase plan services to corporate stock plan participants.

Scudder Kemper Investments, Inc. - E*Trade's Mutual Fund Center offers more than 30 no-load Scudder Funds online.

ShareData, Inc. - E*Trade has acquired ShareData, Inc., the leader in stock plan knowledge-based software and expertise for pre-IPO and public companies. ShareData, Inc. serves more than 2,500 companies and represents more than 2.5 million employee option holders worldwide (E*Trade, 1998c). The post-merger goal is for E*Trade to be able to offer plan sponsors and their employees a completely integrated and automated solution for stock plan management and company stock transaction capabilities. On the acquisition of ShareData, Cotsakos stated, "The acquisition of ShareData reinforces E*Trade's strategy of moving beyond transaction fees to increase the number of ways in which we generate revenue." E*Trade used stock to pay for the estimated $28 million acquisition (Piper Jaffray. 1998c).

Softbank - On July 13, 1998, Japan's Softbank Corp. agreed to buy 15.6 million shares of E*Trade stock for $400 million in cash (E*Trade, 1998f). Much of this cash will be used for acquisitions and to fund E*Trade's growth objectives. The agreement also includes a provision that prevents Softbank from selling its newly acquired shares for two years and prevents Softbank from purchasing additional shares for five years. At the time, Softbank also owned 31% of Yahoo!, 35% of GeoCities, and 71% of Ziff-Davis (Wettlaufer, 1998).

ThirdAge Media - ThirdAge.com, the most comprehensive source of content, community, and commerce on the Web for active older adults, has selected E*Trade to be its exclusive online securities trading partner. ThirdAge.com users will have convenient one-click access to E*Trade throughout the ThirdAge site.

United Airlines - E*Trade customers will have opportunities to earn frequent flier miles on United Airlines.

VeriSign - VeriSign's advanced digital identification technology will be used to simplify and enhance Internet security procedures for E*Trade customers.

VERSUS Technologies - VERSUS Brokerage Services offers online investing services in Canada under the E*Trade name.

WebTV Networks, Inc. - WebTV viewers are able to access E*Trade in the Investing and Brokerage sections of the WebTV Network.

Yahoo! - In August 1998, E*Trade entered into an agreement with Yahoo! Yahoo! has set the standard for Internet companies, and its site is the most trafficked site on the Web. E*Trade's agreement with Yahoo! will substantially increase E*Trade's presence on banners, advertisements, and sponsorships throughout the Yahoo! network. Within the agreement, E*Trade also renews its status as one of Yahoo's premier merchants. E*Trade hopes its agreement with Yahoo! will help achieve its goal of becoming a leading branded, bookmarked financial destination site on the Web.

Zurich Kemper Investments - Zurich Kemper Investments, E*Trade's money market fund provider, offers a combination of competitive current yields, service, pricing, and potential for new-service development to E*Trade customers.

Table 2: Online investing services provided at destination E*Trade Web site

Smart alerts based on price	Portfolio tracking	News updates from Reuters
Smart alerts based on volume	Watch lists	Earnings estimates from Zach's
Secure e-mail	Mutual fund information from Morningstar	A plethora of research report
Free real-time quotes	Company reports	Java-based charting capabilities

Launching "Destination E*Trade"

Although the opening was delayed several times, in September 1998 E*Trade launched the much anticipated "Destination E*Trade" with a celebrity-filled event including Bob Costas and Shaquille O'Neil. Destination E*Trade was intended to play a key role in helping E*Trade reach its ambitious goal of tripling its account base between 1998 and 2000. The new site offered features and content well beyond the reaches of E*Trade's previous site and beyond industry standards, as shown in Table 2.

Destination E*Trade allowed all visitors to view headline news, delayed stock quotes, and other widely available market information. Merely by registering, even without opening an E*Trade account, a visitor could get access to customizable tools, secure e-mail, investment chat rooms, and free real-time quotes. E*Trade targeted the estimated 20 million individual investors who accessed the Web for investment research and portfolio tracking but had yet to open an online investment account (E*Trade, 1998g). E*Trade used these freebies to convince some of its visitors to stick around and open an account. Between September 1998 and January 1, 1999, more than 500,000 visitors became members (E*Trade, 1998i).

By early 1999, E*Trade had established a popular Web site offering self-directed investors the convenience and control of automated stock, options, and mutual fund order placement at low commission rates. In addition, E*Trade had a digital suite of value-added products and services that could be personalized, including portfolio tracking, real-time stock quotes, "smart" alerts, market commentary and analysis, news, investor community areas, and other information services. Exhibit 4 presents a comprehensive list of E*Trade's products, services, and features as of March 1999. Exhibit 5 highlights various measures of E*Trade's rapid growth.

CURRENT CHALLENGES/PROBLEMS FACING E*TRADE

In February 1999, Christos Cotsakos should have been one of the happiest men on the planet. As CEO of E*Trade, he had seen his company grow at an

Exhibit 4: E*Trade's Products (March 1999)

Comprehensive Trading - With an E*Trade account, customers can buy and sell stocks, options, bonds, and more than 4,300 mutual funds directly from their personal computer or by telephone.

Complete Account Management - E*Trade customers can review their portfolio holdings, balances, and outstanding orders online. E*Trade offers unlimited free checking, competitive interest rates on uninvested cash, online cash transfers, and an E*Trade Visa® card.

Free Real-Time Quotes - All E*Trade customers and members are offered free and unlimited real-time quotes.

Mutual Fund Center - Launched on November 3, 1997, E*Trade's Mutual Fund Center offers access to more than 4,300 mutual funds from many popular fund families, including American Century, Baron, Bridgeway, Invesco, Janus, and Vanguard. There are 900 no-load funds to choose from. Custom screening tools and research help guide customers to the funds that are right for them. E*Trade also provides direct access to online prospectuses for all the funds in the network.

Bond Center - Through E*Trade's comprehensive online bond trading capability, individual investors can place online orders for a wide range of fixed-income securities, including U.S. Treasury, corporate, and municipal bonds. The Bond Center also offers analytical tools, commentary, and credit rating information.

Investment Research - E*Trade offers access to investment research and analysis tools. Users can get breaking news, quotes, charts, earnings estimates, company fundamentals, and live market commentary 24 hours a day—all for free.

Power E*Trade - A powerful collection of free tools and services for the active trader. Customers who qualify can maximize their profit potential with ultra-fast order entry, NASDAQ Level II quotes, real-time streaming portfolios, and priority customer service.

Professional Edge - Customers can subscribe to get institutional research reports and real-time buy/sell recommendations before the market opens from the analysts at BancBoston Robertson Stephens. E*Trade expects premium content, such as the Professional Edge, to generate 2% of future revenue (Olmstead, 1998a).

Mortgages - E*Trade offers direct access to comprehensive information on mortgages. Users can compare market rates and apply for a home loan from their PC.

Insurance - Through E*Trade's Insurance Center, users can easily compare coverages and prices of different insurance carriers for policies that fit their individual needs.

Credit Cards - E*Trade offers Platinum and Classic Visa® credit cards at competitive interest rates and no annual fees.

Ideas and Tools - E*Trade provides free investing help and education, including mutual fund screening tools, tech stock analysis, options analysis, and retirement planning calculators.

Personal Market Watch - E*Trade customers can personalize their view of the markets with "My E*Trade," selecting Snapshot, Tech Spotlight, Trader, Portfolio, or Analyst views. The Portfolio Manager feature lets users follow the securities they own or track.

Smart Alerts - This free service allows customers to have stock price, volume, and P/E alerts delivered directly to their inbox on the Web and to any e-mail address or alphanumeric pager.

Discussion Groups - In Community @ E*Trade, members can exchange ideas and discuss hot stocks and investing strategies. E*Trade also offers live celebrity chat events.

E*Station - E*Trade's self-service information center lets customers find answers to their questions. It also allows customers to submit service requests online.

E*Trade Mail - E*Trade's free e-mail service provides customers the security, reliability, and speed to handle all of their e-mail needs free of charge.

Security - All E*Trade transactions over the Internet are secured by Netscape Secure Commerce Server (SSL), the industry's leading technology for Web security. When customers access the E*Trade Web site using either Netscape Navigator or Microsoft Internet Explorer, their communications are automatically protected through server authentication and data encryption.

Note: All these products were available through E*Trade's Destination Web site.

Exhibit 5: Measures of E*Trade's growth (A, B and C)
A) E*Trade's account growth, 1996-1999 (in thousands)

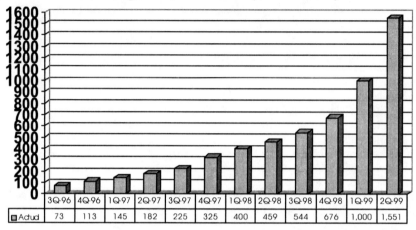

	3Q-96	4Q-96	1Q-97	2Q-97	3Q-97	4Q-97	1Q-98	2Q-98	3Q-98	4Q-98	1Q-99	2Q-99
◻ Actual	73	113	145	182	225	325	400	459	544	676	1,000	1,551

B) E*Trade's average number of online trades per day, 1996-1999.

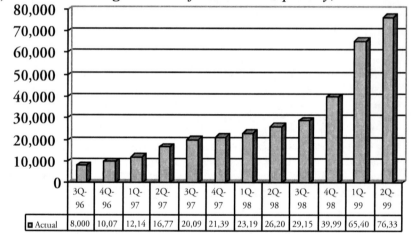

	3Q-96	4Q-96	1Q-97	2Q-97	3Q-97	4Q-97	1Q-98	2Q-98	3Q-98	4Q-98	1Q-99	2Q-99
◻ Actual	8,000	10,07	12,14	16,77	20,09	21,39	23,19	26,20	29,15	39,99	65,40	76,33

Source: Credit Suisse First Boston, Piper Jaffray, and E*Trade's 10K Reports

C)E*Trade's fluctuations in market share, 1997-1999.

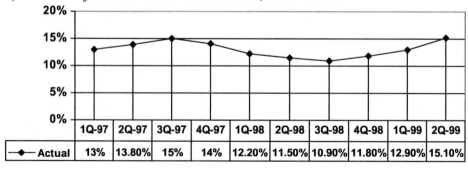

	1Q-97	2Q-97	3Q-97	4Q-97	1Q-98	2Q-98	3Q-98	4Q-98	1Q-99	2Q-99
◆ Actual	13%	13.80%	15%	14%	12.20%	11.50%	10.90%	11.80%	12.90%	15.10%

Source: Credit Suisse First Boston, Piper Jaffray, and E*Trade's 10K Reports

Exhibit 6: E*Trade's annual financial data

Years Ended September 30	1999 (Projected)	1998	1997	1996	1995
(in thousands, except transaction and per share amounts)					
Revenue	$621,402	335,756	$234,128	141,803	108,961
Pretax income	(91,536)	2,151	29,323	3,671	9,446
Net income (loss)	(54,438)	1,927	19,193	4,166	7,333
Income per share					
Basic	(0.23)	0.01	0.14	0.05	0.11
Diluted	(0.23)	0.01	0.13	0.03	0.07
Shares used in computation of income (loss) per share					
Basic	235,926	173,906	133,572	80,554	68,467
Diluted	235,926	185,479	147,833	121,863	111,427
Average transactions per day	68,484	27,620	16,382	6,148	2,335

Years Ended September 30	1999 (Projected)	1998	1997	1996	1995
(in thousands, except account, associate, and per share amounts)					
Active accounts	1,551,000	544,000	225,000	91,000	32,000
Number of associates	1,735	954	698	489	245
Working capital	319,634	615,968	270,778	74,041	22,257
Total assets	3,926,980	2,066,286	1,148,114	397,169	107,212
Shareowners' equity	913,667	734,410	303,694	89,785	27,908
Net book value per share	3.81	3.18	1.85	0.70	0.22

Source: E*Trade Corporate Report 1999

astounding pace, with 1998 revenues reaching $335.7 million and E*Trade's account base climbing to 676,000. (Exhibit 6 presents the company's financial data since 1995.) He had also watched the company's stock price increase 491% between September 30, 1998, and January 29, 1999. In 1998, his company became the first securities and financial services company to be awarded the CPA WebTrust Seal of Assurance by the American Institute of Certified Public Accountants. His efforts had earned him the honor of Ernst and Young as he was named the 1998 National Entrepreneur of the Year for Internet Products and Services Companies.

At the same time, Cotsakos must also have been terrified after watching E*Trade's computer systems shut down on three consecutive days during the week of February 8, 1999. Technological problems crashed E*Trade's entire online trading capacity for hours at a time and led to a class action lawsuit filed against E*Trade on February 9, 1999 (Glasgall, 1999). From February 2 to February 10, 1999, E*Trade's stock value plummeted 35%.

Cotsakos was pleased with the success of E*Trade so far, but he faced several challenges not only from the fiercer competition within an industry shifting toward online trading but also from emerging ethical and operational problems. While he wanted to push forward with international expansion, he wondered whether his company had grown too fast and could even handle its current customer base in the United States. Operating in the ever-changing world of online investing presented enormous challenges, gratification, and headaches for executives like Cotsakos, who were on the front lines of rewriting the rules of the investment world.

An Industry Shift Toward Online Trading

Competition in the online trading segment was fierce. (Exhibit 7 presents several measures of the online trading segment's rapid growth.) What began in 1995 as a few firms competing for a small number of accounts turned into an industry segment with about 80 competitors vying for millions of accounts. In 1998, full-service brokerage firms still accounted for about 80% of dollar commissions generated in the retail brokerage business (Credit Suisse First Boston, 1998b). But as some of their investors began to defect to online trading, full-service firms adjusted (Exhibit 8 depicts investors' primary reasons for trading online). By late 1998, several full-service brokerage firms began planning measures to offer select customers certain aspects of online investing without compromising the tradition of full-service investing. Instead of charging per transaction, the full-service firms began charging a flat percentage-of-assets fee similar to those charged by asset managers. For example, in early 1999, Morgan Stanley Dean Witter began offering online trading to 20,000 of its customers. Investors with $50,000 to $250,000 were charged

Exhibit 7: Measures of online trading growth (A, B, C, D and E)

A) U.S. Online Investment Acount Growth, 1996-2002 (in millions).

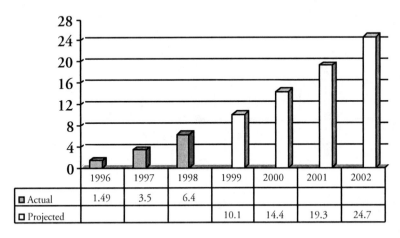

	1996	1997	1998	1999	2000	2001	2002
▪ Actual	1.49	3.5	6.4				
□ Projected				10.1	14.4	19.3	24.7

Source: International Data Corporation, February 1999

B) Average number of online trades per day, 1997-1999 (in thousands)

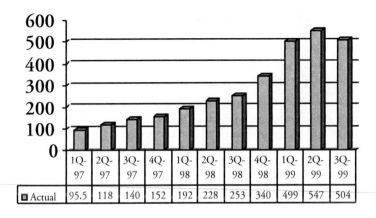

	1Q-97	2Q-97	3Q-97	4Q-97	1Q-98	2Q-98	3Q-98	4Q-98	1Q-99	2Q-99	3Q-99
▪ Actual	95.5	118	140	152	192	228	253	340	499	547	504

Source: Credit Suisse First Boston (1998a)

C) Assets managed in online investment accounts, 1997-2002 (in billions)

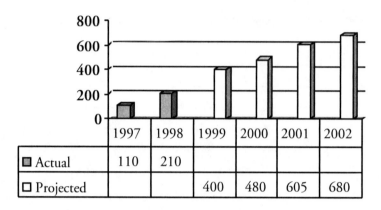

	1997	1998	1999	2000	2001	2002
▣ Actual	110	210				
☐ Projected			400	480	605	680

Source: Pettit (1998)

D) Online trading commissions generated, 1996-2001 (in millions)

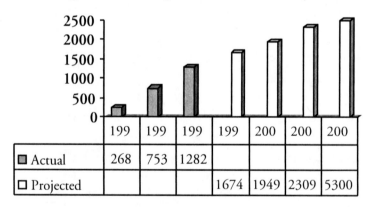

	199	199	199	199	200	200	200
▣ Actual	268	753	1282				
☐ Projected				1674	1949	2309	5300

Source: Credit Suisse First Boston (1999a).

E) Online trades as a percentage of all equity trades, 1997-1999

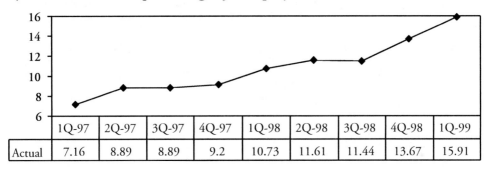

	1Q-97	2Q-97	3Q-97	4Q-97	1Q-98	2Q-98	3Q-98	4Q-98	1Q-99
Actual	7.16	8.89	8.89	9.2	10.73	11.61	11.44	13.67	15.91

Source: Credit Suisse First Boston (1999a)

Exhibit 8: Primary reasons for investing online (According to Jupiter Communications)

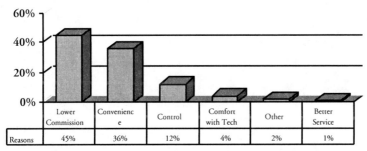

	Lower Commission	Convenience	Control	Comfort with Tech	Other	Better Service
Reasons	45%	36%	12%	4%	2%	1%

Source: International Data Corporation, February 1999.

2.25% of their assets and were granted 56 trades per year (Glasgall, 1999). Prudential Securities was offering a rate of $24.95 per trade to account holders with more than $100,000 in addition to an annual fee of 1%. Merrill Lynch was planning to roll out similar services to 55,000 of its estimated 5 million account holders (*CBS*, 1999). Table 3 depicts the competitive breakdown as of September 2, 1999.

In 1999, Schwab had greater market share than its two nearest competitors combined. It also maintained a relatively high commission level ($29.95), while the average commission charged by the top 10 firms had steadily declined, as shown in Exhibit 9 (Credit Suisse First Boston, 1998b). Because of its well-established brand name, popular mutual fund supermarket, and huge existing account base, Schwab was able to grab an early lead that it never

Table 3: Key players in the online trading industry

Company	Market Share	Assets Controlled	Number of Accounts	Ave. Trades per Day	Ave. Trades per Yr. (per customer)
Charles Schwab	23.3%	$263 billion	3,000,000	117,800	12.7
E*Trade	15.1%	$28 billion	1,551,000	76,333	16
Waterhouse	12.1%	$52.7 billion	877,000	61,031	21.6
Fidelity	11.9%	$202 billion	3,060,000	60,013	4.8
Datek	10.7%	$7 billion	290,000	53,840	59
Ameritrade	9.2%	$22.9 billion	560,000	46,199	26.4
DLJ Direct	3.8%	$14.2 billion	302,000	19,200	19.9

(Source: Credit Suisse First Boston, 1999b; Piper Jaffray, 1999a, 1999b)

Exhibit 9: Average commission charged by the top 10 online trading firms, 1996-1999 (in US dollars)

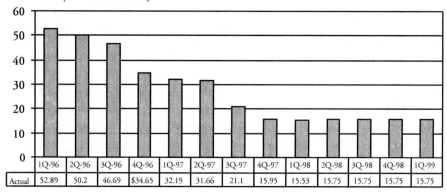

	1Q-96	2Q-96	3Q-96	4Q-96	1Q-97	2Q-97	3Q-97	4Q-97	1Q-98	2Q-98	3Q-98	4Q-98	1Q-99
Actual	52.89	50.2	46.69	$34.65	32.19	31.66	21.1	15.95	15.53	15.75	15.75	15.75	15.75

Source: Credit Suisse First Boston (1999a).

Table 4: Commissions charged by the top players in the online trading industry

Company	9/30/98	12/31/98	Notes
Schwab	$29.95	$29.95	For the first 1000 shares, $0.03 per share thereafter
E*Trade	$14.95	$14.95	$19.95 for limit and NASDAQ orders
Waterhouse	$12	$12	For the first 5000 shares, $0.01 per share thereafter
Fidelity Active Trader	$14.95	$14.95	To qualify, investor must place 36 trades per year
Datek	$9.99	$9.99	All trades up to 5000 shares
Ameritrade	$8	$8	$13 for limit and stop orders
DLJ Direct	$20	$20	For the first 1000 shares, $0.02 per share thereafter
Quick & Reilly	$14.95	$14.95	$19.95 for limit orders, $0.02 per share above 1000 shares
Typical Full-Service Broker	$300-$500		Varies by firm; often at the discretion of individual broker

(Source: Credit Suisse First Boston, 1998a)

Exhibit 10: Actual and projected worldwide Internet users, 1995-2003 (in millions)

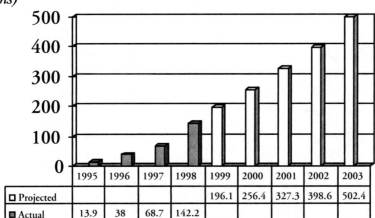

	1995	1996	1997	1998	1999	2000	2001	2002	2003
□ Projected					196.1	256.4	327.3	398.6	502.4
▣ Actual	13.9	38	68.7	142.2					

relinquished. Table 4 lists the commissions charged by the top players in the online trading industry for a typical market order.

The growth in the online trading industry was driven by several key factors:

1. *Increased Internet Usage* - In 1992, there were fewer than 10 million Internet users worldwide. By the end of 1999, that number was projected at 196.1 million (see Exhibit 10 for a chart of actual and projected worldwide Internet users from 1995 to 2003).
2. *Increased Consumer Comfort with Electronic Commerce* - For a while, people had been willing to "surf" the Web but unwilling to conduct business on it. Attitudes had begun to change and confidence was rising in the Internet as an alternate channel for conducting business.
3. *A Roaring Bull Market* - With the strong market run since 1995, online trading emerged at an opportune time. Technology firms' stocks were rising faster than other stocks, and tech investors were predisposed to lead the movement toward online investing (Economist, 1999).
4. *Media Attention* - The mass media had made online trading "chic." Articles in *Business Week*, the *Wall Street Journal*, and *Fortune* had raised awareness about online trading and hyped its potential.
5. *Baby Boomers Approaching Retirement* - As the members of the baby boom generation approached retirement, they were pouring increasing amounts of their income into investments (Credit Suisse First Boston, 1998a). Many of them were shifting their investments toward online brokerage accounts.

6. *Continued International Expansion* - E*Trade and Schwab had led the expansion, but others were ramping up their own efforts. Japan was a prime target as its securities industry was opening to foreign companies, and its citizens had low faith in local firms and high savings account balances.

7. *Partnering with Investment Banks* - Online brokerage firms were rushing to partner with investment banks in hopes of offering their account holders access to initial public offerings (IPOs). Critics charged that these arrangements were one-sided, guaranteeing the online firms very few shares of "hot" IPOs while using the online firms as a distribution outlet for the shares of "weak" IPOs. To mitigate this problem, online firms may begin to develop their own "limited" investment banking operations (Credit Suisse First Boston, 1999a).

8. *Large Banks Entering the Online Trading Industry* - With the banking infrastructure created and refined over the last 100 years, banks felt that they could enter the online trading industry without major obstacles. Banks wanted to have online trading capabilities to help attract and keep customers. Initially, banks wanted to target high-end customers, not day traders. Many saw their advancement into the online trading industry as a defensive move (Piper Jaffray, 1998b).

Ethical Issues within the Online Trading Industry

The following important ethical issues within the realm of online trading were emerging by the end of 1999.

1. *"Know Thy Customer"* - Regulations by the Securities and Exchange Commission of the United States required full-service brokers to monitor their customers' investment activities and prevent them from entering into inappropriate transactions. Online trading firms were subject to the same regulations, but they "complied" by installing monitoring software that tracked their customers' transactions. It was not clear whether or not a software tracking system met the criteria of "know thy customer" (Piper Jaffray, 1998a).

2. *Access in High-Volume Periods* - When market volume was extremely high, access to online trading Web sites could become difficult, with so many users trying to logon at the same time. Several firms were considering buying or developing software that could distinguish whether the person trying to logon to its site had an account value of $5,000 or $10,000,000. The software could then block the $5,000 account holder and permit access to the $10,000,000 account holder. Would such a system be ethical? Would it be legal?

3. *Distribution of IPOs* - Access to IPOs had long been a point of controversy within the world of investing. Who should have access to the precious initial

shares? Institutions always seemed to have access, and so did wealthy brokerage account holders. As IPOs became available to online traders, how could firms decide who would have access? Would it be the wealthiest account holders, those who agreed not to "flip" the shares, or those who were first to request that particular IPO? With more and more IPOs available online, this issue was becoming increasingly important.

4. *Registration* - Securities brokerage companies had to register in other countries before accepting or soliciting customers from there. These firms also had to respect the securities laws of these countries. Since online trading firms had sites on the Internet, and the Internet was available in virtually every country, did this mean online brokerage firms needed to register in every country?

E*Trade's Operational Problems

Some of the most critical problems that E*Trade was experiencing by the end of 1999 included:

1. *Vague and Broad Investment Agreement* - E*Trade customers had voiced concern about the "fine print" in E*Trade's investment agreement. To open an account at E*Trade, the customer had to agree to the terms of the E*Trade Customer Agreement, the introduction of which stated, "*Please note that the information contained herein is subject to change without notice.*" Furthermore, the "General Provisions" section included the following sentence: "In consideration of E*Trade opening and maintaining one or more accounts, you agree to the terms and conditions contained in this Agreement, as amended from time to time."

    This clause gave E*Trade wide latitude to change the terms of its customer agreement. Other agreement clauses allowed blame to be shifted from E*Trade to the market makers when confirmations moved slowly, granted E*Trade "Irrevocable Power of Attorney," and disclaimed liability regarding "losses resulting from a cause over which E*Trade or its affiliates do not have direct control."

2. *Insufficient Capacity* - In December 1997, a class action lawsuit was filed against E*Trade, claiming that customers had lost money because of E*Trade's failure to correctly handle the volatile trading days in October 1997. The complaint alleged that E*Trade knew that its communications systems could handle only 10,000 to 15,000 users, fewer than 7% of its accounts at that time (Iwata, 1997). A similar class action lawsuit was filed on February 9, 1999, after E*Trade's systems crashed three times during one week.

    The 1998 launching of Destination E*Trade brought complaints about the new site's speed and accessibility. Investors continually complained that they could not access the Web site during peak trading periods and that the site loaded very slowly. Since E*Trade's decision to open the site to non-customers had contributed to the problem, customers suggested that E*Trade freeze new accounts until it could service existing accounts properly. Customers also found the new site difficult to navigate, and its error messages confusing.

3. *Poor Trade Executions* - Given that E*Trade was selling its order flow to market makers who were executing orders with their own interests in mind, investors often complained that their "market" orders had been executed at unfavorable prices and at a very slow pace. Investors said that E*Trade shifted the blame over to its market makers, who were looking to make money on each transaction. Unlike Datek, E*Trade did not have a one-minute market order fill guarantee. Customers reported that "market" orders placed at night were not executed until 11 A.M. the following day.[2] There were also complaints about long delays in confirming trade executions—from 10 minutes to 1.5 hours.[3]

4. *Questionable Practices* - One of the investors interviewed, who tired of E*Trade's continual problems, elected to transfer his account to Fidelity. This investor held a risky position in the very volatile Amazon.com. The stock was trading at $135 in the summer of 1998 when E*Trade acted on the transfer order in the *middle* of the trading day. The investor was then blocked from selling his position later that day. Since the account was no longer accessible through the Web site, he had to wait a week until his new account was "live" at Fidelity. By then, the stock had fallen under $100. The investor, an attorney, considered E*Trade's decision to close his account in the middle of the day to be ludicrous and in bad faith. The matter was not resolved by several e-mail messages to customer service, and the investor ultimately sent a formal protest to E*Trade's compliance department. He was informed that the investment contract, in the fine print, gives E*Trade the right to close the account at its discretion. Furthermore, he was told that he could still have placed the trade using E*Trade's $35 broker-assisted trading through its "800" telephone number. The investor was further irritated by this response.

5. *Poor Customer Service* - E*Trade customers complained about "canned" e-mail responses that missed the point of their questions, long waits on calls to the "800" telephone numbers, a confusing telephone menu, waits of over a week for e-mail responses, and customer service representatives with poor attitudes.

During the summer of 1998, E*Trade ran a promotion offering an investor $50 if s/he placed five or more trades between June 16 and June 30. When one of the interviewees for this study complained via e-mail about not receiving his $50, an E*Trade customer service representative sent an e-mail apologizing and confirming that the $50 was being credited to his account. Two weeks later, the customer still had not received his credit and wrote back. The same customer service representative who had confirmed the credit two weeks earlier now explained that the previous e-mail was a mistake and that the customer did not qualify for the $50. (Actually, the customer did not qualify for the $50, but he still felt he deserved it because the customer service representative had confirmed that he would receive it.)

Another customer had trouble with E*Trade's "tell-a-friend" program, which granted a free trade to a customer who referred a friend who ultimately opened an account. This customer recalled, "I referred about fifteen friends, seven of whom have opened an account. However, I had to send several e-mails to E*Trade's customer service to get the proper credit for my referrals. I have never received credit without having to chase E*Trade."

6. *Questionable Security* - Perhaps most troubling of all were E*Trade's sloppy account set-up procedures. A customer from Colorado called several times regarding a trade. Each time, the representative could not find the trade request anywhere in the customer's account record. On the fifth call, the representative finally asked for more detailed information and inquired why the address associated with the account was in Massachusetts. It was revealed that E*Trade had mixed up the two account numbers in its records, a dangerous error. The two customers involved happened not to be active traders, but they had had access to trade on each other's accounts.

FURTHER READING

A definition of the financial elements used in this case: http://www.finpipe.com/.

An Internet broker score card done by Gomez Advisors: http://www.gomezadvisors.com.

Brown, S. A. (2000). *Customer Relationship Management: Linking People, Process, and Technology.* John Wiley & Sons.

Cotsakos, C. M. (2000). *It's Your Money: The E*Trade Step-by-Step Guide to Online Investing.* HarperCollins. (A new book written by E*Trade chairman of the board and CEO).

Dutta, S., Kwan, S., and Segev, A. Transforming business in the marketspace: Strategic marketing and customer relationships. http://inside.insead.fr/rise/papers/tbmfull.pdf.

Hagel III, J. and Singer. M. (1999). *Net Worth: Shaping Markets when Customers Make the Rules*. Harvard Business School Press.

Johnson, D. (2000). *Discount Commodity Brokers Ranked*, February 8. Retrieved on the World Wide Web: http://www.sonic.net/donaldj/futures.html.

Prewitt, E. (1997). Coping with infoglut: What you can learn from the folks in financial services. *Harvard Management Update*, August 1997.

Serwer, A. (1999). A nation of traders. *Fortune,* October, 116-120.

Shapiro, C. and Varian H. R. (1999). *Information Rules.* Harvard Business School Press.

U.S. Securities and Exchange Commission. Learn about Investing. Retrieved on the World Wide Web: http://www.sec.gov/consumer/jneton.htm.

REFERENCES

Buckman, R. (1998). E*Trade expects its stock price will benefit from losses but the market seems to disagree. *Wall Street Journal*, July 30.

Byron, C. (1997). Flame your broker! *Esquire*, May.

CBS. (1999). Merrill Lynch tiptoes into online trading. *CBS MarketWatch Report*, March 4.

CNN. (1998). *Online Trading–A Special Report*, August 22.

Credit Suisse First Boston. (1998a) *Online Trading Quarterly: June.* August.

Credit Suisse First Boston. (1998b). *Online Trading Quarterly: 3rd Quarter,* November.

Credit Suisse First Boston. (1999a). *Online Trading Quarterly: 4th Quarter,* January.

Credit Suisse First Boston. (1999b). *Online Trading Quarterly: 4th Quarter,* September.

Dalton, G. (1998). Chief information officer of the year: Debra Chrapaty. *InformationWeek,* December 21/28.

Economist. (1999). When the bubble burst, January 30, 23-25.

E*Trade. (1998a). E*Trade signs second international joint venture agreement in seven days. *Company Press Release*, June 11.

E*Trade. (1998b). E*Trade offers customers platinum and classic Visa card. *Company Press Release*, June 26.

E*Trade. (1998c). E*Trade to acquire ShareData, Inc. *Company Press Release*, July 6.

E*Trade. (1998d). E*Trade enters Korean market as international expansion moves forward. *Company Press Release*, July 9.

E*Trade. (1998e). E*Trade makes strategic investments in high technology companies. *Company Press Release*, July 14.

E*Trade. (1998f). E*Trade reports third quarter earnings of 114 percent on revenue growth of 68 percent. Company Press Release, July 21.

E*Trade. (1998g). E*Trade expands marketing and commerce agreement with Yahoo! *Company Press Release*, August 6.

E*Trade. (1998h). E*Trade launches new destination Web site and Stateless Architecture (SM) to empower individual investors. *Company Press Release*, September 10.

E*Trade. (1998i). E*Trade's new destination financial services Web site attracts more than 500,000 members since September. *Company Press Release*, December 28.

Glasgall, W. (1999). Who needs a broker? *Business Week*, February, 22.

Iwata, E. (1997). Online brokerage sued for being slow; ads were deceptive, some customers say. *Seattle Post-Intelligencer*, December 4.

Kane, M. (1998). E*Trade to offer financial services. *Yahoo! News*, July 8.

Lipton, B. (1998). E*Trade launches portal site. *CNET News*, September 10.

Olmstead, A. (1998a). "Investors have high hopers for E*Trade's new site. *Online Broker*, September 14.

Olmstead, A. (1998b). Storming the borders. *Online Broker*, October 22.

Pettit, D. (1998). Logged on. *Wall Street Journal*, September 8.

Piper, J. (1997). *E*Trade*. August.

About the Authors

EDITOR

Mahesh S. Raisinghani is a faculty member at the Graduate School of Management, University of Dallas, where he teaches MBA courses in Information Systems and E-Commerce, and serves as the Director of Research for the Center for Applied Information Technology. He is also the President and CEO of Raisinghani and Associates International, Inc., a diversified global firm with interests in software consulting and technology options trading. Dr. Raisinghani earned his Ph.D. from the University of Texas at Arlington and is a Certified E-Commerce Consultant (CEC). Dr. Raisinghani was the recipient of the 1999 UD Presidential Award and the 2001 King Hagar Award for excellence in teaching, research and service. As a global thought leader on E-Business and Global Information Systems, he has served as the local chair of the World Conference on Global Information Technology Management in 2001 and the track chair for E-Commerce Technologies Management at the Information Resources Management Association since 1999. Dr. Raisinghani has published in numerous leading scholarly and practitioner journals, presented at leading world-level scholarly conferences and has served as an editor of two books, i.e., E-Commerce: Opportunities and Challenges and Cases on Worldwide E-Commerce: Theory in Action. He serves as the associate editor for JGITM and IRMJ and is a member of the editorial review board of leading information systems/e-commerce academic journals. He has also served as the editor of three special issues of the Journal of Electronic Commerce Research on Intelligent Agents in E-Commerce and eBusiness Security. Dr. Raisinghani was also selected by the National Science Foundation after a nationwide search to serve as a panelist on the Information Technology/E-Commerce Research Panel and Small Business Innovation Research panel. He has also been involved in consulting activities and frequently participates in news media interviews on IS issues. Dr. Raisinghani serves on the board of directors of Sequoia, Inc. and is included in the millennium edition of Who's Who in the World, Who's Who Among America's Teachers and Who's Who in Information Technology.

CONTRIBUTING AUTHORS

Dale A. Bondanza. Since receiving his BS in Computer Science from Rochester Institute of Technology, Dale Bondanza has held increasingly responsible positions in the Information Systems industry through senior management. Dale's interest in the Celtic Tiger was fostered while pursuing his MBA in MIS and E-Business at St. Joseph's University. Dale's IS background has primarily concentrated on financial applications in a variety of industries including banking, pharmaceutical, and financial services. Dale is currently consulting as a Program Manager for a financial services company in Philadelphia, PA. When not working Dale is an active volunteer firefighter as well as a dedicated weekend golfer.

Debabroto Chatterjee is Assistant Professor and Boeing Fellow in Management Information Systems at Washington State University. He received his Ph.D. in Business, with a specialization in Management Information Systems (MIS) and Strategic Management, from Florida State University in 1997. He also holds MBA, CPA (Chartered Accountant) and B.Com. (Bachelor's in Commerce) degrees. Dr. Chatterjee's research interests lie at the interface between information technology and strategy. He is currently pursuing research in the area of electronic commerce—the goal being to understand and explain how companies are leveraging Web and Internet-related technologies to facilitate business activities and strategies.

Antonio Díaz holds an MBA from Escuela de Administración de Negocios para Graduados (ESAN) in Lima, Perú and a B.Sc. in aeronautical-mechanical engineering from Escuela de Ingeniería Aeronáutica in Córdoba, Argentina. His areas of interest are e-business and the strategic use of information systems for supporting organizational planning and control. As a former officer, he worked in flight simulators projects for the Peruvian Air Force and was the Quality Control Department Deputy Manager at Servicio de Mantenimiento (SEMAN-PERU). Currently, he works as a Research Assistant in the information technology area at ESAN.

Adam T. Elegant graduated from Washington University (St. Louis) in 1995, with a B.A. in Political Science. After college he worked for American International Group (AIG) and Templeton Funds. In 1999, he earned his M.B.A. from the University of Colorado at Boulder in Finance and Technology & Innovation Management. He currently works for Goldman Sachs in

San Francisco, focusing on institutional on-line trading and venture investments related to financial services. He can be reached at Adam.Elegant@gs.com.

David Gordon is a Professor of Management, and has been affiliated with the University of Dallas as a faculty member of the Graduate School of Management since 1969. During this period, he has functioned in several management roles including that of Associate Dean. Currently, he serves as Director of MBA Programs in Engineering and Industrial Management. Prior to receiving his doctorate in Industrial Engineering from the University of Oklahoma and joining the Graduate School of Management, Dr. Gordon held a broad range of industrial management positions.

Hanns-Christian L. Hanebeck, Director of Enterprise Applications at GlobeRanger Corporation, is an expert in supply chain management, marketing and business strategy. Prior to joining the company as one of the first employees Mr. Hanebeck worked extensively as a consulting director in the U.S., Europe, and Asia. His professional experiences include founding and management of joint ventures, establishing strategic alliances and key account management as well as project leads in business process engineering, enterprise resource planning and software implementations. His areas of interest are focused on electronic commerce, inter-company collaboration, corporate performance management, supply chain planning and optimization, and knowledge management.

Leonard M. Jessup is the Philip L. Kays Distinguished Professor of MIS and is the Associate Director for the School of Accounting, Information Systems, and Business Law at Washington State University. Professor Jessup received his B.A. in Information and Communication Studies in 1983 and his M.B.A. in 1985 from California State University, Chico, where he was voted Outstanding MBA Student. He received his Ph.D. in Organizational Behavior and Management Information Systems from the University of Arizona in 1989. His primary areas of research are electronic commerce, computer-supported collaboration, and technology-supported learning.

Stanley L. Kroder is an Associate Professor, Graduate School of Management, University of Dallas and founding Director of both the MBA Program in Telecommunications Management and the Center of Distance Learning. He joined the University in 1989 after a 29-year career with IBM. In 1993, he received the Douglass Award for teaching excellence and entrepreneurial spirit for the Graduate School of Management. In 1999, he was chosen as the

Michael A. Haggar Fellow, one of the two top honors for faculty of the entire university. Dr. Kroder received a Bachelor of Science degree in Industrial Management from MIT's Sloan School of Management and a Master of Science in Operations Research from Case-Western Reserve University. He holds a Ph.D. in Organization Theory, Business Strategy and International Management, from the School of Management, University of Texas at Dallas

Ook Lee is a Professor of Information Systems in the Department of Business Administration at Hansung University in Seoul, Korea. Previously, he worked as a project director at Information Resources, Inc, in Chicago, Illinois, and as a senior information research scientist at Korea Research Information Center in Seoul, Korea. His main research interests include electronic commerce, digital libraries, expert systems, neural networks, and critical social theory. He holds a B.S. in Computer Science and Statistics from Seoul National University in Seoul, Korea, and an M.S. in Computer Science from Northwestern University in Evanston, Illinois. He also earned an M.S. and Ph.D. in Management Information Systems from Claremont Graduate University in Claremont, California. His email address is leeo@hansung.ac.kr.

Ramiro Montealegre received his Doctorate in Business Administration from the Harvard Business School in the area of management information systems. His Master's degree in computer science is from Carleton University, Canada. He holds a Bachelor in Engineering degree from the Francisco Marroquin University, Guatemala. Currently, he is an Assistant Professor of Information Systems at the University of Colorado, Boulder. He is regularly an Invited Lecturer at Case Western Reserve University, Instituto de Centro America de Administracion de Empresas (INCAE) in Costa Rica, the Instituto Tecnologico y de Estudios Superiores de Monterrey in Mexico, Instituto de Altos Estudios Empresariales (IAE) in Argentina, and Universidad Pablo Olavides in Spain. His research focuses on the interplay between information technology and organization transformation in highly uncertain environments. He has been involved in studying projects of organizational change in the United States, Canada, Mexico, and the Central and South American regions. His research has been published in MIS Quarterly, Sloan Management Review, Journal of Management Information Systems, IEEE Transactions on Communications, Information & Management, Information Technology & People and other journals.

John H. Nugent serves as an Assistant Professor in the Graduate School of Management at the University of Dallas, Irving, TX, where he teaches in the telecommunications and entrepreneurship concentrations. Dr. Nugent concurrently serves as CEO of the Hilliard Consulting Group, Inc., a leading strategy consulting firm in the telecommunications and IT industry segments. Previously, Dr. Nugent served as president of a number of AT&T subsidiaries where he won the Defense Electronics "10 Rising Stars" award.

Margaret T. O'Hara is an Assistant Professor of MIS at East Carolina University. After considerable work experience as a CIO, she completed her Ph.D. in MIS at The University of Georgia. She specializes in understanding the impacts of technology-driven change, including the changes brought about by data warehousing. Maggie has also done considerable research in Information Systems education, including on-line learning and curriculum. She has published articles in both academic and practitioner journals, including *Management Decision, The Journal of Computer Information Systems, Information Management,* and *Computerworld*, and has presented her work at numerous national and international conferences.

David Paper is an Associate Professor at Utah State University in the Business Information Systems and Education Department. His academic credentials include a Bachelor of Arts in Computer Science from Southern Illinois University, a Master of Business Administration from Arizona State University, and a PhD. in Business from Southern Illinois University. He has several refereed publications appearing in journals such as *Communications of the AIS, Journal of Information Technology Cases and Applications, Journal of Computer Information Systems, Long Range Planning, Creativity and Innovation, Accounting Management and Information Technologies, Business Process Management Journal* and many others. He has also spent time in industry and consulting with Texas Instruments, DLS, Inc., the Phoenix Small Business Administration, the Utah State University Research Foundation, and the Utah Department of Transportation. His teaching and research interests include database management, e-commerce, business process reengineering, organizational transformation, and change management.

J. Martín Santana is Associate Professor of MIS and the Director of the Center for Information Technology at the Escuela de Administración de Negocios para Graduados (ESAN) in Lima, Perú. He received his Ph.D. in Business Administration from Florida International University in 1997. He also holds a M.Sc. in Management Information Systems from École des Hautes Études Commerciales in Montreal and a B.Sc. in Industrial Engineering from Universidad de Lima. His current research interests are in electronic business, systems development (especially for the web-centric applications) and technology-supported learning. He has published in the areas of international use of information technology, methods in software development, and strategic management of information systems.

Joseph Sarkis is currently an Associate Professor at the Graduate School of Management at Clark University. He earned his PhD from the State University of New York at Buffalo. His research interests include manufacturing strategy and management, with a specific emphasis on performance management, justification issues, enterprise modeling and environmentally conscious operations and logisitics. He has published over 120 articles in a number of peer reviewed academic journals and conferences. He is a member of the American Production and Inventory Control Society (APICS), Institute for Operations Research and Management Sciences (INFORMS), the Decision Sciences Institute (DSI), and the Production and Operations Management Society (POMS). He is also a certified production and inventory manager (CPIM).

Jaime Serida is an Associate Professor of Information Systems at the Escuela de Administración de Negocios para Graduados (ESAN) in Lima, Perú. He received his Ph.D. in business administration from the University of Minnesota. His research interests include electronic business, strategic impact of information technology, group support systems, and the adoption and diffusion of information technology in organizations.

Sabine Seufert, born 17th of April in Lahr, Germany, is senior lecturer and MBA study director at the University of St. Gallen in Switzerland. She studied business administration, computer science, psychology and pedagogic at the University of Erlangen-Nuremberg, Germany and received her Ph.D. in business administration of the University of Muenster, Germany in 1996. From 1997 to 1999 she has worked as a co-founder and project manager for the Learning Center at the Institute for Information Management at the University of St. Gallen in Switzerland. Since 1999 she has been working as study director of the Executive MBA in New Media and Communication (www.media-mba.unisg.ch) at the mcm Institute at the University of St. Gallen. Her research focus lies in the area of E-Learning, collaborative learning, organizational learning and knowledge management. From August to December 2000 she stayed as Visiting Scholar at the Stanford Learning Lab to investigate learning technologies and Communities.

James E. Skibo is an Adjunct Professor of Industrial Management at the University of Dallas, Graduate School of Management. He is the Director of Cooperative Advertising for the Army & Air Force Exchange Service in Dallas, Texas. His areas of expertise include an extensive range of business and operations management.

R. P. Sundarraj is an Associate Professor of Information Systems at Clark University in Worcester, MA. He obtained his Bachelor's in Electrical Engineering from the University of Madras, India, and his MS and PhD in Management Science from the University of Tennessee, Knoxville. Professor Sundarraj's research encompasses the development of methodologies for the efficient design and management of emerging information systems, as well as the use of massively parallel computing for solving large-scale problems. His research has been accepted in journals such as *Information Systems Management*, *IEEE Transactions*, *ACM Transactions* and *Mathemtical Programming*. In addition, he has consulted with Fortune 100 companies on the development of decision support and other software systems for materials and marketing management.

Kenneth B. Tingey is a doctoral student at Utah State University in the Business Information Systems and Education Department. He has over twenty-five years experience in industry, working as a venture capital fund founder and general partner, entrepreneur, general and line manager, and executive staff assistant. He is founder, Chairman, and CEO of OpenNet Corporation, an enterprise software developer. His academic credentials include a Master's Degree in Pacific International Affairs from the University of California, San Diego, a Master of Business Administration from Brigham Young University, a Bachelor of Arts in Music Education from Utah State University, and a Baccalaureate Major in Accounting from Brigham Young University. His professional affiliations include Strategic Information Division of Ziff-Davis Publishing Company, the Ventana Growth Fund, and Sunrider International. In addition, he has conducted many business consulting and systems development projects on contract with direct selling companies, software development companies, and government contractors. Mr. Tingey has engaged in many enterprise-level systems development projects with special emphasis on requirements of supporting the mission of institutions by means of information processing models and information technology tools. Mr. Tingey is the author of Dual Control, a book on the need to support top-down policies and horizontal processes in a unified system environment.

Roberto Vinaja is Assistant Professor of Computer Information Systems at the University of Texas Pan American and has a Ph.D. from the University of Texas at Arlington. He has published in the *Handbook of IS Management,* presented at international/national conferences, and developed software for EDS, Mattel Toys and AETNA.

Hugh J. Watson is a Professor of MIS and a holder of a C. Herman and Mary Virginia Terry Chair of Business Administration in the Terry College of Business at the University of Georgia. He is the author of 22 books and over 100 scholarly journal articles. He is recognized for his work on decision support systems, executive information systems, and most recently, data warehousing. Hugh has consulted with numerous organizations, including the World Bank, Intel, IBM, Arthur Andersen, Conoco, and Glaxo. He is the senior editor of the *Journal of Data Warehousing* and a Fellow of The Data Warehousing Institute. He is the consulting series editor for John Wiley & Sons' Computing and Information Processing series.

Ira Yermish is an Assistant Professor of Management and Information Systems at St. Joseph's University in Philadelphia. His teaching and research areas include systems analysis and design, data base management, data communications, information resource management, and strategic management. In addition to his current academic activities, he is an active management and information systems consultant. Dr. Yermish earned degrees from Case Western Reserve University, Stanford University the University of Pennsylvania. His early professional experience included positions with UNIVAC, Control Data, RCA Corporation, the Institute for Scientific Information, and founder of MagnaSystems, Inc. When not teaching or consulting, Dr. Yermish is an avid cyclist, runner, photographer, choral singer and arts board member.

Index

A

accounting 137
active investors 230
advertisement 193
agents 202
Alma Mater Multimedialis 74
America Online 108
application development 205
Application Service Provider (ASP) 6
audit 35

B

B2B market 4
B2C market 4
banner ads 192
bricks and clicks 152
broadband communications 187
brokerage industry 222
budgetary 143
business model 71
business plan 172
business strategy 151

C

central database 4
change management 36
channel of distribution 203
charting 224
competition 234
configuration 34
consultants 172
consumer-centric 136

corporate brochure 206
corporate universities 72
credit card penetration 102
credit cards 187
cultural differences 99
currency 95
customer relations 199
customer service 227
customer-managed orders 39
customers 201, 221
customization 204
cyberspace 191
cyberspace marketing 190

D

daily e-mail service 186
deployment 138
direct e-mail advertisement 192
direct marketer 193
direct sales 204
discount brokerage firms 223

E

E*Trade 221
e-commerce 32, 95, 186
e-learning 70
e-mail 195
E2B 75
E2C 75
E2E 75
education consortiums 74
education providers 74
effective commercial activity 191

El Sitio 107
electronic business 152
electronic commerce 113
electronic data interchange (EDI) 38
electronic forms 208
electronic marketing 152
eLocate™ 2
ENI Company 186
enterprise resource planning 7, 32, 33
entrepreneurs 171
European Union 171
extranet 207

F

fiberoptic computer networks 198
financial portal 224
financial services industry 201
Fortune 500 136
future-proofing 6

G

global business processes 37
global ecommerce setting 32
global Internet strategy 48
"global" model 51
GPS (Global Positioning System) 1

H

heuristic "rules of thumb" 48
hybrid model 53

I

implementing technologies 201
information infrastructure 186
information-based services 201
infrastructure 98
insurance 204
insurance and financial services industry
      201
insurance industry 203
Internet 3, 39
Internet commerce 115
Internet industry 188
Internet marketing 192
Internet Service Providers 196

Internet trading 221
Internet-based globalization 48
intra-industry competition 204
investors 221

J

justification 35

K

key metrics 40
Korea information infrastructure 191

L

lack of growth 204
language 95
location devices 4
logistics 137
logistics systems 2
Lycos 106

M

management support 44
market analysis 6
mass customization 39
metrics 33
Microsoft 108
modem-based bulk mailing 197
multi-functional teams 143
multiple instance 40

N

narrowband wireless standard 5
national IT infrastructure 186, 190
non-customers 224

O

on-line trading 223
one-company image 206
one-stop shop 221
online service 222
operational problems 221
organizational structures 136
outsourcing 33

P

personalization 204
portals 96
price 195
privacy 193
process change 40
product 186
project management 33
promotion 193
PUSH technology 192

Q

Quepasa.com 107
quotes 224

R

reengineering 35
research 224
retail 114
retail traders 230
retailers 117
reverse auction 204

S

Safeco 201
satellite communication 5
Sears 96
securities brokerage industry 221
securities industry 222
segmentalism 142
shareholders 203
single-instance implementation 38
smart money 8
SQL 210
StarMedia 96
stock screening 224
straddlers 229
strategic 32
strategic alliances 226
strategic information systems 34
strategic justification 35
strategic planning 34
strategic systems 33
supplier-managed inventory 39

supply chain 32
supply chain management function 2
system configuration 35
system evaluation 35
system outages 227
systems integration 36

T

T1MSN 108
technological glitches 227
telephone lines 187
Telmex 103
Terra Networks 106
three-tiered approach 51
time-to-market 2
tracking 1
Trade*Plus 223
"transnational" e-commerce model 51

U

university networks 74

V

value-added services 207
virtual supermarket 119
virtual universities 74

W

Web application development 205
Web developers 210
Web technologies 201
Web-based education 70
wireless communications 3
wireless modem 4
wireless networks 4
wireless technologies 3
workable payment method 187
worker-computer industry 188
World Wide Web 198

Y

Yahoo! 108
Yupi 106